D1613450

Financial Stability and Central Banks

Recent events remind us how crucial it is that the banking and payments system should be protected from risks and crises. The difficulties that beset Indonesia, South Korea and Thailand in 1997 are a vivid example, as are the acute problems that confronted Russia in 1998, and the chronic financial malaise that underlay Japan's macroeconomic underperformance throughout the 1990s. Even more dramatic was the banking and economic collapse in the US and much of Europe in the 1930s.

It is a prime responsibility for central banks to try to prevent and contain the financial crises that could precipitate such a calamity. This book, developed from the Central Bank Governors' Symposium on Financial Stability and written by current policy-makers, offers a highly informed account of contemporary policy issues and explores the legal, regulatory, managerial and economic issues that affect central banks, including:

- banking crises
- regulatory and supervisory regimes
- the role of central banks
- crisis management
- the role of bank capital
- capital flows and capital controls

Financial Stability and Central Banks provides an up-to-date and comprehensive overview that will prove invaluable to economists, researchers, bankers, policy-makers and students in this field.

Central Bank Governors' Symposium Series

Lavan Mahadeva and Gabriel Sterne (eds) (2000) *Monetary Frameworks in a Global Context*, Routledge.

Maxwell Fry, Isaack Kilato, Sandra Roger, Krzysztof Senderowicz, David Sheppard, Francisio Solis and John Trundle (1999) *Payment Systems in Global Perspective*, Routledge.

Charles Goodhart, Philipp Hartmann, David Llewellyn, Liliana Rojas-Suárez and Steven Weisbrod (1998) *Financial Regulation; Why, How and Where Now?* Routledge.

Maxwell Fry (1997) *Emancipating the Banking System and Developing Markets for Government Debt*, Routledge.

Maxwell Fry, Charles Goodhart and Alvaro Almeida (1996) *Central Banking in Developing Countries; Objectives, Activities and Independence*, Routledge.

Forrest Capie, Charles Goodhart, Stanley Fischer and Norbert Schnadt (1994) *The Future of Central Banking; The Tercentenary Symposium of the Bank of England*, Cambridge University Press.

Financial Stability and Central Banks

A global perspective

Richard A. Brealey
Alastair Clark
Charles Goodhart
Juliette Healey
Glenn Hoggarth
David T. Llewellyn
Chang Shu
Peter Sinclair
Farouk Soussa

London and New York

First published 2001
by Routledge
11 New Fetter Lane, London EC4P 4EE

Simultaneously published in the USA and Canada
by Routledge
29 West 35th Street, New York, NY 10001

Routledge is an imprint of the Taylor & Francis Group

© 2001 Bank of England

Typeset in Times by Wearset, Boldon, Tyne and Wear
Printed and bound in Great Britain by TJ International Ltd,
Padstow, Cornwall

British Library Cataloguing in Publication Data
A catalogue record for this book is available from the British Library

Library of Congress Cataloging in Publication Data
Financial stability and central banks / Juliette Healey ...[et al.].
    p. cm.
  Includes bibliographical references and index.
  1. Banks and banking, Central.   I. Healey, Juliette.

HG1811 .F56 2001
332.1'1–dc21   200101929

ISBN 0-415-25775-1 (hbk)
ISBN 0-415-25776-X (pbk)

This book is dedicated with affection to the memory of our friend and colleague Maxwell John Fry, Director of the Centre for Central Banking Studies from 1997 to 1999

Contents

Charts

Tables

Contributors

Richard A. Brealey is Special Adviser to the Governor, Bank of England.

Alastair Clark is Executive Director for Financial Stability, Bank of England.

Professor Charles Goodhart, Financial Markets Group, London School of Economics, and formerly Monetary Policy Committee Member, Bank of England.

Juliette Healey is Adviser for Financial Stability at the Centre for Central Banking Studies, Bank of England.

Glenn Hoggarth is a Senior Manager in the Financial Industry and Regulation Division, Bank of England.

David T. Llewellyn is Professor of Money and Banking at Loughborough University and President of SUERF (Societe Universitaire Europeenne de Recherches Financieres).

Chang Shu is a Manager at the Hong Kong Monetary Authority, and formerly a research analyst at the Centre for Central Banking Studies, Bank of England.

Peter Sinclair is Director at the Centre for Central Banking Studies, Bank of England, and Professor of Economics at the University of Birmingham.

Farouk Soussa is a financial stability expert, Bank of England.

Foreword

In June 2000 the Bank of England hosted its seventh Central Bank Governors' Symposium. The monograph presented at this symposium and the discussion which followed form the basis for this book. Since the Bank of England's 300th birthday celebrations in 1994, its annual Central Bank Governors' Symposium has developed into a structured investigation of particular central banking topics. Our first two symposia looked at the history and nature of central banking, first in the industrialised countries and then in developing countries. Subsequent symposia have examined the implications of government borrowing for central banks, financial regulation, payment systems, and, in 1999, monetary policy frameworks in a global perspective. The full list of resulting publications is provided on page ii.

The 2000 symposium turned to financial stability and the role of central banks. I asked Professor Peter Sinclair, the new Director of the Bank of England's Centre for Central Banking Studies to co-ordinate the project involving authors from the Bank and from academia.

The maintenance of financial stability is complementary to the pursuit of monetary and price stability and a principal concern of central banks the world over. Price stability is imperilled if the financial system is in crisis, and price instability will warp and threaten the stability of the financial system. So financial stability and price stability go hand in hand. You cannot really expect to have one without the other. Both are key ingredients for the economic confidence upon which investment, prosperity and growth depend.

One thing all central banks have in common is an interest in financial stability as a public policy objective, as a key factor influencing macroeconomic performance and the potential for systemic disturbances. But the precise institutional arrangements vary widely country by country, and are also changing rapidly in many cases. How is financial stability secured? There are numerous factors that affect it. The public authorities have a range of tools they can use to influence these structural factors and to address crises when they occur. Some of these factors and tools were explored and discussed during a research workshop and project at our

Centre for Central Banking Studies at the end of 1999. But there was a range of issues that we wanted to follow up.

I asked the authors to look at topical issues in a global perspective so that challenges facing all types of economies – industrial, transition and developing – were addressed. In this complex field, cross-country comparisons are particularly valuable. This volume certainly aspires to add to our stock of knowledge.

The papers in this volume explore the changing environment in which we operate, and discuss the range of policy reponses and which might be most appropriate. The papers cover a wide range of issues. After setting out the questions being addressed and a summary of the papers, Chapter 1 looks at financial crises and the experience of bank failures, the trade-off between competition and safety, the links between financial stability and monetary policy and the roles played by various agents. Chapter 2 sets out the results of a survey of thirty-seven central banks – from industrial, transition and developing economies – comparing their responsibilities across a spectrum of 'financial stability' tools. It examines the background to central bank involvement in regulation and supervision, and current and likely future changes in the institutional structure. Some central banks regulate and supervise, others do not, but all are involved in promoting a robust infrastructure for the financial system, the surveillance of risks to stability and crisis management. As the financial system changes, the authorities need to respond. Chapter 3 further explores the debate over whether it makes any difference where bank supervision occurs, and what its organisational structure is. This topic attracted a good deal of attention at our symposium and is clearly of interest to many countries.

What suits one country may not suit another. Another area where we have seen change is in the 'regulatory regime', which goes much wider than regulation *per se*. This is the theme of Chapter 4. Increasingly the focus is on how to structure incentives to promote market discipline. Chapter 5 explores the role of bank capital, particularly in terms of protecting against bank failure and its contribution to economic activity. The Basel Accord is an important feature of international bank regulation. The principles underlying it, and the modifications proposed to it, are examined in depth in this chapter.

No discussion of financial stability would be complete without a look at financial safety nets, not just regulation and supervision but also crisis management and deposit insurance. Chapter 6 describes the various roles the authorities undertake and the issues facing them. Central banks have long held the role of lender of last resort but as the financial system evolves so must our forms of response. Increasingly we operate at an international level with new levels of 'connectedness' across the global financial system. The book moves on in Chapter 7 to review the role of international capital movements – both benefits and drawbacks – and includes an analysis of the literature and some of the practical details. This is a topical issue for many countries. And, finally, the last chapter highlights several issues that are currently occupying the policy arena and looks at the changing role of central banks.

There is a great current interest in financial stability issues, both at a national and international level. We hope that this volume will contribute to the continuing debate.

Sir Edward George
Governor of the Bank of England

Acknowledgements

We wish to thank the Governor of the Bank of England and the Governors of central banks from around the world who participated in the Bank of England's 7th Central Bank Governors' Symposium for sharing their insights on the issues raised in the preliminary papers upon which this book is based. In particular, we are indebted to our three official discussants at the Symposium, Governors Tito Mboweni of South Africa and Carlos Massad of Chile, and Deputy Governor Stephen Grenville of Australia.

We are also most grateful for the care and attention with which central bankers from thirty-seven countries completed the questionnaire described in Chapter 2, and commented on earlier drafts. We would like to offer our sincerest gratitude to each of the following:

Alejandra Anastasi (*Central Bank of Argentina*), Christopher Kent (*Central Bank of Australia*), Antonio Monteiro (*Bank of Brazil*), Victor Yotzov (*Bulgarian National Bank*), Sean O'Connor (*Bank of Canada*), Felipe Morande (*Central Bank of Chile*), A.J. Philippou (*Central Bank of Cyprus*), Jiri Boehm (*Czech National Bank*), Karsten Biltoft (*Danmarks Nationalbank*), Indrek Saapar (*Bank of Estonia*), Jukka Topi and Kimmo Virolainen (*Bank of Finland*), Julia Leung (*Hong Kong Monetary Authority*), Aniko Turjan (*National Bank of Hungary*), R. Kannan (*Reserve Bank of India*), Hartadi Sarwono (*Bank of Indonesia*), Mary O'Dea (*Central Bank of Ireland*), Jeonghwan Cho (*Bank of Korea*), Guntis Valujevs (*Bank of Latvia*), Prakash Kannan (*Central Bank of Malaysia*), W.R. Milonde (*Reserve Bank of Malawi*), Alfred Demarco (*Central Bank of Malta*), Lic Javier Guzman Calafell (*Banco de Mexico*), Reinder Van Dijk (*De Nederlandsche Bank*), Margaret Griffin (*Reserve Bank of New Zealand*), Henning Strand (*Norges Bank*), Hugo Perea (*Banco Central de Reserva Del Peru*), Marta Golajewska (*National Bank of Poland*), Vladimir Smenkovsky (*The Central Bank of Russia*), Lim Soon Chong (*The Monetary Authority of Singapore*), Gordana Ilc Krizaj (*Bank of Slovenia*), Hugo Stark (*Reserve Bank of South Africa*), C.I. Fernando and L.K. Gunatilake (*Central Bank of Sri Lanka*), Felice Marlor (*Sveriges Riksbank*), Paiboon Kittisrikangwan (*Bank of Thailand*), E. Katimob-

Mugwanya (*Bank of Uganda*) and W. Manungo (*Reserve Bank of Zimbabwe*). Also Toshio Tsuiki (*the Bank of Japan*) and John Dearie and Ed Steinberg (*Federal Reserve Bank of New York*) who kindly provided comments on the summaries of the position in Japan and the USA.

We also wish to thank all those who participated in the Bank of England's Centre for Central Banking Studies' research workshop and project on 'Central Bank Responsibility for Financial Stability, September–December 1999' and upon whose discussions and research we built.

This volume would not have been possible without the support and patience of our publishers, Routledge – special thanks go to our editors Robert Langham and Heidi Bagtazo and their colleagues. Also thanks to our colleagues at the Centre for Central Banking Studies.

Many others have commented on drafts of individual chapters and assisted in the production of the papers published in this volume. Thanks are given by individual authors at the beginning of each chapter.

The views expressed in this book do not necessarily reflect those of the Bank of England or any individual acknowledged within. All errors remain the sole responsibility of the authors.

Juliette Healey
Peter Sinclair

1 Financial stability and central banks

An introduction

Peter Sinclair[1]

1.1 Background

The collapse of a country's payment and banking system is a terrible disaster. It would spell closure for many of its firms, ruin for many of its inhabitants. It is a prime responsibility for central banks to try to prevent and contain the financial crises that could precipitate such a calamity.

But financial stability is not the central bank's sole concern – safeguarding the nation's currency is at least as important a task. Nor is the central bank the only body with financial stability responsibilities. Finance ministries share this role, as do regulators and supervisors of financial firms, when housed outside the central bank.

Recent events remind us how crucial it is that the banking and payments system should be protected from risks and crises. The difficulties that beset Indonesia, South Korea and Thailand in 1997 are a vivid example. So too were the acute problems that confronted Russia in 1998, and the chronic financial malaise that underlay Japan's macroeconomic underperformance throughout the 1990s. Even more dramatic was the banking and economic collapse in the United States and much of Europe in the 1930s.

Without trying to understand such phenomena, whenever and wherever they occur, we can have little hope of preventing their repetition. Sharing knowledge of different central banks' experiences, and debating their implications in the never-ending search for improved monetary and financial policy, is undertaken in a variety of fora. One such is the Central Bank Governors' Symposium, held annually in London since 1994. The Bank of England's Centre for Central Banking Studies presents a set of papers to this annual Symposium.

The subject for the Central Bank Governors' Symposium in June 2000 was 'Financial Stability'. A written report was provided, *Financial Stability and Central Banks*. This contained six papers, each devoted to a different aspect of the subject. The present volume is a revised and expanded version of that report. Together with the report's six chapters, it contains a chapter by Charles Goodhart (Chapter 3), a concluding note by Alastair

Clark (Chapter 8), and a record of the discussion at the Symposium on 2 June.

Section 2 of the present chapter presents a summary of the volume, and Section 3 poses twelve key questions about financial stability to which its contributors offer answers. Section 4 takes a brief look at the incidence of bank failure. Some aspects of the trade-off between safety and competition are examined in Section 5. Sections 6 and 7 identify certain links between financial stability policy and monetary policy, and some aspects of the character of the work of those charged with responsibility for financial stability policy. Section 8 concludes.

1.2   Summary of the volume

After his precis of the key points of other chapters in this volume, Peter Sinclair, in this chapter, presents a list of twelve questions about financial stability that he posed to the contributors before we began our work. He goes on to sketch what history tells us about the mortality probabilities of financial institutions. He emphasises the tendency of bank deaths to cluster, to vary over space and time, and to respond (somewhat weakly) to the character of the regulatory regime.

Despite undoubted advantages, liberalisation and intensified competition among banks have a worrying tendency to raise the frequency of failures. Reasons for this are discussed. Various linkages between monetary policy and financial stability policy are identified, linkages that point strongly to preserving the latter as a core function for the central bank, even if and where supervision and regulation are undertaken elsewhere.

Numerous and often conflicting pressures confront those charged with safeguarding the financial system, be they within or outside the central bank. They also face the misfortune of attracting blame when troubles arise, while appearing redundant in quieter periods. Their value in containing or preventing costly crises is not easy to quantify.

The extent and character of central banks' involvement in safeguarding financial stability varies greatly from one country to another. It has also been subject to some radical recent changes. Establishing an up-to-date picture across a wide range of central banks is therefore particularly valuable. This is done in Chapter 2.

After a brief historical review of the evolution of central banks, which have multiplied from ten in 1870 to nearly 180 today, Juliette Healey examines the current spectrum of financial stability activities of thirty-seven central banks across a range of economies, drawing on responses to a CCBS questionnaire. All but one of the thirty-seven deem the promotion of financial stability, and the stability of settlement and payments systems, as core elements in their mandates. While the wide variety of institutional arrangements suggests there is no single 'optimal' model, the responses may shed light on how an effective framework can be developed.

One topical issue is whether the efficiency of regulation and supervision of individual institutions may be influenced by the particular institutional structure in which they are conducted. Juliette Healey explores the issues that have prompted change in this area, the different ways in which authorities from industrial, transition and developing countries have responded, and what further changes might be expected and why. She also explores the principal arguments on whether a central bank should carry out regulation and supervision in addition to its monetary policy role. Evidence from the survey is included.

There is also a brief look at the correlation between the degree to which a central bank enjoys independence in its monetary policy, and the extent of its responsibility for prudential regulation and supervision. Taking a wider sample than the survey, of eighty-three (about half the world's central banks), she finds a statistically significant negative association between independence and supervision: the greater a central bank's autonomy in monetary policy, the less likely it is to conduct supervision and regulation. The chapter ends with some observations about establishing an effective regulatory institutional structure, and notes that not all current movement is towards integrated supervision outside the central bank: some central banks have expanded, or seem set to expand, their regulatory role. The institutional structure is a topic for lively debate; but there are few grounds for thinking that one structure is unambiguously better than another for all countries in all circumstances.

With the present facts summarised in Chapter 2, Chapter 3, by Charles Goodhart, carries forward the discussion about whether, in fact, it makes any difference where bank supervision occurs, and what its organizational structure is. The central bank would have to work closely with bank supervisors and regulators wherever they were located. The disappearance of boundaries between different kinds of financial institution, and the growth of multi-function financial firms, renders the old system of separate supervision for each obsolete. The growth of multi-country banks complicates supervision and implies that it is increasingly Finance Ministries, not the private sector, that fund any rescues of troubled firms.

Possible conflicts of interest, the need to amalgamate supervision, and concerns about excessive concentrations of power, might argue for taking supervision outside central banks, although the first of these three was not compelling by itself. The central bank's Lender of Last Resort function argued in favour of keeping supervision inside the central bank, though perhaps less so when the Ministry of Finance also becomes involved in the resolution of banking crisis. Information flows point to the same conclusion. Supervisory data can assist monetary policy, for example. The central bank can choose what data to look at, and not just rely on information, however full and timely, passed on by another institution. Notwithstanding these points, the combination of blurred boundaries in financial markets (making separate supervisors for separate types of institution anachronistic) and the political disquiet about concentrating excessive power within the (increasingly independent) central bank point in favour of external supervision in many developed countries.

As far as developing and emerging countries are concerned, Charles Goodhart concludes, keeping (or integrating) banking supervision within the central banks has particular appeal: supervision would be better funded, better conducted, more dependable, and less open to outside pressures.

What matters is not regulation *per se*, David Llewellyn argues in Chapter 4, but the *regulatory regime*. This has seven key elements. Three relate primarily to regulated financial firms: how they govern themselves, how the market disciplines them, and the structure of incentives for staff and others within them. Then there are four elements for the regulators – the rules they set, how they monitor and supervise, their intervention, and their own accountability.

It is wrong to focus on just one element, such as monitoring and supervision. Tradeoffs and interactions between all seven elements need to be recognised. The optimum mix of the seven elements is liable to change over time and differ across firms. One promising concept is 'contract regulation'. The regulator sets objectives and principles; the firm chooses how best to satisfy them, entering a contract with the regulator with penalties for infringements.

There is no single course of bank distress or crises. Strict, precise rules have numerous drawbacks. Regulation should reinforce discipline by the market, not replace or distort it. Market discipline is insufficient by itself (externalities, state-owned banks with soft budget constraints, restrictions on takeovers). A rules-based approach to intervention has merit, with a bias against (but no bar on) forbearance. Shareholder monitoring is an important adjunct to regulator supervision. Oversight by directors and senior management is crucial.

There are two extreme views, both of them unsatisfactory. One says that banks should be told in detail what to do, watched continuously, and punished for any transgression. The other claims that supervision should be left to shareholder audit and internal monitoring, with the threat of takeover to punish inefficiency. It is far better, Llewellyn argues, to have complementary, flexible external regulation, possibly of the 'contractual' type. Llewellyn sees merit in the recommendations of the 1999 Basel Committee on Banking Supervision, which:

a   emphasise internal risk analysis and control, and market discipline;
b   suggest a role for market-based risk ratings; and
c   strengthen the capital adequacy framework for supervision with extended, revised and improved systems of risk weighting.

Economic growth depends on an efficient financial system, Richard Brealey argues in Chapter 5. Particularly in developing countries, banks play a central role by providing liquidity services to savers and allocating capital to productive uses. Yet their ability to fulfil these functions has been hampered by widespread bank failure, which typically results from a decline in economic activity and sharp falls in asset prices and foreign exchange reserves.

Although banks are not the sole providers of capital, and therefore are not alone in suffering periodic losses, falls in asset prices are generally thought to have more serious consequences if they occur in the banking system rather than elsewhere in the economy. There are three reasons for this view. The first arises from banks' role in the payments system. The second arises because banking crises may restrict credit and accentuate the fall in economic activity. The third comes from the fragility of bank deposits and the costs of monitoring bank solvency. These externalities provide the justification for bank regulation.

There are many ways to protect a bank against failure, but bank equity constitutes a general-purpose buffer against failure from any source. Thus capital requirements have played a central and increasing role in regulation. However, they are effective only if prompt corrective action is taken when capital is becoming exhausted. Capital requirements can trigger a credit crunch when constraints bind, but most G-10 banks, at least, now hold more than the statutory minimum. Riskier banks require more capital.

The international standard for bank capital was set by the Basel Accord. Because the values of bank assets do not evolve smoothly and cannot be observed continuously, banks with risky assets should hold more capital. An important contribution of the Accord was that, in computing capital ratios, the Accord made formal allowance for risk.

The Basel system of credit risk weightings suffers from two weaknesses. First, it focuses on the risk of individual loans and ignores the diversification of the loan portfolio. Second, it applies a broad bush treatment to the classification of loans. The proposed revisions to the Accord will tackle the second weakness, but the diversification problem may prove less tractable. This raises two issues. The first is the need to value bank assets at their true value, and the second is the appropriate level of bank capital. Decisions on the latter question depend on a better understanding of the cost of capital. Bank equity is commonly thought to be very costly, but the source of these costs is unclear.

Confidence in a bank can crumble quickly, and its failure can generate large external costs. This is why Glenn Hoggarth and Farouk Soussa argue, in Chapter 6, that central banks cannot ignore the threat to financial stability posed by a troubled bank.

The financial safety net of regulation, supervision and deposit insurance will prevent some crises and contain others. But the risk of failure cannot be wholly removed, not least because deposit insurance discourages depositor monitoring and the safest types of bank lending.

Honest brokering by the central bank can facilitate and co-ordinate a private sector rescue or takeover of a financial institution in distress. Private sector solutions may require central bank involvement, particularly when competition between financial institutions intensifies.

The central bank is lender of last resort, meeting regular liquidity needs for the market, and occasionally, and temporarily, providing discretionary emergency lending in response to exceptional strains. Inter-bank markets should satisfy normal liquidity demands of an individual bank, backed up by central bank lending on very rare occasions if and when these markets malfunction. While too high a price for official lending may induce gambling for resurrection, risking taxpayers' funds is potentially very costly. Official emergency lending should be limited in size, highly infrequent, on tight terms, collateralised, and not mechanical. An element of ambiguity reduces moral hazard problems, especially when supported by other types of punishment for deficient management.

Current trends to larger, conglomerate and global banks complicate crisis prevention and management practices. This is recognised, in part, in the current Basel proposals that place an increased emphasis on the need for market discipline and supervision of banks' management systems and controls, rather than formulaic capital standards. The importance of timely information sharing and cooperation between central banks and (bank and non-bank) supervisors within and across countries is also recognised. These may, however, need to be enhanced in the future.

International capital movements may damage output, and employment or wages, in the source country, and profit incomes and competitiveness in their destination. Despite these drawbacks, Peter Sinclair and Chang Shu argue, in Chapter 7, that they should in principle increase national income in both countries. International capital migration also provides valuable opportunities for smoothing consumption, diversifying risk and intertemporal trade; and despite the problems they pose for central banks, they accommodate imbalances in the current account of the balance of payments. The presumption of positive net effects on social welfare constitutes a general case against capital controls.

Temporary controls may be helpful in crises, however. From many standpoints inflow controls are preferable to outflow controls, and both tend to outrank the blunt instrument of prohibition. Currency crises may stem from fundamentals (such as inconsistencies between exchange rate and macroeconomic policies), but information disparities and asymmetries, together with mimicry by imperfectly informed investors, play important roles. While this may justify intervention, capital controls have not prevented crises, and their anticipation may provoke them.

A survey of the evidence and literature on capital controls reveals several general insights. First, they tend to be most effective under sound macroeconomic policies. Further, their impact diminishes rapidly, as agents learn how to bypass them. Next, their ability to insulate the domestic economy from financial developments abroad is qualified, and comes at the price of costly distortions. Finally, they are no alternative to wise prudential regulation and prompt corrective action.

The final contribution to this volume, by Alastair Clark, concludes by selecting a group of important policy questions for special scrutiny.

1.3 Twelve questions about financial stability

All contributors to the volume were shown a list of questions about financial stability, which the author of this chapter drew up before we embarked upon our work. Twelve questions came to the fore as our research progressed. Here they are:

1 Can or should central banks have responsibility for financial stability, if regulation of financial firms has passed to another authority? Or is it best to split prudential regulation from business-conduct or consumer-protection regulation, with the former remaining with central banks?

2 Can we learn anything (yet) from the experience of countries where central bank responsibilities (no longer) include bank regulation? Is there (so far) any discernible difference in stability between those countries and others?

3 How could we attempt to measure the (marginal) benefits and costs of central bank actions to promote financial stability? How could we tell if a central bank was doing too much or too little in this regard? What in principle determines the optimum level and character of financial protection by a central bank?

4 Why can't the financial system 'look after itself' – or are there parts of it that can or could?

5 Is 'financial protection' a strict public good, that the market would underprovide, if left to itself, or not provide at all?

6 Does public financial protection make private sector actors significantly more careless, and if so does this matter? Is there a satisfactory and workable practical distinction between systemic and asystemic risk?

7 What are the precise differences, boundaries, and overlaps between monetary policy and operations on the one side, and policy or operations to promote financial stability on the other?

8 In financial markets, is there a trade off between safety and competition? If there is, what determines the ideal point of balance between the two?

9 Does evidence suggest that financial instability is mainly a cause or mainly a consequence of business cycle fluctuations, to the extent that the two are correlated at all?

10 How should a central bank decide when to pull the plug on a troubled financial institution, as opposed to awaiting news, or committing to brokering a rescue?

11   Is the present structure of international monetary and financial institutions appropriate, in the face of globalisation and mounting threats to financial stability?

12   Are there any good reasons for restricting international capital movements? If so, what are they, when do they apply and what form should restriction best take?

Ch 7

The volume does not examine all these questions, and some others are investigated. Nonetheless, many are considered in the pages that follow. Key aspects of questions 1, 2 and 3 are examined in Healey's survey in Chapter 2. In Chapter 3, Goodhart provides important insights, *inter alia*, into question 1. Questions 4, 5 and 6 are all addressed by Llewellyn in Chapter 4. Brealey (Chapter 5) and Hoggarth and Soussa (Chapter 6) throw interesting light, between them, on questions 9, 10 and 11. Sinclair and Shu (Chapter 7) address question 12 directly, and touch upon others. In Chapter 8, on Challenges for the Future, Clark provides some powerful insights on several questions, particularly 11. The two remaining questions, 7 and 8, are considered below in later sections of the present chapter.

1.4   Financial crises and the morbidity of banks

The most obvious symptom of a financial crisis is a bank failure. So it is useful to give a broad indication of financial institutions' survival rates. Each year, on average, about 960 financial firms out of 1,000 survive as independent entities. Thirty-four in a thousand join a larger institution as a result of takeover or merger. Finally, the remaining five or six in a thousand perish and vanish, with uninsured depositors standing to lose some of their funds.

These figures are widely drawn averages. They relate to the past century's experience in Western Europe and North America, much of which is described, for example, in Heffernan (1996) and sources cited therein. The annual mortality hazard faced by a financial institution is, on this showing, less than one-third of that now confronting a person in those countries; financial institutions are more like Galapagos turtles or oak trees in this regard – they appear to have a half-life of about 115 years. If survival is defined more strictly as neither death nor absorption into a larger company, morbidity worsens to give a half-life of some twenty-four years.

Averages such as these conceal large disparities. Clearing banks have somewhat better survival prospects than other financial institutions. In finance, just as in the wider economy, large firms are less prone to death or takeover than smaller ones. Probably the highest mortality rates have been recorded recently for new small banks in the Czech Republic: Mantousek and Taci (2000a, b) show that only two out of nineteen of these institutions, founded after the Velvet Revolution of 1989, had survived the decade to 1999.

Death rates, on broad and narrow definitions, are apt to vary across countries. They also show a very pronounced tendency to cluster in time. The early 1930s witnessed a massive rash of bank closures, especially in the United States, when both nominal bank deposits, and the number of banks, shrank by more than one-third. Severe recessions, and large falls in the prices of equity and real estate, almost invariably accompany increased risks of bank failure. Although cause and effect are hard to identify here, Richard Brealey, in his contribution to the volume (Chapter 5), cites important evidence that demonstrates that downturns in industrial production and equity prices tend to lead banking failures by about three-quarters.

The rate of bank failure also appears to be sensitive to the character of the supervision and regulatory regimes. Tighter supervision and stiffer requirements for reserves and capital should succeed in prolonging a financial institution's expectation of life (but the evidence does not testify to a robust link, as Brealey shows). More intense competition between financial institutions on the other hand – which may result from changes in the regulatory regime – is apt to have the opposite effect. Davis (1999) provides valuable evidence testifying to this, and other concomitants or precipitators of bank failure, in his analysis of macro prudential indicators of financial turbulence. Demirgüç-Kunt and Detragiache (1998a, b) provide further empirical support.[2]

1.5 Competition and safety

The simplest view of financial markets is that they are perfectly competitive. In perfectly competitive markets, all financial institutions would take the prices of their products as given, outside their control. No retail bank could influence the interest rates on its deposits or advances, for example. Profits would vary as market conditions fluctuated, around a level that gave a 'normal' rate of return on capital. Margins and spreads would be narrow, even wafer-thin. Very large numbers of banks, none of them large enough to exert any influence upon prices, should lead to such an outcome.

It would not be necessary to have a large number of banks, however, to achieve theses results. There could be intense competition between just two banks, or even, in the very special conditions of 'perfect contestability',[3] there might be just one incumbent bank, forced by a hypothetical entrant to price its products at cost. Alternatively, there could be just one bank, or more, owned by its customers, and setting its interest rates to maximise their welfare.[4]

At the opposite extreme, we could have monopoly. A single bank, immune from entry, could set its prices at will, presumably to maximise its profits. If it could price-discriminate perfectly in all its markets, and set out to maximise profit, its total volume of activity would resemble that of a perfectly competitive banking industry, although profits would then be very large. Short of perfect price discrimination, both the volume of activity and profits would be somewhat smaller. In comparison with perfect competition, we would see lower activity and larger profit levels. Such an outcome would occur with one firm, but it could arise under other circumstances. There might be two, three or many banks, as long as all of them acted as one and colluded in all their decisions (much as Charles Goodhart considers in Chapter 3, when discussing the segmented financial markets typical of the UK up to the 1970s). The risks of insolvency would be smallest in the case of monopoly, and highest under perfect competition.

Between these extremes lies a huge range of intermediate possibilities, best described as oligopoly. One type of banking oligopoly would see banks as independent quantity-setters in their deposit and loan markets, taking the actions of their competitors as given. This is known as *Cournot* oligopoly. A model of Cournot oligopoly, or strictly speaking oligopsony from the standpoint of deposits, is the most natural starting place for economists thinking about banks.

In an oligopoly satisfying Cournot's assumptions, total deposits and loans will be smaller than under perfect competition, but higher than under (non-price-discriminating) monopoly. Profit and spreads will lie between these two extremes. The critical variable in Cournot oligopoly is the number of banks: output is larger and spreads and profits smaller, the greater the number banks participating in the market. More banks imply more competition, but also, as we shall see, greater risks of financial fragility.

The number of banks is also critical in other circumstances. The more banks there are, the harder it is for them to reach an understanding to limit competition. It is far easier for two banks to collude effectively than three or four. And if banks are characterised by quite intense price competition, but vary in costs, the prices of financial products may tend to gravitate towards the unit costs of the bank with the second-lowest cost. Add another bank, and some incumbents may have to shave their margins further. They could be driven out of business if they fail to reduce their costs to match. Widening access to financial markets (permitting foreign banks to establish themselves in the domestic market, or removing territorial boundaries between financial institutions previously specialised in different markets, for example) will be good for competition but bad for incumbents' profits.

If there were no fixed costs, introducing another firm would bring more extra benefit to banks' customers, in the form of keener prices, than the cost to banks' owners in the form of lower profits. So in that case, the optimum number of banks would be limitless; and free entry would make for perfect competition by driving profits to zero.

In the presence of fixed costs, an equal amount let us say for any firm, the picture changes completely. Free entry would make the number of banks finite. Depositors would have to receive lower interest than the rate the banks could earn on assets, in order to pay for the overhead costs. And the *optimum* number of banks, the number that maximised the sum of customers' welfare and owners' profit, would be smaller still. Free entry would lead to overcrowding: getting rid of a bank or two at this point would typically save more in total costs than the accompanying sacrifice in consumer welfare. The reason for this is, at this point, the departure of one bank would raise the sum of all banks' profits by more than it would reduce the surplus of banks' customers. The deterioration in depositors' interest would be very small, in comparison to the gain in the profits earned by the owners of all the banks taken together.

This finding about Cournot oligopoly, which can easily be extended to banks, is due to Mankiw and Whinston (1986). The same result is often (but not invariably) encountered under another market form intermediate between perfect competition and monopoly. This is monopolistic competition, which arises when the characteristics of banks' products differ, say by location.[5] The fact that the number of firms is socially excessive under Cournot oligopoly with free entry follows for sure in tranquil conditions, when financial markets are not subject to random shocks. It is displayed even more forcefully in a stochastic environment, when banks' fixed costs are liable to random movement, for example; furthermore, Bolton and Freixas (2000) show that it will be the riskiest borrowers that opt for bank loans, as opposed to equity or debentures (bonds), for external finance.

In a simple case, the optimum number of firms plus one equals the number of firms under free entry, plus one, raised to the power of two-thirds – so if free entry gave room for eight banks, for example, the social ideal would be just three. With random shocks, and the risk of socially costly insolvency, the ideal number of banks shrinks still further. These arguments are explored in detail, for the Cournot oligopoly case, by Mullineux and Sinclair (2000).

Further light on the trade-off between competition and safety in banking is thrown by the observation that a troubled bank, desperate to survive if it possibly can, will be tempted to take great risks. Failure is an awful prospect, but it really makes no difference how large the bank's debts are in the event of failure. Going bankrupt because net liabilities are £1 is as bad as bankruptcy with net debts of £1 billion. The downside risk is effectively truncated. A large gamble, if successful, could pull the bank off the rocks towards which it may be heading. So, in an instance like this, an extra gamble would be cheap or even free. There is no extra cost to the gambler if it fails, and a very large gain, in the form of survival, if it succeeds.

The damaging social consequences of an incentive to take free bets constitute the key argument for making the punishment fit the crime. A death penalty for minor theft might discourage minor theft, but it will induce some malefactors to substitute into more heinous activities. In adverse circumstances, bankers taking free bets – 'gambling for resurrection', or gambling to survive – may become a much likelier phenomenon as the number of banks increases. This is because profits will fall, and each bank will edge closer to the region where bets for survival become cheap or free. If emergency lending assistance is given to a bank close to the edge, monitoring by those providing it needs to ensure that the aid is not frittered on gambles that could make the financial system less secure, not more.[6]

Technically, the free (cheaper) bets on (near) a bank's survival boundary represent a convexification of returns. An otherwise risk-neutral individual is encouraged to gamble, and the incentive to gamble is stronger, the greater the likelihood of being at the point of kink for returns. The key point here is not just that more banks and greater competition raise the chance that one or more banks might slip into insolvency, but, still more important, that the risk of this is increased because of the greater incentive to take a gamble in this region.

Free bet incentives also qualify the case for deposit insurance: fully insured depositors need no longer worry about where they lodge their funds, so riskier banks prosper at the expense of the taxpayers or shareholders of safer banks, and each bank is itself encouraged to take on more risk too. As Hoggarth and Soussa argue in Chapter 6, free bet incentives raise problems for the lender of last resort as well. They can even affect the regulator, who may share a sick bank's inclination to wait for the chance of better news, and be tempted into forbearance or procrastination.

A banking system with fewer banks may well be a safer one. Yet safety is not everything. Competition brings undoubted benefits. Barriers to entry, official or natural, can act as a screen behind which collusion, inefficiency and unhealthy lending practices flourish. The admission of another bank, a foreign one perhaps, may blow away the cobwebs of cronyism.

There are also growth effects. Most models of endogenous growth ultimately reduce to two fundamental equations linking the rates of growth and real interest.[7] One equation is positive: higher real interest for households that save implies a faster long-run growth rate of consumption and income. The other is often negative: higher real interest rates for corporate borrowers deter innovation and invention. Greater competition between banks narrows the gap between interest rates facing lenders and borrowers, and should therefore make for faster long-run growth.[8]

So policy-makers face an intriguing dilemma. Fewer well-padded banks make for a safer, but growth-stifling financial environment. The faster growth that comes from keener competition among banks makes for a bumpier ride. The agency entrusted with regulation and supervision faces conflicting pressures. At one end, there is the risk of capture by the incumbent banking interest. At the other, the constituencies of borrowers and depositors may take over, forcing narrow interest spreads and imperilling financial stability.[9] Fashions change: in the early days of Britain's privatisations in the 1980s, regulators appointed to oversee utility pricing may have been lenient to profit (Vickers and Yarrow 1988); later, under political pressure, most of them appear to have become much tougher. History might repeat itself in the banking arena.

The complex dilemma of safety versus competition confronting financial regulators is modulated, of course, by BIS capital adequacy and risk arrangements, which are currently under review.[10] Many difficult choices remain. Hellman, Murdock and Stiglitz (2000) show that capital adequacy ratios by themselves will establish Pareto-inefficient outcomes, when interest rates on deposits are determined by unfettered competition between banks. The problem arises because competition and capital adequacy ratios together undermine franchise valuations, and this undoes some of the reduction in the incentive to gamble that higher ratios bring. One instrument that could be valuable here, as Hellman *et al.* show, is a ceiling on deposit interest rates. Furthermore, as Brealey emphasises in Chapter 5, neither regulation, nor the imposition of capital standards, succeeds in *preventing* financial crises.

There are certainly powerful arguments for resolving the safety versus competition dilemma within the confines of a single institution, which might be, but need not be, the central bank itself.

1.6 The links between financial stability policy and monetary policy

One important argument for preserving a financial stability function in a central bank, even when regulation of financial firms passes to another institution, is that monetary and financial stability policy are intertwined.

Monetary policy can have important implications for financial stability; financial stability decisions will also have implications for monetary policy. Some of these links are investigated below. We consider first the effects of monetary policy on financial stability.

If monetary policy is mishandled, inflation may become rapid and volatile. Positive inflation surprises redistribute real wealth from lenders to borrowers contracting in nominal (unindexed) loan instruments. Negative inflation surprises have the opposite effect. The size of this redistribution is greatest when the instruments are at fixed, as opposed to floating, interest. Redistribution in either direction may provoke bankruptcy, with serious implications for the quality and performance of banks' loans. Since inflation surprises, negative and positive, increase with the variance of inflation, and since the variance of inflation appears apt to increase with its speed, these risks are liable to increase with average rate of inflation.

There is also some risk attached to a very tight, sustained monetary policy that pushes inflation to very low, even negative levels. The lower the rate of inflation, the greater the attraction of holding cash in comparison with interest-bearing bank deposits. Any switch away from bank deposits is liable to reduce the profits earned by banks, and particularly so in an oligopolistic setting of the Cournot type described above when the number of banks is given. Reducing banks' profits implies a greater chance, in a stochastic environment, however remote, that one or more banks will sooner or later run into insolvency. At sufficiently modest rates, inflation does not just bring seigniorage gains to the government or the monetary authorities. If imperfectly competitive, the banks tend to share some of this seigniorage as well. Charles Goodhart, in Chapter 3, stresses the fact that tight monetary policy is often associated with high incidences of failures of financial firms.

A third link running from monetary policy to financial stability policy stems from interest rate setting. Above all, monetary policy aims at stabilising inflation, with short-run nominal interest rates now widely accepted as the instrument of choice. Sharp, temporary alterations in short nominal rates may add to uncertainties in financial markets. Particularly when delayed – so that the magnitude (and duration) of the alterations, when they come, is greater than it otherwise could have been – interest rate swings tend to increase the variance of the rate of business failures. This has adverse effects on the balance sheets of banks at times of credit crunch. These effects are greatest when monetary policy is 'too much, too late'. Timely, modest interest responses to inflation surprises can contribute powerfully to long-run financial stability.

So much for the impact of monetary policy upon financial stability. What of the reverse? More effective supervision, to reduce the risks of bank failures, increases confidence in banks' liabilities. Widely defined money demand should go up. This has no persistent effect on the rate of inflation, but the transition to a 'safer' regime of financial control will imply lower equilibrium inflation for any given path of nominal monetary aggregates, as velocity subsides. Put another way, policy decisions that make the banking system look more hazardous could generate a flight from broad money, and exacerbate the rate of inflation in the short run through a variety of mechanisms (not least via the foreign exchange rate). A lender of last resort function, wisely deployed, may also enhance confidence in the liabilities of banks. So its removal could conceivably trigger a transitory burst of inflation in extreme circumstances.

The intense debate between the Banking and Currency Schools in the era of the 1844 Bank of England Act also throws light upon these issues. The Currency School, widely seen as the antecedent of modern monetarists, was alarmed that a Lender of Last Resort mechanism might ultimately endogenise the supply of money. If liquidity is continually pumped into commercial banks at modest rates of interest, the monetary authorities could ultimately lose control over the price level, Currency School adherents argued. Their opponents stressed the case for the central bank to meet the legitimate needs of commerce: acting as Lender of Last

Resort, the monetary authority could stabilise the business cycle, contributing to greater stability in not just the real variables of the macroeconomy, but possibly the nominal variables as well.

On the other hand, financial stability concerns may translate into greater aversion to wobbles in aggregate output relative to wobbles in inflation. Any resulting shift from stabilising the price level to stabilising output is likely to generate greater volatility in inflation, and quite possibly higher average expected and actual rates of inflation as well. Rogoff's (1985) plea for monetary policy to be conducted by a conservative central banker could be compromised if financial stability concerns made the central banker less averse to inflation or inflation swings.

If the central bank has no responsibility for financial stability *per se*, these numerous linkages between financial and monetary policy are liable to be disregarded. Serious conflicts of interest could arise between the central bank and the agency, or agencies, charged with protecting the stability of the financial system. Organising cooperation between distinct institutions is awkward. It becomes progressively harder, if the central bank has shed these functions, as staff turnover effaces old habits of consultation between erstwhile colleagues. Significant delays could ensue, particularly if channels of information are subject to filtering or blockage. Inefficient outcomes might easily result. Those who argue that the central bank should retain some financial stability responsibilities would stress the advantages of internalising, within a single institution, the discussions that relate to these financial–monetary policy links.

These observations do not, however, imply that all aspects of regulation and supervision belong within the central bank.[11] The 'narrow model', with its separation of supervision and regulation from the central bank's core functions, brings the advantage of a clean, sharp delineation of responsibilities between distinct institutions. The fact that countries' institutional arrangements differ so widely in this respect should not be taken to suggest that some are right and others are mistaken. What is best for one country may well be less than best for another.

1.7 Bakers and firefighters

Bread, and those who bake it, are in continuous demand. Firefighters are needed only in emergencies. Monetary policy-makers are like bakers. A continuous watch on macroeconomic and monetary conditions must be kept. Interest rates need to be reset, even if only to be confirmed at unchanged levels, at regular and frequent intervals. Financial stability experts, by contrast, are primarily firefighters. Part of this work involves surveillance, and trying to prevent or contain fires by the building of fireproof structures. This relates to the design of the payments system, minimum capital accords, and – since fires do not respect country borders – the international financial architecture as well. A general oversight of financial conditions needs to be maintained at all times, but really close monitoring and intervention is reserved for financial institutions in serious trouble. Checking that fire extinguishers and alarms are in place and in working order, and that fire breaks and walls and regulations are respected, is an important recurrent task, but fighting fires that break out is the prime responsibility. Even in a large economy, it is not as if little fires are happening much of the time. Fires, especially big fires, are occasional events. And just as the externality of fire damage is the central argument for suspecting that individuals will take inadequate precautions if left to themselves, the web of adverse externalities and risks of contagion in financial crises provides the key case against pure *laissez-faire*. The externalities that go with systemic risk are the principal reason why a central institution is needed to help ensure the stability of the financial system.

While the need for an institution to formulate and operate monetary policy is beyond doubt, some observers are apt to be sceptical about the usefulness of those responsible for maintaining financial stability. When financial stabilisers, if we may call them this, succeed in *preventing* fires, their value is invisible to the naked eye. If they succeed in *containing* a fire, it is hard to establish that the fire would have been worse in their absence. Worse, ill-informed popular opinion seeks scapegoats. Any fire may see them blamed for having, allegedly, allowed it to start in the first place. Like an ailing financial institution, financial stabilisers may be tempted to delay intervention, in the hope that tomorrow brings better news. Rain, or a change in wind direction, might snuff out an incipient fire before any damage is done. The need for timely information sharing between the supervisor and the financial stabiliser, and for prompt corrective action, is stressed in many contributions to the book – and particularly by Hoggarth and Soussa in Chapter 6.

Firefighting is no simple task. Nor is fire-watching. There is a grey area between performing and non-performing loans. Valuing collateral or unquoted assets takes time. The markets for many types of debt are thin. Future debt serviceability is never known. The variances and covariances[12] of returns on all assets are notoriously non-stationary. Brokering an urgent informal auction or rescue of a troubled institution is never straightforward, nor is weighing the benefits and costs of emergency assistance under extreme time pressure, or countering the temptation for lenders to preserve goodwill or stay alive by rolling over suspect debts. All these factors pose real challenges. The value of experienced staff, and the awkward tendency for financial crises to cluster over time, make it very unwise for those in authority in tranquil periods to dispense with their financial firefighters, tempting though that might sometimes be.

Whatever the institutional arrangements a country has established for safeguarding its financial stability, there are powerful practical reasons for not altering them without due cause. There are costs and risks associated with the transition from one regime to another. If a new institution, with some inexperienced personnel, is entrusted with financial stability issues, it may be tempted to rely heavily on the rule-book. New rules are cheap to write, but they are costly to learn, interpret, obey and enforce.[13] In the absence of compelling reasons to the contrary, a country may do better to refine its existing arrangements than to import an alien model to which its particular circumstances are ill-suited. So wherever the firefighters work, alongside the bakers or elsewhere, rehousing them may well not prove advantageous.

1.8   Conclusions

Safeguarding financial stability is a core function of the modern central bank, no less than market operation and the conduct of monetary policy. This is evident from a detailed survey of thirty-seven central banks, drawn from a wide variety of industrial, transition and developing countries. For those central banks that have never acted as regulator or supervisor of financial institutions, and for those that have recently shed these roles, financial stability responsibilities may be shared with other agencies, but the central bank is still very much in the game. This is particularly true in circumstances where bank failure would pose systemic risk. Threats to financial stability may arise from many sources, including excessive competition or overcrowding in the banking sector, misguided or mis-applied regulation or lending to troubled institutions, undue forbearance, and currency crises. Financial stability impinges upon monetary policy and reacts to it. There are therefore powerful arguments for retaining responsibility for both within the central bank.

Notes

1 The author of this chapter thanks co-authors of this volume, Bill Allen, Charles Bean, Alex Bowen, Alastair Clark, Alec Chrystal, Gill Hammond and Gabriel Sterne for very helpful comments on a previous draft.
2 In their contribution to the volume (Chapter 6), Hoggarth and Soussa also stress the argument that central bank involvement in support of troubled finan-cial institutions is liable to become more necessary as competition intensifies.
3 These conditions include: (a) the absence of sunk costs, specific to current operations, which cannot be recouped on exit; (b) no incumbent able to change prices until after consumers have had a chance to switch suppliers; and (c) all firms, incumbents and outsiders alike, with access to the same technology and the same price and quality of inputs. The threat of entry then forces an incum-bent to price at average cost, which will equal marginal cost if average cost is flat. Consumers' costs of switching banks, freedom to reprice almost instanta-neously, the sunk costs of acquiring information and the obstacles to hiring specialised personnel make banking less than perfectly competitive in practice.
4 A firm owned by its customers would seek to maximise their welfare, not their profit income; this should result in prices at marginal cost. Mutual institutions have been long-established in the financial sector, but rarely among market leaders, and current trends are against them.

5   In Salop (1979), for example, free entry leads to twice as many firms as the social ideal.

6   Mitchell (2000) and Aghion, Bolton and Fries (1999) explore some of the implications of these ideas, and the incentives for banks to roll over doubtful loans.

7   For example, Aghion and Howitt (1992, 1998) and Romer (1990).

8   King and Levine (1993) were the first to argue this; see also Fry (1995).

9   Boot and Thakor (2000) show that increased interbank competition must benefit some borrowers, but not necessarily all of them.

10 Richard Brealey, in his contribution to the volume (Chapter 5), has numerous pertinent observations upon them. He commends the proposed adoption of explicit market value accounting as a solution to the problem of forbearance towards suspect loans, but queries popular reasons for opposing an expansion of banks' capital on the ground that it is unclear why equity should be much more expensive than debt.

11 The 'broad model' described by Healey in Chapter 2.

12 Omission of covariances across different risky assets is one of the unfortunate features of the Basel Accord rules as they stand at present; this is one of several reasons why those monitoring financial stability need to do much more than merely check whether these rules are obeyed.

13 As David Llewellyn stresses in his contribution to the Symposium.

2 Financial stability and the central bank

International evidence

Juliette Healey[1]

2.1 Introduction

Safeguarding financial stability is a multi-faceted task that requires action at both the micro and macro level and can involve a number of institutions which share the responsibilities – the central bank, other regulatory and supervisory bodies and the government. While there is much commonality across countries in the financial stability responsibilities of public authorities, the way in which they are assigned to particular public institutions differs considerably. This chapter looks at institutional arrangements for safeguarding financial stability, with a particular focus on the evolving role of central banks in this area.

The principal objective of this chapter is to set out the facts about central bank involvement in financial stability functions in a systematic and concise way, drawing on the responses to a CCBS questionnaire from thirty-seven central banks from industrial, transition and developing countries (see Table 2.1).[2] The wide variety of institutional arrangements suggest that there is no single 'optimal' model. Nevertheless, the responses may shed light on how an effective framework can be developed.

First, we look briefly at the evolution of central bank responsibilities (Section 2.2). This provides the historical context against which we set out the current spectrum of activities that central banks undertake to support and promote financial stability across a diverse range of economies (Section 2.3). One topical issue is whether the efficiency of regulation and supervision of individual institutions may be influenced by the particular institutional structure in which they are conducted. Although it is still most common for the central bank to also be the banking supervisor, over the last decade a number of countries have consolidated supervisory functions, often in an agency (or agencies) outside the central bank. Other countries are planning or considering an institutional reorganisation of financial regulation and supervision along similar lines. As we look at the variety of central bank models in Section 2.3 we highlight the issues that have prompted changes in this area and the different ways in which authorities have responded. One particular aspect of the debate is the implications for

Table 2.1 Countries included in the survey[3]

Industrial	Transitional	Developing
Australia	Bulgaria	Argentina
Canada	Czech Republic	Brazil
Denmark	Estonia	Chile
Finland	Hungary	Cyprus
Hong Kong	Latvia	India
Ireland	Poland	Indonesia
Netherlands	Russia	Malawi
New Zealand	Slovenia	Malaysia
Norway		Malta
Singapore		Mexico
South Korea		Peru
Sweden		South Africa
UK		Sri Lanka
		Thailand
		Uganda
		Zimbabwe

monetary policy and Section 2.4 briefly explores the principal arguments about whether a central bank should carry out regulation and supervision in addition to its monetary policy responsibilities. Included is evidence from our survey and a brief look at whether there is a correlation between the degree to which a central bank may be 'independent' and whether it has responsibility for prudential regulation and supervision. We make some observations about establishing an effective regulatory institutional structure in Section 2.5. The final section provides some brief concluding comments.

2.2   The evolution of responsibilities

Central banks come in all shapes and sizes, and each central bank has developed in its own particular political, economic and cultural context. To understand the role of central banks today, and to contemplate their future, it is useful to track their development. There follows a very brief general description of the evolution of central bank responsibilities with a particular focus on financial stability.[4]

With respect to monetary policy, the main objective of central banks, over the centuries, has been the maintenance of the internal and external value of the currency. However, the interpretation of this objective has changed over time. Under the classical gold standard the objective was cast in terms of metal convertibility. With the gradual erosion of the gold standard throughout the first half of the twentieth century, and its replacement by a pure fiat standard, the objective of central bank policy was recast in terms of price stability (Capie *et al.* 1994). Within this, the framework and the intermediate target may vary considerably.[5] Most, if not all, central banks would agree that monetary stability is one of the most important contributors to financial stability; and conversely, a properly functioning financial system, in particular the banking system, will enhance the transmission and efficacy of monetary policies. Central banks have long recognised that they have a role in maintaining financial stability, which stems from their function in managing the domestic currency liquidity of the commercial banking system. Their role in safeguarding financial stability has evolved as financial systems have developed.

Earlier-established central banks were founded as special *commercial* banks and their changing relationship with other commercial banks has been a key part of the development of their financial stability responsibilities. They were special because they received a charter from government and the role of (principal) banker to the government. In some countries, notably Scandinavia and the Netherlands, these government chartered banks were effectively the only commercial bank in existence when first founded and one of the incentives for their establishment was to encourage the provision of commercial banking services where there previously were none. Other central banks were established for a variety of other reasons. For example, to raise money to fund national wars (e.g. Bank of England in 1694) or to restore monetary stability after wartime expenditures had been funded by excessive issue of government paper currency (e.g. Norges Bank in 1816, Reichsbank in 1876, Danmarks Nationalbank in 1818). At the time of their establishment there was no concept of 'central banking'. So when did these special commercial banks become central banks? Capie *et al.* (1994) apply a functional definition, identifying a central bank as the government's banker, monopoly note issuer and lender of last resort. They found that, strictly speaking, prior to the 1820s none of the institutions then in existence were central banks.

Table 2.2 provides a chronology of central banks established prior to the twentieth century. The table shows their original date of founding and also the decade within which each is identified as becoming a central bank in the modern sense of the term. However, identifying a single significant date in the evolution of an individual central bank is not easy. The earlier central banks gained monopolistic powers, for example over the note issue, often gradually. Also, an institution may have undertaken lender of last resort operations and bank rescues several times before it fully accepted its responsibility as lender of last resort. In the early 1900s, the common, standardised role for the central bank which became generally adopted among all the main industrialised countries included occasional emergency liquidity support to banking institutions, but on an *ad hoc*, co-operative basis without general commitment and without accepting any formal regulatory or supervisory role. Thereafter central banks accepted the role of lender of last resort as a core function. Central banks had also

Table 2.2 Central banking institutions before 1900†

Bank	Founded	Lender of last resort (decade)
Sverige Riksbank	1668	1890
Bank of England	1694	1870
Banque de France	1800	1880
Bank of Finland	1811	1890
Nederlandsche Bank	1814	1870
Austrian National Bank	1816	1870
Norges Bank	1816	1890
Danmarks Nationalbank	1818	1880
Banco de Portugal	1846	1870
Belgian National Bank	1850	1850
Banco de Espana	1874	1910
Reichsbank	1876	1880
Bank of Japan	1882	1880
Banca D'Italia	1893	1880

† The table excludes central banking institutions of the Netherlands Antilles (est. 1828), Indonesia (1828), Bulgaria (1879), Romania (1880) and Serbia (1883).
Source: Capie *et al.* (1994).

become the bankers' banker and were gradually withdrawing from commercial activities. This helped avoid conflicts of interest and shifted the relationship between central banks and commercial banks from a competitive, often adversarial, relationship towards acceptance of the central bank as the guardian of the financial system as a whole.

By the beginning of the twentieth century, there were eighteen institutions and, using Capie *et al.*'s functional definition, all of them were central banks. As the concept gained popularity and many previously colonial countries gained independence, the numbers of central banks burgeoned. With the establishment of numerous independent states in the early 1990s the numbers have continued to rise. Today we have more central banks than ever before. Chart 2.1 shows the growth in the number of central banks over the last century.

The involvement of central banks in their lender of last resort role and monetary policy objectives has led central banks to be intrinsically interested in the stability and general health of the financial system. Concerns over the moral hazard which might result from emergency assistance and the potential costs of financial instability[6] in turn led central banks to take a closer interest in the behaviour of individual banks. Often, but not always, this resulted in the central bank supervising and, if necessary, regulating the banking system. While in nearly all cases regulation and the accompanying supervision is the consequence of crises, the allocation of those responsibilities and the way in which they have evolved in various countries differs markedly.

For example, in the UK, for many years the Bank of England had no

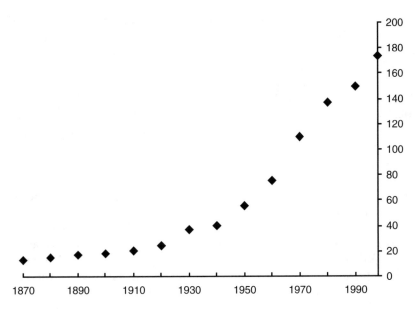

Chart 2.1 The number of central banks 1870–2000

formal powers. The Bank had commercial leverage, via its market operations and supervised, without statute, the accepting and discount houses before the clearing banks. The Governor's eyebrows were famous for wielding the Bank's considerable influence. But it was not until 1979, following the secondary banking crisis, that the Bank was first given statutory responsibilities for the regulation and supervision of banks and, for the first time, a mandate to protect depositors. In contrast, Mexico established a regulatory system long before there was a central bank. An 1897 statute established the Ministry of Finance as the body responsible for banking supervision while the central bank was not created until 1925. In the USA, the creation of the Federal Reserve System in 1913 was prompted by frequent banking panics and a particularly severe crisis in 1907. From the very beginning the Fed's functions included the regulation and supervision of member banks.

Certain other central banks, notably the Scandinavian central banks (Finland, Denmark, Sweden, Norway), some Latin American central banks (Chile, Mexico, Peru) and the Canadian central bank have never been responsible for prudential banking regulation or supervision. Typically in these countries the government carried out some form of supervision initially before delegating responsibility to a separate agency.

Financial supervision and regulation were not part of early central banking but, in common with many other forms of state intervention (such as the nationalisation of previously privately owned central banks), they came in the more collectivist years after 1939. The reliance on self-regulation versus formal supervision depended very much on the state of the domestic banking system. The more cartelised and protected the banking system, the easier it was to maintain stability with self-regulation (Capie *et al.* 1994).

Over the last few decades competition, enhanced by information technology, and driven on by monetary and financial instability and de-regulation, has changed the financial landscape. Increasingly, concerns about financial stability have gained prominence, largely as a result of the growing number, breadth and severity of bouts of financial distress. As the financial environment changes it is appropriate that policy-makers review current arrangements to determine what changes should be made. One such area is that of institutional structure and how it can contribute to effective and efficient regulation and supervision.

One of the most noticeable changes over the last decade or so has been the move to consolidate financial supervision in a separate agency – Norway (1986), Canada (1987), Denmark (1988), Sweden (1991) and most recently Hungary (April 2000) – and in some cases this involved a transfer of responsibilities out of the central bank, e.g. Australia (1998), UK (1998), Japan (1999), Korea (1998), Iceland (1999). Others are in the process of implementing such changes – Latvia is setting up a consolidated supervisory agency by mid-2001 and Indonesia plans to establish an independent supervisory board by the end of 2002. Yet more countries, such as Cyprus, Estonia, Ireland, Israel, Malta and South Africa, are known to be considering a similar move (See Table 2.6 for a summary). In the next section we set out the financial stability activities of central banks from the thirty-seven survey countries plus the USA and Japan, and some of the key issues in deciding whether to integrate financial supervision in a separate agency outside the central bank.

2.3   The current spectrum of central bank financial stability activities

To safeguard financial stability, the authorities need to have adequate and timely information about behaviour and leverage on it. Central banks will typically have both direct and indirect access to information and influence, depending on their particular institutional context. We also need to keep in mind that what happens in practice may be different from the formal arrangements. Central banks may have considerable influence even in areas where they have few or no powers. Whatever the institutional model employed, the central bank's objective should be to maximise information and influence subject to achieving an optimal balance between safety and competition in the financial sector.[7]

As stated at the outset, safeguarding financial stability is a multi-faceted task that requires action at both the micro and macro level. So what range of levers are at the disposal of central banks? For central banks the macro-economic levers are the instruments of monetary policy. However, the provision of a safety net for depositors and prudential controls over banks may also have macroeconomic implications, as well as constituting part of the central bank's armoury of micro levers. Another lever might be the publication of macroprudential assessments which alert financial players to incipient risks. In addition, central banks may wish to influence institutions, markets and infrastructures. The levers related to these micro areas that are covered by our survey relate primarily to infrastructure and institutions; the payment and settlement systems, elements of the provision of a safety net for depositors and procedures for resolving crises, the regulation and supervision of individual institutions and the formulation of uniform accounting conventions. There are, of course, additional micro level activities in which some central banks may be directly involved that are not specifically covered here. Examples include aspects of the legal framework (insolvency, company, contract law, etc.), financial market surveillance and macroprudential assessments. All these levers can be used both to prevent financial instability and to manage it once it emerges.

The rest of this section is divided into small parts. In Section 2.3.1 we look at the range of 'models' of central banks and how to interpret the main tables. We look briefly at financial stability mandates in Section 2.3.1.1, payment and settlement systems in Section 2.3.1.2, safety net provision/crisis resolution (under headings of emergency liquidity assistance (ELA), honest brokering and deposit protection schemes) in Section 2.3.1.3, and finally regulation and supervision of individual institutions in Section 2.3.1.4.

2.3.1 Involvement in financial stability functions: evidence across countries

Tables 2.3, 2.4 and 2.5 summarise a spectrum of financial stability 'activities' for thirty-seven central banks from industrial, transition and developing economies respectively, based on responses to a questionnaire circulated in February 2000 and updated in November 2000. The thick black vertical line in each table segregates countries whose central banks exercise prudential supervisory functions to the left, from those that do not to the right. The tables suggest that, very roughly, countries can be divided into three basic models. The 'narrow' model central bank focuses on the overall stability of the financial system, including core financial stability functions such as payment system oversight, some payments processing and occasional emergency liquidity assistance (Australia, Canada, Hungary, the Nordic countries and the UK). Under this model the remaining financial stability functions listed are carried out by other government entities or sometimes private entities, for example, deposit insurance. An 'intermediate' model includes the core functions plus some role in crisis resolution, but excludes supervision and regulation of individual financial institutions (a number of the industrial countries and Latin American countries). At the other end of the spectrum, the 'broad' model central bank includes the core functions plus various safety net/crisis resolution functions as well as some role, if not the sole responsibility, for the regulation and supervision of banks and some non-bank financial institutions. The majority of transition and developing country central banks are, for instance, of the broad model.

INTERPRETING THE TABLES

While it is useful to identify general structures across economies and geographic areas, in presenting the results for the thirty-seven central banks we are very conscious of what might be termed an 'interpretation spread' in the various activities listed. Terms and functions may be interpreted differently by different central banks. Also, the questionnaire was simplistic in that it required either a tick or a cross to indicate whether or not the central bank is involved in that function. However, in practice, in each 'financial stability function' there is a range of possible degrees of involvement. For example, one central bank may be the sole agency responsible for prudential supervision while another central bank may share responsibility with another agency, and yet both will show a tick on the table for that function.

We asked each respondent to complete the table indicating which functions were *currently* or *potentially* performed by the central bank. As well as overlap in functions with other agencies, there may be an element of speculation, for example, where a central bank has a facility that has in fact never been used (one or more forms of emergency liquidity assistance) or a historic role that may not be called upon in the future, but which the central bank is happy to perform if required (e.g. honest brokering).

In some functions, the central bank's role may not be precisely defined: practice may be evolving; the central bank may advise, or exercise influence upon policies set by government or other agencies, or may be called upon to assist in their implementation; and in some instances the central bank may be given wider discretion than in others. For example, central banks, even if not directly involved in the formulation of accounting rules, are often invited to offer their views.

INDUSTRIAL ECONOMIES

Among the industrial economies included in Table 2.3 all three models are represented. Australia, Canada, Denmark, Finland, Norway, Sweden and the UK can be roughly described as narrow model central banks,[8] while South Korea follows the intermediate model and Ireland, the Netherlands, Hong Kong and Singapore the broad model.

Both Bulgaria and Estonia currently operate currency boards, which do not allow for an independent monetary policy or emergency liquidity assistance except in extreme circumstances. All of the transition central banks shown in Table 2.4, apart from Hungary, are the primary prudential regulator and supervisor for banks. Otherwise, the functional responsibilities of the transition countries are very similar and, except for Hungary which probably belongs to the narrow model, fall largely into the broad model category despite their narrow range of crisis management functions.

DEVELOPING ECONOMIES

Of the developing countries shown in Table 2.5, apart from Chile, Peru and Mexico, where the central banks have never had responsibility for prudential regulation and supervision, all follow a broad model. However, there is much more variation in the safety net/crisis resolution activities and the scope of their regulatory and supervisory responsibilities than there is among transition countries.

2.3.1.1   *Financial stability mandates*

While there appears to be widespread intellectual consensus about the monetary policy objectives which central banks should pursue, it is more difficult to define a measurable objective for financial stability. Not surprisingly, there is also less consensus about the means by which central banks should pursue their financial stability 'objectives', than there is over their monetary policy responsibilities.

In our survey, all but one of the respondent central banks had some responsibility for financial stability.[9] Generally, the legal basis lies in interpretations of central bank laws and/or in banking laws. However, there are large differences in the breadth and specificity of the mandate.

Where central banks have a role in the regulation and supervision of individual institutions, this is usually specified by statute, but in some cases central banks carry out these functions as a delegated authority (Malta, Thailand). Elsewhere, the clarity of the mandate varies. In a number of cases the legal provisions explicitly refer to responsibility for promoting 'financial system stability' (UK, Finland). In other cases the responsibility is inferred from phrases such as promoting 'a sound financial structure' (Singapore). In the majority of developing and transition economies, the statutory mandate for central banks does no more than specify the regulatory and supervisory function, although in a few countries there is also a specific remit to 'safeguard the smooth functioning of the payment system' (Uganda, Zimbabwe, Bulgaria, Russia). In some countries where the central bank does not carry out prudential supervision, the statute may specify responsibility for ensuring the smooth and/or efficient functioning

Table 2.3 Industrial economies: degree of central bank involvement in financial stability 'functions'

Financial stability function	Description	Singapore	Netherlands	Ireland	Hong Kong	New Zealand	Finland	Denmark	Sweden	Canada	South Korea	Australia	Norway	UK
Payments System Services	Some or all of: Currency distribution and provision of settlement balances, electronic payments, cheque clearing and general oversight of payments system.	✓	✓	✓	✓	✓	✓	✓	✓	✓	✓	✓	✓	✓
Safety net provision/crises resolution														
Emergency liquidity assistance to the market[1]	Provision of liquidity to the money markets during a crisis.	✓[2]	✓[1]	✓[1]	✓	✓	✓[1]	✓	✓	✓	✓	✓	✓	✓
Emergency liquidity assistance to depositories	Direct lending to individual illiquid depositories.	✓	✓	✓	✓	✓	✓	✓	✓	✓	✓	✓	✓	✓
Emergency solvency assistance to depositories	Direct lending to individual insolvent depositories.	✗	✗	✗	✗	✗	✗	✗	✗	✗	✗	✗	✗	✗
Emergency liquidity assistance to non-depositories	Direct lending to individual illiquid non-depository institutions.	✗	✗	✗	✗	✓	✗	✓	✓[9]	✗	✓	✓[9]	✓	✗
Emergency solvency assistance to non-depositories	Direct lending to individual insolvent non-depository institutions.	✗	✗	✗	✗	✗	✗	✗	✗	✗	✗	✗	✗	✗
Honest brokering	Facilitating or organising private sector solutions to problem situations.	✓	✓	✓	✓	✓	✓[7]	✓	✓[7]	✓[7]	✓	✓[7]	✓	✗
Resolution	Conducts, authorises or supervises sales of assets and other transactions in resolving failed institutions.	✓	✓	✗	✗	✗	✗	✗	✗	✗	✗	✗	?	?
Legal	Resolves conflicting legal claims among creditors to failed institutions.	✗	✗	✗	✗	✗	✗	✗	✗	✗	✗	✓[7]	✓[7]	✗[7]
Deposit insurance	Insures deposits or other household financial assets.	✓[3]	✗	✗	✗	✗	✗	✗	✗	✗	✗	✗	✗	✗

Regulation and supervision

Bank regulation	Writes capital and other general prudential regulations that banks (and other deposit-taking institutions) must adhere to.	✓	✓	✓	✓	✗	✗	✗	✗	✗	✗
Bank supervision	Examines banks to ensure compliance with regulation.	✓	✓	✓	✓	✗[6]	✗	✗	✗	✗	✗
Bank business code of conduct	Writes, or monitors banks' compliance with, business codes of conduct	✓	✓	✓	✗	✗	✗	✗	✗	✗	✗
Non-bank financial regulation	Writes capital and other general prudential regulations that non-banks must adhere to.	✓	✓[4]	✓[5]	✗	✗	✗	✗	✗	✗	✗
Non-bank financial supervision	Examines non-banks (although not necessarily all) to ensure compliance with regulation.	✓	✓[4]	✓[5]	✗	✗	✗	✗	✗	✗	✗
Non-bank business code of conduct	Writes, or monitors non-banks' compliance with, business codes of conduct	✓	✓[4]	✓[5]	✗	✗	✗	✗	✗	✗	✗
Chartering and closure	Provides authority by which a banking entity is created and closed.	✓	✓	✓	✓	✗	✗	✗	✗	✗	✗
Accounting standards	Establishes/participates in establishing uniform accounting conventions.	✓	✓	✗	✗	✗	✗	✗	✗	✗	✗

Notes:

1 For Euro-Zone countries, in the context of Euro-system co-ordination.
2 The MAS will assess the situation should it arise. Systemic risk is not an unconditional call on emergency liquidity assistance.
3 The deposit insurance scheme has been set up by the banking sector. The central bank is responsible for implementation.
4 De Nederlandsche Bank is also responsible for investment institutions and exchange offices, but not insurance or securities sector.
5 Excluding insurance companies only.
6 The Reserve Bank is the banking supervisory agency but in 1996 introduced a regime based on disclosure and market discipline. The RBNZ does not conduct on-site inspections as a matter of course but has the power to require independent reports on a bank. Directors of institutions are primarily responsible for ensuring compliance with regulation and are required to provide regular attestations on compliance.
7 Most likely to be carried out by the supervisory authority or the deposit insurance agency but the central bank might assist, particularly in systemic circumstances.
8 The Bank of Korea may require the supervisory agency to examine banking institutions and to accept the participation of central bank staff on joint bank examinations.
9 In principle, emergency liquidity support is available to any institution supervised by the Finansinspektionen or APRA, respectively, provided the institution is solvent and failure to make its payments poses a threat to the stability of the financial system, and there is a need to act expeditiously.

Table 2.4 Transition economies: degree of central bank involvement in financial stability 'functions'

Financial stability function	Description	Bulgaria[1]	Estonia[1]	Czech Rpblc	Poland	Slovenia	Latvia	Russia	Hungary
Payments System Services	Some or all of: Currency distribution and provision of settlement balances, electronic payments, cheque clearing and general oversight of payments system.	✓	✓	✓	✓	✓	✓	✓	✓
Safety net provision/crises resolution									
Emergency liquidity assistance to the market	Provision of liquidity to the money markets during a crisis.	✗	✗	✓	✓	✓	✓	✓	✓
Emergency liquidity assistance to depositories	Direct lending to individual illiquid depositories.	✗	✗	✓	✓	✓	✓	✓	✓
Emergency solvency assistance to depositories	Direct lending to individual insolvent depositories.	✗	✗	✗	✗	✗	✗	✗	✗
Emergency liquidity assistance to non-depositories	Direct lending to individual illiquid non-depository institutions.	✗	✗	✗	✗	✗	✗	✗	✗
Emergency solvency assistance to non-depositories	Direct lending to individual insolvent non-depository institutions.	✗	✗	✗	✗	✗	✗	✗	✗
Honest brokering	Facilitating or organising private sector solutions to problem situations.	✗	✗	✗	✗	✗	✗	✗	✗
Resolution	Conducts, authorises or supervises sales of assets and other transactions in resolving failed institutions.	✗	✓[2]	✗	✗	✗	✗	✗	✗
Legal	Resolves conflicting legal claims among creditors to failed institutions.	✗	✗	✗	✗	✗	✗	✗	✗
Deposit insurance	Insures deposits or other household financial assets.	✗	✗	✗	✗	✓[3]	✗	✗	✗

Regulation and supervision

Bank regulation	Writes capital and other general prudential regulations that banks (and other deposit-taking institutions) must adhere to.	✓	✓	✓	✓	✓	✓[5]	✗
Bank supervision	Examines banks to ensure compliance with regulation.	✓	✓	✓	✓	✓	✓[5]	✗[6]
Bank business code of conduct	Writes, or monitors banks' compliance with, business codes of conduct.	✓	✓	✗	✗	✓	✓	✗
Non-bank financial regulation	Writes capital and other general prudential regulations that non-banks must adhere to.	✗	✗	✗	✗	✗	✓	✗
Non-bank financial supervision	Examines non-banks (although not necessarily all) to ensure compliance with regulation.	✗	✗	✗	✗	✗[4]	✗	✗[6]
Non-bank business code of conduct	Writes, or monitors non-banks' compliance with, business codes of conduct.	✗	✗	✗	✗	✗[4]	✗	✗
Chartering and closure	Provides authority by which a banking entity is created and closed.	✓	✓	✓	✓	✓	✓	✓[7]
Accounting standards	Establishes/participates in establishing uniform accounting conventions.	✓	✓	✓	✓	✓	✓	✗

Notes:
1 Bulgaria and Estonia currently operate currency boards which prohibits the lender of last resort function except in the most extreme circumstances.
2 Limited role, primarily stipulated in the Act on Banks 1992.
3 A deposit guarantee scheme, administered by the Bank of Slovenia will start operating on 1 January 2001.
4 However, the Bank of Slovenia supervises foreign exchange offices and monitors their compliance with business codes of conduct.
5 Including non-bank credit institutions.
6 Limited to legal regulations specified in the Central Bank Act and National Bank of Hungary decrees on money circulation, foreign exchange, data supply and minimum reserves (credit institutions).
7 The NBH issues licences for exercising certain financial services and is involved, with the Hungarian Financial Supervisory Authority, in the issuance and withdrawals of other licences.

Table 2.5 Developing economies: degree of central bank involvement in financial stability 'functions'

Financial stability function	Description	Malaya	Malta	India	Sri Lanka	Uganda	Malawi	Argentina	Brazil	South Africa	Thailand	Zimbabwe	Cyprus	Indonesia	Mexico	Chile	Peru
Payments System Services	Some or all of: Currency distribution and provision of settlement balances, electronic payments, cheque clearing and general oversight of payments system.	✓	✓	✓	✓	✓	✓	✓	✓	✓	✓	✓	✓	✓	✓	✓	✓
Safety net provision/crises resolution																	
Emergency liquidity assistance to the market	Provision of liquidity to the money markets during a crisis.	✓[1]	✓	✓	✓	✓	✓	✓[5]	✓	✓	✓	✓	✓	✓	✓	✓	✓[13]
Emergency liquidity assistance to depositories	Direct lending to individual illiquid depositories.	✓[1]	✓[1]	✓	✓	✓	✓	✓[5]	✓	✓	✓	✓	✓	?✗	✓	✓	✓[13]
Emergency solvency assistance to depositories	Direct lending to individual insolvent depositories.	✗	✗	✗	✗	✗	✗	✗	✗	✗	✗	✗	✗	✗	✗	✓[10]	✗
Emergency liquidity assistance to non-depositories	Direct lending to individual illiquid non-depository institutions.	✗	✓	✓[3]	✗	✗	✗	✗	✗	✗	✗	✗	✗	✗	✗	✗	✗
Emergency solvency assistance to non-depositories	Direct lending to individual insolvent non-depository institutions.	✗	✗	✗	✗	✗	✗	✗	✗	✗	✗	✗	✗	✗	✗	✗	✗
Honest brokering	Facilitating or organising private sector solutions to problem situations.	✓	✓	✓	✓	✓	✓	✓	✓	✓	✓	✓	✓	✓	?	✗	✗
Resolution	Conducts, authorises or supervises sales of assets and other transactions in resolving failed institutions.	✓	✓	✗	✓	✓	✓	✓	✓	✓	✗	✗	✗	✗	✗	✗	✗
Legal	Resolves conflicting legal claims among creditors to failed institutions.	✗	✗	✓	✓	✓	✓	✓	✓	✓	✓	✓	✓	✓	✗	✗	✗
Deposit insurance	Insures deposits or other household financial assets.	✗	✗	✓	✓	✓	✓	✓	✓	✗	✓	✗	✓	✓	✗	✓	✗

Regulation and supervision

Bank regulation	Writes capital and other general prudential regulations that banks (and other deposit-taking institutions) must adhere to.	✓	✓	✓	✓	✓	✓	✓[6]	✓[7]	✓[8]	✓	✓	✓	✓	X[9]	X[11]	X
Bank supervision	Examines banks to ensure compliance with regulation.	✓	✓	✓	✓	✓	✓	✓[6]	✓[7]	✓[8]	✓	✓	✓	✓	X[9]	X	X
Bank business code of conduct	Writes, or monitors banks' compliance with, business codes of conduct.	✓	✓	✓	✓	X	X	✓	✓[7]	X	✓	X	X	X	X[9]	X	X
Non-bank financial regulation	Writes capital and other general prudential regulations that non-banks must adhere to.	✓	✓[2]	✓[4]	✓[4]	✓	X	✓	X	X	X	X	X	X	X[9]	X[12]	X
Non-bank financial supervision	Examines non-banks (although not necessarily all) to ensure compliance with regulation.	✓	✓[2]	✓[4]	✓[4]	✓	X	✓	X	X	X	X	X	X	X[9]	X	X
Non-bank business code of conduct	Writes, or monitors non-banks' compliance with, business codes of conduct.	✓	✓[2]	✓[4]	✓	✓	X	✓	X	X	X	X	X	X	X[9]	X	X
Chartering and closure	Provides authority by which a banking entity is created and closed.	✓	✓	✓	✓	✓	✓	✓	✓	✓	✓	X	✓	✓	X	X	X
Accounting standards	Establishes/participates in establishing uniform accounting conventions.	✓	X	✓	✓	X	✓	✓	✓	✓	✓	X	✓	✓	X	X	X

Notes:
1 Subject to the prior approval of the Minister of Finance.
2 Excluding investment services, insurance companies and offshore banks.
3 Primary dealers in domestic money markets.
4 Development finance companies and non-bank financial companies (see also Box 2.5 on India).
5 Within the terms set out in the Convertibility Law (which sets out Argentina's currency board regime). The central bank may inject liquidity into the banking system in a variety of ways; 20 per cent of the deposit base in the form of liquidity requirements, 10 per cent excess reserves above the Convertibility Law and 8 per cent of the deposit base from a contingent liquidity facility with international banks. Any additional amounts would have to be funded by the Treasury.
6 Including non-bank deposit-taking institutions.
7 Including Consortium Management Companies.
8 Including certain Financial Co-operatives.
9 The Banco de México regulates and supervises financial market activities only. Capital and other prudential regulation and supervision is carried out by other supervisory agencies.
10 As part of the crises management process set out in the General Law on Banks, if necessary, to cover the 100 per cent central bank guarantee on demand deposits.
11 Prudential regulation and supervision is carried out by the SBFI. However, the Banco Central de Chile can determine limits for the asset liabilities risks exposures.
12 The Banco Central de Chile determines the portfolio limits for the Pension Funds Administrators.
13 According to the central bank law, credits to commercial banks are only for monetary regulation. The central bank should not be involved in bailout programs.

of the payment system and/or responsibility to monitor developments in the money, credit and foreign exchange markets (Norway, Sweden, Chile, Hungary). In many countries the objective and role of the central bank can be inferred from the law; for example, phrases such as 'facilitate payment transactions' and 'provision of services to support financial transactions' are interpreted to give the central bank responsibility for the oversight of payment and settlement systems. In some cases there are separate statutes covering payment and settlement systems which give the central bank very detailed and explicit responsibilities (Australia, Canada, Norway). There appears to be a trend in recent legislation to specify a central bank's responsibility for the oversight of payment and settlement systems more clearly, reflecting increasing importance of payment and settlement systems in ensuring overall financial stability (and the efficacy of monetary policy).

For members of the European System of Central Banks (ESCB) the financial stability mandate is included in Article 3.3 of the ESCB statutes: 'In accordance with Article 105(5) of this Treaty, the ESCB shall contribute to the smooth conduct of policies pursued by the competent authorities relating to the prudential supervision of credit institutions and the stability of the financial system.' The institutional responsibility for prudential regulation and supervision is left to national discretion and varies across member countries.

While the scope of mandates varies, practically all central banks consider the promotion of 'systemic stability' and the stability of payment and settlement systems as part of their core mandate.

2.3.1.2 Payment and settlement systems

Not surprisingly, all central banks responding to the survey say that they have a role in the oversight of key payment and settlement systems, whether or not their statutes give them an explicit mandate. The reduction of risk and the promotion of efficiency of key payment and settlement systems are important means of preventing financial instability and helping to contain it when it arises. Central bank involvement is greatest in the 'core' inter-bank large value funds transfer systems, which central banks in many cases own or operate and whose risk-management features they can strongly influence or control. While all central banks have an oversight role, the degree of operational involvement differs widely, largely reflecting the development of their financial systems.

In *industrial* economies some central banks have increasingly withdrawn from operational involvement in payment and settlement systems to focus on ensuring the maintenance of an effective service and protection against systemic financial risk.[10] For example, Fry et al. (1999), found that for industrial countries, operational involvement did not fully reflect strong formal oversight responsibilities, even in the large value transfer systems. In some countries, such as the UK, the motivation has partly reflected broader public policy principles – that the markets are most likely to provide the optimal solution.

In general, the oversight responsibilities of central banks in *transition* and *developing* economies tend to be more formal than in industrial economies, either under the authority of the central bank law and/or banking laws. Not surprisingly, there is considerably more central bank ownership and operational involvement in key systems in transition and developing countries than in industrial countries. Fry *et al.* (1999) show that around 60 per cent of central banks in industrial countries own or part-own their country's Real Time Gross Settlement (RTGS) systems, compared with 100 per cent in transition and developing countries. Similarly, 50 per cent of deferred net settlement systems were entirely privately owned in industrial countries, while over 80 per cent were owned or part-owned by their central banks in transition and developing countries.

These differences are not surprising given the relative development of financial systems. In particular, transition countries have been faced with the challenge of building new payment systems and developing competitive market-based financial sectors. Although the starting point may be different in developing countries, the challenges may also be large if the financial sector is uncompetitive and dominated by state-owned banks. The commercial banking sector may not have the resources, skills or incentives to develop new payment and settlement systems on their own. Given their concerns to reduce risk and promote the efficiency of a country's payment system it is not surprising if central banks in both transition and developing countries are likely to play a prominent role in the development of all systems. As financial sectors and market forces develop, central banks may be able to withdraw gradually.

There is no obvious optimal model for the division of responsibilities for payments systems between the authorities and the private sector. However, as the pace of technological innovation continues and the demand for cross-border services grows, the role of the private sector may grow as the provision of services becomes more cost effective and incentives for private sector involvement increase.[11] What is clearly core is the position of settlement bank services to the banking system, reflecting the special role of central bank money. This role gives central banks a direct interest in the stability, integrity and effectiveness of payment systems and the nature, extent and distribution of payment system credit and liquidity risks.

2.3.1.3   Safety net provision/crisis resolution

The roles of lender of last resort and crisis manager are discussed in Chapter 5 in this volume. They do not, therefore, require detailed treatment here. However, there are several interesting comparisons that come out of Tables 2.3–2.5.

EMERGENCY LIQUIDITY ASSISTANCE (ELA)

Nearly all central banks accept the possibility of providing emergency liquidity assistance to the market or to individual institutions where failure would lead to systemic effects. There are three exceptions, shown on Tables 2.4 and 2.5 – Bulgaria and Estonia operate currency boards which inhibit last-resort lending and Peru's central bank is restricted to monetary regulation, specifically excluding rescues.

Nearly all central banks do not, in principle, lend to insolvent institutions. However, a liquidity problem may become a solvency problem, particularly in a severe crisis. As a result, central banks sometimes find themselves in the position of having provided emergency solvency assistance even if that was not the intention. There may also be circumstances in which it is thought desirable to extend emergency assistance to an institution which is insolvent, for example to ensure that deposits can be repaid. In such cases the central bank may come under pressure to provide assistance, although usually the government would provide the funding or a guarantee. This is most likely in financial systems which include state-owned banks. In some countries that have experienced a severe and widespread crisis, special restructuring agencies have been created which have taken on some of the central banks' traditional roles in crisis resolution, e.g. Mexico. Among our survey countries, only the Bank of Chile is obliged, under the crisis management process laid out by the General Law on Banks, to provide assistance if the institution's 'technical reserves' are insufficient, to cover the 100 per cent central bank guarantee on demand deposits. However, the Bank of Chile then has first call on the remaining assets of the institution, and since term deposits are only protected to 90 per cent up to US$300, it is other creditors, rather than the central bank, who will probably bear the burden of any losses.

The tables also highlight that there are some central banks which recognise the possibility, at least in principle, of *providing emergency liquidity assistance to non-depository institutions* (Australia, Denmark, India, Malta, New Zealand, Norway, South Korea and Sweden). In the case of India and Malta it is likely that the non-depositories would only be those institutions subject to the regulation and supervision of the central banks. However, this group of central banks is clearly dominated by industrial countries where the growth of financial conglomerates has prompted the integration of regulation and supervision of financial, both depository and non-depository, institutions (Australia, Denmark, Norway, South Korea and Sweden). In some cases the recognition of the possibility of providing ELA to non-banks reflects a formal arrangement, either set out in statute (Norway, South Korea)[12] or public policy statements (Australia).[13] However, *in practice*, ELA to non-banks is less likely than for banks because they are less likely to be systemic and/or illiquid.[14]

Other differences that emerge from Table 2.3 include the fact that central banks who are members of the Euro area operate under a co-ordinated framework, e.g. Finland, Ireland and Netherlands. In a financial crisis where the need to provide lender of last resort facilities had to be considered, the main guiding principles would be:

- the appropriateness of the provision of emergency liquidity assistance is primarily a national responsibility;
- the associated costs and risk of such a funding should be borne at the national level; and
- mechanisms ensuring an adequate flow of information are in place so that 1) any potential liquidity impact can be managed in a way consistent with the maintenance of the appropriate Euro area monetary policy stance, and 2) any cross-border implications can be dealt with by the competent authorities.

HONEST BROKERING

Most central banks are willing to perform the role of 'honest broker' by facilitating a private sector solution to a problem situation. A private sector solution is usually preferred to official assistance as it carries less risk of moral hazard. There are, however, differences in practice across countries. Most noticeable is the fact that none of the transition central banks shown in Table 2.4 perform the role of 'honest broker'. In these countries the view is that it is for shareholders (including the state, where it is a shareholder) to find potential investors, although the central bank may have an advisory role. Another noticeable difference is a shift in countries that have established an integrated supervisory agency outside of the central bank. In most (if not all) of these countries, it is likely that either the supervisory authority, the deposit insurance agency, or the central bank could fulfil the 'honest broker' role, depending on the circumstances.

DEPOSIT PROTECTION SCHEMES

While the provision of deposit insurance schemes around the world has increased, the desirability of deposit insurance remains a matter of controversy among economists. According to economic theory, deposit insurance may increase bank stability by reducing depositor runs but it may decrease bank stability by encouraging risk taking by the banks. A discussion of the widely differing views on the optimal structure for the coverage, funding and management of deposit insurance is beyond the scope of this chapter.[15]

Not surprisingly, there is considerable variation in the provision of, and the involvement of central banks in, deposit insurance schemes across countries.[16] In nearly all of the industrial countries represented in the survey there is some form of deposit protection scheme, usually compulsory, operated either by the supervisory agency or by a separate body (the exceptions are Australia, Hong Kong and New Zealand). In the surveyed transition countries, nearly all of the countries have separate entities which operate a deposit insurance scheme. Of the remainder, Russia and Slovenia, a scheme is under development in Slovenia which will operate from January 2001. The scheme is established under the Banking Act and the Bank of Slovenia had responsibility for laying down the operational regulations for the implementation of the deposit insurance scheme. The widest variation in practices is among developing countries. Some countries are developing deposit insurance schemes (Malta, South Africa), have recently introduced them (in Cyprus operations started in November 2000) or are strengthening existing ones (Sri Lanka). In several countries there are separate deposit insurance agencies (Brazil, Mexico). In Malaysia, during the recent crisis, the government announced that it would guarantee all conventional and Islamic banking deposits; while in Chile it is the central bank who provides the guarantee.

2.3.1.4   *Regulation and supervision of individual financial institutions*[17]

A survey of 123 countries, published by Central Banking Publications (1999), found that, in nearly three-quarters of them, prudential banking supervision was the responsibility of the central bank. Furthermore, the most common model, which makes up around 50 per cent of supervisory structures, is for the central bank to supervise banks only. Similarly, it is still most common to have separate supervisory agencies for each of banks, insurance companies and securities firms. However, this overall picture masks a diverse range of institutional structures for the regulation and supervision of individual financial institutions and some significant changes. This sub-section attempts to explore some of these alternative structures and the reasons behind the variations.

One recent feature has been the increased interest in integrating the supervision of different financial sectors. Goodhart *et al.* (1998) identified six reasons for this:

- The rapid structural change that has taken place in financial markets spurred by the acceleration in financial innovation. This has challenged the assumptions behind the original structuring of regulatory organisation. The question that arises here is how institutional structure should mirror the evolution of the structure of the financial sector.
- The realisation that financial structure in the past has been the result of a series of *ad hoc* and pragmatic policy initiatives raising the question of whether, particularly in the wake of recurrent banking crises and dislocation, a more coherent structure should be put in place.

- The increasing complexity of financial business as evidenced by the emergence of financial conglomerates. This has raised the issue of whether a series of agencies supervising parts of an institution can have a grasp of developments in the institution as a whole.
- The increasing demands being placed on regulation and its complexity, in particular the development of a need for enhanced regulation of 'conduct of business' (e.g. covering financial products like pension schemes and insurance offered to consumers).
- The changing risk characteristics of financial firms occasioned by financial innovation.
- The increasing internationalisation of banking which has implications for the institutional structure of agencies at both the national and international level.

When trying to assess the costs and benefits of a supervisory structure, policy-makers have to take a number of factors into account, including:

- the cost of performing regulation and supervision;
- the efficiency of supervision;
- the effectiveness of supervision; and
- the implications for co-ordination with the central bank.

The judgements on the above factors are not easy and will vary from country to country. However, it may be interesting to look at the considerations and frameworks adopted in a range of countries in order to identify key elements for success and whether there are any lessons for those countries currently considering such a move.

INDUSTRIAL ECONOMIES

The majority of industrial countries in Table 2.3 do not have prudential regulation and supervision within the central bank – Denmark, Sweden, Canada, Korea, Australia, Norway and the UK. However, these central banks may still retain a role, be it formal or informal, in the design of the regulatory framework. All these countries now integrate the prudential supervision of banking, securities and insurance sectors within a single separate supervisory agency (but with significant variations between each country).[18] Although this is a recent phenomenon in countries such as Australia, Korea and the UK, the other countries – Canada, Denmark, Norway and Sweden – have been moving in this direction for several decades, and adopting variants of the integrated supervisor model since the mid-1980s.

Norway was the first country to establish an integrated agency in 1986, followed by *Denmark* in 1988 and *Sweden* in 1991. In all three countries, the Banking and Insurance Inspectorates had long histories and none had ever been part of the central bank's responsibilities, thus the consolidation process of supervisory responsibilities outside the central bank did not involve any obvious dilution of the central bank's powers.[19] As Taylor and Fleming (1999) point out, there were strong similarities between these countries' economic and financial systems, as well as their political systems and cultures. This has produced many similarities in terms of the basic structure and organisation of their integrated regulatory agencies. The countries also point to common issues as motivation for the move towards an integrated regulator, namely a desire 1) for more effective supervision of financial conglomerates, and 2) to obtain economies of scale in the use of scarce regulatory resources in a comparatively small, highly concentrated financial system in which financial conglomerates predominated.

It is interesting to note that *Finland*, despite having a similar system of regulation to that of Norway, Denmark and Sweden until the late 1980s, went in a different direction. Following their banking crisis, the Finnish authorities concluded that there was a need to enhance the linkages between its banking supervisors and the Bank of Finland. They moved the Banking Supervision Office away from the Ministry of Finance and established an agency governed by an independent board, the Financial Supervision Authority, but which is administratively connected with the central bank. This arrangement, while different from that followed by Norway, Denmark and Sweden, also exploits economies of scale. However, supervision across the financial spectrum is less integrated as Finland retains a separate insurance regulator.[20]

The change in *Canada*'s regulatory institutional structure was driven by similar considerations and again, the central bank had never had responsibility for prudential regulation and supervision. However, Canada's economy and financial system is large, and has a complex structure which operates at both a federal and a provincial level. Canada combined banking supervision and insurance regulation but has left securities supervision with the provincial authorities. Box 2.1 describes the regulatory institutional structure in Canada and the framework which has been developed to co-ordinate policies and their implementation across the financial system.

Both the UK and Australia transferred banking regulation and supervision out of their central banks and created integrated supervisory agencies in 1998, closely followed by Korea in 1999. In *Australia* the move was preceded by extensive public debate and the Wallis Report's recommendation for the establishment of the Australian Prudential Regulation Authority (APRA) revolved around the changing structure of the financial industry.[21] They opted for a 'twin peaks' model under which APRA covered prudential regulation and supervision while the Australian Securities and Investments Commission was responsible for conduct of business regulation and supervision. At the same time, the Reserve Bank of Australia (RBA) retained responsibility for monetary policy and for overall

Box 2.1: Canada – institutional responsibility for financial stability

Who is involved: a number of agencies are involved in financial stability in Canada at both federal and provincial level. At the federal level, the responsibility is shared between four public sector bodies: the Department of Finance which is the policy-making authority; the Office of the Superintendent of Financial Institutions (OSFI) which is the supervisory authority; the Canada Deposit Insurance Corporation (CDIC) which is the deposit-insurance authority; and the Bank of Canada (BOC). At a provincial level, each province has the equivalent of a superintendent of deposit-taking institutions, a superintendent of insurance, and a securities commission. The system is further complicated by the fact that many financial institutions may be incorporated at either provincial or federal level. Institutions incorporated at the federal level may be subjected to further regulation by provincial authorities in areas such as conduct of business and consumer protection. Securities dealers, even if incorporated at the federal level, are subject to provincial regulation.

Bank of Canada's role: the Bank's broad objective with regard to financial stability is the promotion of a safe and sound financial system (including payment and clearing and settlement systems, financial institutions and financial markets). This broad objective is stated in its 'Commitment to Canadians' and the preamble in the Bank of Canada Act (1934) requires the Bank 'to promote the economic and financial welfare of Canada'. More specifically, the BOC contributes to financial stability with the provision of:

- a risk-free asset to settle financial obligations among financial intermediaries;
- lender of last resort services;
- oversight of systemically important clearing and settlement systems for the purposes of encouraging the efficient and effective control of systemic risk;
- policy advice leading to good financial system design and development;
- monitoring the financial system for signs of potential major disruptions, from both domestic and international sources; and
- collaboration on financial stability work through domestic and international forums.

In terms of **legislation**, the Bank of Canada Act empowers the BOC to provide deposit accounts to members of the Canadian Payments Association (CPA), as well as collateralised loan facilities to banks and other CPA members, to facilitate settlement of payments. The BOC's role was formalised further by the CPA Act 1980. The BOC Act also permits the Bank to transact in foreign currencies and securities, which can affect the level and distribution of liquidity among the key participants in these markets. The Bank's oversight role regarding systemically important clearing and settlement systems was formalised by the Payment Clearing and Settlement Act

1996 (PCSA). The PCSA provides the Governor of the Bank with the power to designate, oversee, and if necessary direct actions of major clearing and settlement systems that may pose a systemic threat to the financial system.

Relationships between the agencies: the BOC's policy development role is primarily consultative and advisory. In addition to advising the Minister of Finance on financial sector policies, the Governor of the BOC, in accordance with the OSFI Act 1987, participates with the other three federal bodies in the Financial Institutions Supervisory Committee (FISC), chaired by the Superintendent of Financial Institutions. This interagency committee aims to ensure consultation and information exchange on supervisory matters that have implications for solvency, last-resort lending and the risk of deposit insurance payout (including issues of prudential regulation, the practices and condition of individual institutions, and the co-ordination of action when dealing with troubled institutions). Hence, the FISC is intended to give the Superintendent, who is responsible for judgements pertaining to the viability and solvency of federal financial institutions, the full benefit of views from the deposit insurer and the lender of last resort when making supervisory decisions. The same group of federal agencies also participate in the Senior Advisory Committee (SAC). This is an informal committee (i.e. not established by legislation) chaired by the Deputy Minister of Finance and is used as a forum for the discussion of financial sector policies and legislation. In addition, the Superintendent of Financial Institutions, a Deputy Superintendent of Financial Institutions, the BOC Governor of the Bank of Canada, and the Deputy Minister of Finance are *ex officio* members of the CDIC Board of Directors.

The BOC also provides input into the design and operating policies of payment clearing and settlement systems operated by the CPA through its participation on the CPA Board, which is chaired by a BOC senior official in accordance with the CPA Act, and on various CPA committees. Less formally, in its capacity as fiscal agent for the government, the BOC consults with securities regulatory agencies and industry bodies on issues related to market arrangements for government securities.

Data collection/exchange: according to the statutes establishing the FISC, every member of the Committee is entitled to any information on matters relating directly to the supervision of financial institutions that is in the possession or under the control of any other member (all information received by any member is treated as confidential). The Financial Information Committee (FIC), which is a subcommittee of the FISC, is responsible for a joint reporting system administered by OSFI, CDIC and the BOC, collecting data from federally regulated financial institutions. It uses a common reporting format for deposit-taking institutions which suits the needs and purposes of the participating agencies (e.g. the BOC uses these data for monetary and credit aggregates, while the OSFI and CDIC use the data for supervisory purposes).

The BOC has the power under the Bank Act to request data from the banks, directly, other than information related to the accounts or affairs of

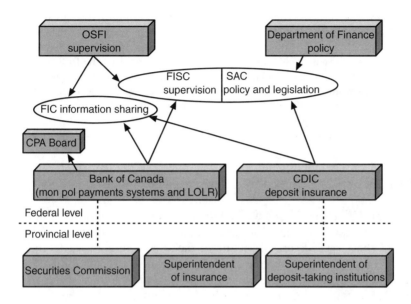

Financial regulation and supervision in Canada

particular persons. Both the BOC and the CDIC have the power to require the OSFI to inspect institutions.

In the case of provincially incorporated trust and loan companies, the BOC receives some information from CDIC. CDIC also works closely with OSFI and provincial regulators.

Crisis management: meetings of the FISC are held at least bi-monthly and special meetings may be held as required. Crisis management responsibilities reflect the statutory responsibilities and powers of the four participating agencies. There are formal and informal arrangements, which can be used to deal with the emergence of crises. The FISC, for example, is an important forum for discussing, planning, and/or co-ordinating actions among the various agencies. In the case of a troubled financial institution, OSFI and CDIC published a 'Guide to intervention for federal financial institutions' (the Guide) in 1996. The document summarises the circumstances under which certain intervention measures may be expected, and it describes the co-ordination mechanisms in place between OSFI and CDIC when dealing with federally regulated deposit-taking institutions. The Guide stresses that OSFI is the regulator of federal financial institutions and is responsible for taking supervisory actions and CDIC is the insurer. OSFI is a primary source of information for CDIC and CDIC relies on OSFI to examine and report annually on the financial condition of CDIC's federally regulated member institutions.

In the case of provincially regulated member institutions, CDIC receives

> information directly from provincial authorities. The Guide also indicates at which points the intervention process would involve the other FISC members. As regards the BOC, the BOC Act gives the central bank discretion in discharging its lender of last resort responsibilities. The BOC's policy is to lend only to banks that are considered solvent. The determination of solvency would be provided by the Superintendent of Financial Institutions but the BOC has the discretion to accept or refuse applications for such loans.

financial system stability and was given enhanced regulatory powers in the payment system, exercised by a new Payments System Board within the RBA.

In the *UK*, a single agency, the Financial Services Authority (FSA), was created by amalgamating ten different supervisory bodies/agencies across one of the largest financial sectors in the world. In contrast to the Australian model, both prudential and business conduct regulation are carried out by the one agency. The move was motivated by a host of factors. The most important were: 1) the growth of conglomerates and the blurring of distinctions between financial services carried out by different types of institutions; and 2) a desire for a less costly and a more co-ordinated supervisory structure. Several high profile financial failures in the proceeding years had increased the call for change. Several models had been put forward: a 'twin peaks' model by Michael Taylor in 1995, six regulators by Goodhart in 1996 and a three-peaked system.[22] The then-new government, elected in May 1997, decided on a new single regulator while the Bank of England would retain responsibility for overall financial stability. Two weeks before announcing the change, the government had given the Bank of England an independent role for the maintenance of price stability, as defined by the inflation target set by the government.

South Korea and *Japan*[23] adopted a similar model to the UK by integrating the supervision of banks, securities and insurance in a single agency outside the central bank, the Financial Supervisory Commission and the Financial Services Agency respectively (although the Bank of Japan retains a banking supervision department). One notable difference is that while both the UK and Australia have agreed Memoranda of Understanding (MOUs) between the relevant public policy institutions, outlining topics such as the division of responsibilities, information sharing and crisis management protocol, Korea and Japan have yet to do so.[24]

Now let's look at the industrial country central banks who have responsibility for regulation and supervision of individual financial institutions. The *Hong Kong* Monetary Authority follows the most common central bank model in that it is responsible for supervisory deposit-taking institutions but not other financial institutions. The Reserve Bank of *New Zealand* is also the banking regulator and agency responsible for supervision, and on that basis could probably be classified as an instance of the broad model. However, New Zealand has introduced a supervisory regime that emphasises the responsibilities of the private sector to supervise compliance through disclosure and transparency, and there are no routine on-site inspections by the Reserve Bank. However, the RBNZ has the power to require independent reports on a bank and, in situations where a bank is in difficulty, may appoint a person to investigate the bank's affairs.

Two of the three eurozone countries, the *Netherlands* and *Ireland*, both have supervisory responsibilities in the central bank. In the Netherlands, the central bank is also responsible for investment institutions and exchange offices but not the insurance or securities sector. In the Netherlands, the authorities strengthened relationships by establishing, in July 1999, the Council of Financial Supervisors as a co-ordinating body on cross-sector policy issues. It consists of executive directors of all three supervisory bodies. In Ireland, financial regulation and supervision has largely been consolidated within the central bank, at least for the time being. A Bill to transfer the supervision of insurance intermediaries to the central bank is to take effect in April 2001. Only insurance companies will be regulated and supervised by a separate body (the Department of Enterprise, Trade and Employment). The Irish government has indicated an intention to fully integrate financial regulation and supervision within a single agency. However, the decision on whether this will be located permanently inside or outside the central bank has not yet been made. Given the potential growth of conglomerates in the European financial system, there is considerable debate over the future structure of financial regulation and supervision across Europe,[25] with some commentators calling for a more integrated institutional structure. An ECOFIN working group, chaired by Dutch Deputy Governor Henk Brouwer, published a report in April 2000 on whether the existing regulatory and supervisory structures in the EU can safeguard financial stability, particularly in the context of a rapidly changing financial environment. The report concludes that no institutional changes are necessary but that improvements are needed in the level of cooperation, including between supervisors and central banks.

In the *USA*[26] the Federal Reserve System (Fed) is the primary regulatory and supervisory body of banking entities, but in many cases shares responsibilities with other agencies (see Box 2.2 for a fuller description). In addition, the Gramm–Leach Bliley Act of 1999 superseded the 'Glass–Stegall' Banking Act of 1933, authorising a wider spectrum of activities and set out a supervisory framework which combines umbrella supervision of the consolidated entity by the Fed, oversight of the depository institutions by their primary bank regulators, and functional regulation of some non-bank entities by their respective specialised regulators. As a result of this framework and the growing complexity of banking organisations, cooperation and co-ordination between supervisors is an increasingly important issue. Policy is co-ordinated via the Federal Financial

Box 2.2: USA – institutional responsibility for financial stability

Overview: the system of financial regulation and supervision in the US is very complex and has a range of agencies, including several self-regulatory bodies. The supervisory structure is related to the status of the institutions, with a notable division between state and national banks and between banks and other financial firms. There is a degree of overlap between regulators, with often several being responsible for overseeing the same institution. Firms have a choice of regulator only through the way they organise their activities, such as whether they hold a state or federal charter, or whether they belong to the Federal Reserve system. This complex and rather duplicative structure is the result of a number of uniquely American political realities, including a deep-rooted historical aversion to concentrations of political, economic or financial power, the tension between state and Federal powers, and political sensitivities that followed the financial upheaval of the Great Depression.

Who is involved: at federal level, the Congress has the legislative role and has delegated rule-writing authority to the regulatory agencies. Often, the responsibility for writing the regulations to implement parts of legislation is shared with the Treasury.

Banks and Holding Companies: at the federal level banks are regulated by:

- the Federal Reserve System (Fed), including twelve regional federal reserve banks, which is the primary regulatory and supervisory body of Financial Holding Companies (FHCs); Bank Holding Companies (BHCs); state chartered, Federal System member banks; and aims to maintain the stability of the financial system;
- the Office of the Comptroller of the Currency (OCC) which is responsible for the regulation and supervision of banks with national charters;
- the Office of Thrift Supervision (OTS) which oversees savings and loan associations and savings banks across the US;
- the Federal Housing Finance Board which supervises the Federal Home Loan Banks created in 1932;
- the National Credit Union Administration which oversees the federal credit union system and its federal insurance fund; and
- the Federal Deposit Insurance Corporation (FDIC) which aims to maintain stability and public confidence in the financial system by administering the Bank Insurance Fund which backs up insured deposits, assisting troubled banks under the Federal Deposit Insurance Corporation Improvement Act of 1991 (FDICIA) and being the federal primary regulator for state-chartered banks which are not members of the Fed.

In addition, each state also has a Banking Department, which supervises state-chartered banks.

Banking regulation: federal supervisor and regulator of banking organisations in the US

Type of banking organisation	Supervisor and regulator
Financial holding companies	Fed as 'Umbrella Supervisor'
Bank holding companies	Fed
National banks	OCC
State banks: Members of Federal Reserve System	Fed/State Banking Departments
Non-members	FDIC/State Banking Departments
Industrial banks (if insured)[1]	FDIC
Thrift holding companies	OTS
Savings banks	OTS/FDIC
Savings and loan associations	OTS
Edge Act and agreement corporations	Fed
Foreign banks:[2] Branches and agencies[3]	
State licensed	Fed/FDIC/State Banking Departments
Federally licensed	OCC/Fed/FDIC
Representative offices	Fed

N.B. Some institutions fall into several categories.

1 Uninsured industrial banks are supervised by the states.

2 Applies to direct operations in the United States. Foreign banks may also have indirect operations in the United States through their ownership of US banking organisations.

3 The FDIC has responsibility for branches that are insured.

Other financial institutions are regulated by:

- the Securities and Exchange Commission (SEC) which administers the federal securities laws, serves as adviser to federal courts in corporate reorganisation proceedings under Chapter 11 of the Bankruptcy Reform Act of 1978 and has certain oversight and other responsibilities with respect to the Securities Investor Protection Corporation;
- the US Commodity Futures Trading Commission (CFTC), which regulates the commodity futures and options markets;
- the Municipal Securities Rulemaking Board, a self-regulatory organisation, which writes rules for securities firms and banks acting as dealers in municipal securities (these must be approved by other bodies before they are enforceable);
- the National Association of Securities Dealers (NASD), a self-regulatory organisation, which has assumed a substantial portion of their parent organisation's responsibilities of being the securities industry's primary self-regulator;
- the National Futures Association, another self-regulatory organisation, devoted to helping the futures industry meet its regulatory responsibilities.

There are also state insurance regulators (the National Association of Insurance Commissioners is a co-ordinating body for this group).

Federal Reserve's role: in terms of legislation, the Fed operates under a whole raft of laws, the most recent being the Gramm–Leach–Bliley Act (GLBA) of 1999. The Act supersedes previously enacted legislation, most notably the 'Glass–Steagall' provisions of the Banking Act of 1933, and enables bank holding companies that are well-capitalised, well-managed, and that maintain a 'satisfactory' CRA (Community Reinvestment Act) rating, to become 'financial holding companies'. FHCs are, in effect, privileged bank holding companies. Under provisions of the GLBA, FHCs may engage in a broader range of activities, including banking, securities and insurance activities, and merchant banking. The Act also sets out a two-tiered supervisory framework which combines umbrella supervision of FHCs and BHCs by the Fed, oversight of the depository institutions by their primary bank regulators (OCC, Fed, and/or the relevant state banking department), and 'functional regulation' of FHCs' non-bank entities by their respective regulators (SEC, CFTC, or the relevant state insurance department).

The Fed's broad objective with regard to financial stability is to promote the safety and soundness of the regulated banking institutions, stability in the financial markets, and fair and equitable treatment of banking consumers in their financial transactions. There is a division of responsibility between the Board of Governors and the twelve reserve banks. The Board of Governors adopts regulations to carry out statutory directives, establishes system supervisory and regulatory policies, and enforces compliance by state member banks with the federal banking consumer protection laws. The reserve banks, under authority delegated by the Board, conduct on-site examinations and inspection of state member banks and bank holding companies, review applications for mergers, acquisitions and changes in control from banks and bank holding companies, and take formal supervisory actions. In addition to its monetary policy and banking regulatory and supervisory responsibilities, the Fed also plays the role of 'lender of last resort', sets margin requirements, which limit the use of credit for purchasing or carrying securities, and plays a key role in assuring the smooth functioning and continued development of the nation's payments system.

Relationships between the agencies: given the sharing of regulatory and supervisory responsibilities across the financial sector, co-ordination is extremely important. A key part of that co-ordination is the Federal Financial Institutions Examination Council (FFIEC), established in 1978, consisting of the Chairpersons of the FDIC and the National Credit Union Administration, the Comptroller of the Currency, the Director of the OTS, and a Governor of the Federal Reserve Board appointed by the Board Chairman. The FFIEC's purposes are to prescribe uniform federal principles and standards for the examination of depository institutions, to promote co-ordination of bank supervision among the federal agencies that regulate financial institutions, and to encourage better co-ordination of federal and state regulatory activities. Through the FFIEC, state and federal regulatory agencies may exchange views on important regulatory issues, for example, Interagency Staff Groups work on common policy, standards and training. Among other things, the FFIEC has developed uniform financial reporting forms for use by all federal and state banking regulators. Mutual board membership between FFIEC members is limited to the Comptroller of the Currency and the Director of the OTS sitting on the Board of Directors of the FDIC. There is also an *ad hoc* group that provides legislative recommendations to Congress on supervisory matters; it is called the President's Working Group on Financial Markets, and consists of the heads of the Fed, Treasury, SEC, and Commodity Futures Trading Commission. In addition, in selected areas examination teams may include staff members from different supervisory agencies, e.g. when a large firm has borrowed from a consortium of lending institutions with different primary supervisory agencies.

The wider scope of financial activities for FHCs authorised by the Gramm–Leach–Bliley Act makes the cooperation and co-ordination between supervisors an increasingly important concern. Also, as Fed Governor Meyer has pointed out,[27] 'There are potential tensions in the interaction between the Federal Reserve as umbrella supervisor, on the one hand, and the specialised functional regulators of non-bank activities – the SEC and the state insurance commissioners – on the other. Moreover, the increased complexity of banking organizations requires improved cooperation and co-ordination between the Federal Reserve as umbrella supervisor and the primary bank supervisor, particularly the OCC, given that most Large Complex Banking Organizations have lead banks with national charters.'

Data exchange: under provisions of the GLBA, the Fed must rely, to the fullest extent possible, on publicly available information, externally audited financial statements, and reports that a functionally regulated subsidiary must provide to its regulator. This is to avoid duplication, minimise regulatory burden and respect individual responsibilities. The Fed can examine such functionally regulated entities only if 1) the Fed Board has reasonable cause to believe that the entity is engaged in activities that pose a material risk to an affiliated depository institution, 2) the Board determines an examination is necessary to inform the Board of the risk management systems of the company, or 3) the Board has reasonable cause to believe the entity is not in compliance with the banking laws. However, given the systemic risks associated with the disruption of the operations of large banks – and the role of the bank within the broader banking organisation – the Fed is of the view[28] that it needs to know more about the activities within large insured depository institutions than can be derived from access to public information or from the reports of the primary bank supervisor. Similarly, the primary bank regulator needs information about the activities of a bank's parent company and its non-bank affiliates to protect the bank from threats that might arise elsewhere in the consolidated organization. To effectively carry out their respective responsibilities as mandated by the GLBA, the Fed and the functional regulators are presently establishing cooperation and information sharing agreements.

In addition, the Fed's National Information Center of Banking Information is available to all and is based on Call Reports and other financial data. The FFIEC's Task Force on Information Sharing maintains a data-exchange inventory of all data files shared among its regulatory agency members.

Crisis management: these are dealt with on a case-by-case basis. However, the FDICIA of 1991 mandates a least-cost resolution method and prompt resolution approach to problem and failing banks (and ordered that the deposit insurance assessment scheme be risk-based). It greatly increased the powers and authority of the FDIC. The FDIC acts as the 'receiver' for banks that fail or are closed, which effectively means co-ordinating and overseeing the valuation and sale of those banks' remaining assets. The FDIC has the authority to recommend that the primary federal regulator of an institution take specified enforcement action against any insured depository institution or affiliate of the institution. If a federal banking agency fails to take the recommended action or an acceptable alternative within 60 days, the FDIC may step in and take action. The Fed, as 'lender of last resort', stands ready to provide temporary or long-term liquidity to any depository institution that meets its criteria for discount window borrowing. This role, coupled with its role as primary supervisor of BHCs and umbrella supervisor of FHCs, gives the Fed a major responsibility for early intervention in problem situations and in managing crises, particularly for large financial institutions. However, there are restrictions; for example, FDICIA stipulates that the Fed may not lend to a critically undercapitalised institution for more than five days beyond the date on which it became critically undercapitalised without incurring a potential liability to the FDIC.

In addition, in principle, in very unusual circumstances, a Reserve Bank may, after consultation with the Board of Governors of the Fed, advance credit to individuals, partnerships, and corporations that aren't depository institutions, if the Reserve Bank determines that credit isn't available from other sources and that failure to provide that credit would adversely affect the economy. However, this authority has not been utilised in more than sixty years.

Institutions Examination Council and a Presidents Working Group. However, further cooperation has been identified as needed, for example, by Fed Governor Meyer (see Box 2.2).

Of the industrial countries, *Singapore* has assigned the largest role to its central bank. They, like others, have integrated financial supervisory roles. But instead of an agency outside of the central bank responsibility for regulating and supervising all financial institutions in Singapore (banking, insurance and securities) has been transferred to the Monetary Authority of Singapore (MAS). This was largely motivated by the desire to benefit from economies of scale and improved co-ordination by centralising responsibilities. It is also relevant that while the MAS has independence in the formulation and implementation of monetary policy, its relationship

Box 2.3: Japan – institutional responsibility for financial stability

Who is involved: the institutional structure of financial regulation in Japan has been and is in the process of comprehensive reform. Prior to 1998 the Ministry of Finance (MoF) was directly responsible for supervising the whole financial system with the Bank of Japan (BoJ) and the Securities and Exchange Surveillance Commission (SESC) both providing subsidiary roles in supervision. In June 1998 the Financial Supervisory Agency (FSA) was established, as a government agency separate from the MoF and accountable to the Diet, to be the regulatory authority over the financial sectors of banking, insurance and securities, to have integrated responsibility for financial system planning, the inspection and supervision of financial institutions,[29] and the surveillance of securities transactions. The SESC was attached to the FSA and shared responsibility for supervising securities markets with the MoF. In December 1998, the Financial Reconstruction Commission (FRC) was established to dispose of bankrupt financial institutions and the recapitalisation of financial institutions with public funds. At that time, responsibility for financial system planning and for drafting legislation rested with the Financial System Planning Bureau of the MoF. In 2000 further reorganisation took place: the MoF's financial planning role was transferred to the FSA and the FSA was renamed the 'Financial Services Agency' (established July 2000). At the time of writing it was also planned to transfer the MoF's Local Finance Bureau to the FSA – this bureau undertakes the inspection and supervision of regional private financial institutions – and to merge the FSA and the FRC in January 2001. The Bank of Japan continues to carry out supervision of financial institutions which have accounts with the BoJ (Article 44 of BoJ Law) on the grounds that they need to assess key settlement system transactors (Article 39) and, like the US Fed, the BoJ believes that the hands-on experience of supervision and regulation provides them with a base of essential knowledge for monetary policy deliberations and aids its financial crisis management role (Articles 37 and 38). The Ministry of Finance retains responsibility for financial system crisis management insofar as this has budgetary implications. The Deposit Insurance Corporation (DIC), established in 1971, continues to operate although various amendments to the insurance of deposits were made during the crisis (see section on Crisis Management below).

Bank of Japan's role: the BoJ's broad objective with regard to financial stability is to maintain price stability and to ensure the stability of the financial system, thereby laying the foundations for sound economic development. More specifically, the Bank of Japan works to maintain the payment and settlement services infrastructure, operates an electronic settlement system for transfers between banks (BoJ–Net), is scheduled to launch an RTGS system in January and continues to carry out supervision of both banks and non-bank financial institutions. It focuses on the risk management of banks and has a role as 'lender of last resort' working with other agencies in crisis resolution.

In terms of *legislation*, the BoJ operates under the Bank of Japan Law 1998. It also plays a role in providing liquidity in conjunction with other financial agencies under the Financial Reconstruction Law and the Financial Early Strengthening Law (which were enacted in October 1998 as a new framework to cope with the financial crisis and to restore the soundness of the financial system).

Relationships between the agencies: during 1998–2000 there was extensive cooperation between the FSA and the BoJ, the FRC and the DIC in inspecting and assessing the situation of financial institutions and the resolution of problem cases. There is no explicit framework for cooperation and only a limited exchange of staff.

Data collection/exchange: both the BoJ and the FSA carry out on-site examinations and receive data directly from financial institutions. The BoJ carries out on-site inspections of financial institutions which have accounts with the BoJ (i.e. city banks, regional banks, shinkin banks, Tanshi brokers and security companies). The commissioner of the FSA may request that the BoJ share the results with the FSA. The MoF regional offices assist the FSA with their on-site inspections of regional banks and regional financial institutions.

Crisis management: following Japan's extensive and expensive financial crisis, a crisis resolution framework was drawn up, to be implemented in April 2001. Also, the current regime of 100 per cent deposit insurance is scheduled to be replaced by partial deposit insurance from April 2002, though liquid deposits will remain fully protected until end-March 2003. There are two parts to the new framework, depending on the systemic implications of the situation, 1) a general quick resolution at lowest cost possible approach applicable in non-large-scale systemic situations, and 2) a coordinated resolution in the event of large-scale systemic situations. A brief description follows:

A *'purchase and assumption'* method to transfer insured deposits and portions of business allows for: (a) prior failure preparations such as the grouping of deposits held by the same depositor and the precise evaluation of assets as soon as a problem is found by the authorities; (b) administering failed institutions by a Financial Reorganisation Administrator; (c) transferring portions of business in steps at an early stage. As the primary regulatory body the FSA would normally be in the lead in coordinating official responses to a problem situation. Also, in order to encourage healthy financial institutions to assume the business of a failed financial institution, the DIC is authorised to inject capital to the acquiring institutions and share a portion of the loss realised after the assets are transferred. When no rescuer comes forward, the DIC is empowered to set up a bridge bank to temporarily assume the business of a failed financial institution. The aim is to promote speedy resolutions, if possible, over a (long) weekend.

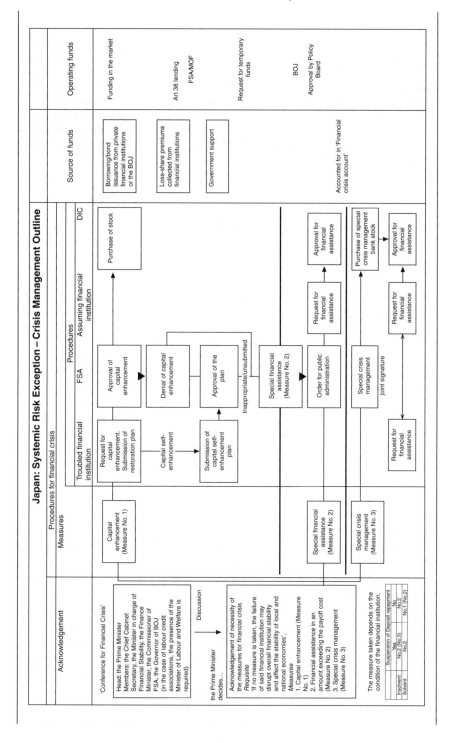

Japan: Systemic Risk Exception – Crisis Management Outline

In the case of *large-scale systemic risk,* the new framework allows exceptional measures such as a capital injection, the full protection of all liabilities
of a failed financial institution, and the nationalisation of a failed institution.
It is the Prime Minister (PM) who may authorise these measures after discussion at a Financial Crisis Management Council, which consists of the PM,
the Finance Minister, the Minister in charge of the financial system and the
Governor of the BoJ. This process is outlined in the diagram on page 53.
The BoJ's role is primarily as LOLR, providing funds to troubled institutions and/or the DIC. The DIC can also currently borrow from elsewhere
although their funding arrangements are under review with the MoF.

with government is a close one. The MAS is a statutory board under the
Ministry of Finance the current MAS Chairman is also the Deputy Prime
Minister, and top civil servants attend the top level management meeting
of the MAS.

TRANSITION ECONOMIES

Table 2.4 shows that, apart from Hungary (see Box 2.4), central banks in
transition countries undertake a similar range of financial stability activities. All of them are responsible for the regulation and supervision of
deposit-taking institutions (in many countries these are banks only).
However, this grouping may change significantly over the next few years
as some countries, such as Estonia and Latvia, are implementing plans to
establish an integrated supervisory agency outside the central bank.

Countries which have established an integrated supervisory agency
have done so largely to benefit from economies of scale and to respond to
the formation of financial conglomerates. Several emerging countries are
becoming increasingly developed so that the emergence of financial conglomerates and pressures for the integration of financial regulation and
supervision may differ markedly amongst transition and developing countries. Where financial conglomerates are not widespread, the case for an
integrated supervisory agency is less strong.

Nevertheless, even in less developed transition and developing countries, integrating financial regulation and supervision could yield
economies of scale (similar to the small financial sectors of Denmark,
Norway and Sweden) and consistency of regulation. Also, since staff
resources are always scarce, one of the key issues that any country faces is
the need to attract, train and retain good staff. In economies where human
capital is still being built up there may be significant advantages to creating
a more integrated organisation for regulatory professionals.

The degree of concentration in the financial services sector may also be
an issue. In some transition and developing economies, financial systems

Box 2.4: Hungary – institutional responsibility for financial stability

Who is involved: there are a number of public sector agencies involved in financial stability in Hungary. Although the National Bank of Hungary (NBH) is not responsible for prudential regulation and supervision, it still retains a role in the regulation and surveillance of financial markets. Capital and other prudential supervision has always been carried out by a separate supervisory agency. Initially within a department of the Ministry of Finance, then by the State Banking Supervisory Authority (1991–6), and subsequently by the Hungarian Banking and Capital Market Supervision agency (HBCMS) which also subsumed the Securities Supervisory Authority. From April 2000, the HBCMS merged with the insurance supervisory agency and the State Private Fund Supervision to create the Hungarian Financial Supervisory Authority (HFSA) which supervises the whole of the Hungarian financial sector. While the HFSA prepares regulation, it is the Ministry of Finance that is the regulatory body and participates in the withdrawal of licences.

National Bank of Hungary's role: the main supervisory responsibilities are monitoring: compliance with reserve requirements; foreign exchange transactions, for which licences are granted by the HFSA only with the agreement of the NBH; compliance by credit institutions, clearing and investment houses with the regulations on money circulation and data supply; and compliance with refinancing loans provided by the NBH. In this context the NBH may conduct on-site supervision. Over recent years the overlap in activities between the supervisory authority and the NBH have been reduced. For example, the NBH's role in licensing has declined although, in principle, licences for banking business, or for changes in the scope of activity of a financial institution should be issued in consultation with the NBH. Instead, the NBH focuses on analysis of the soundness, stability and effectiveness of the whole banking sector (within the Banking Department) and on supervision of compliance with NBH areas of responsibility (Banking Supervision Department). The NBH plays a role in the development of the payment and settlement systems (e.g. the NBH operates the RTGS system, holds a 14.6 per cent share of the operator of the interbank clearing system and owns 50 per cent of the securities clearing and settlement body) and contributes to the formulation of legislation affecting the financial sector.

Relationships between agencies: in addition to legislation governing the respective roles of the agencies, there is a formal cooperation agreement between the NBH and the HFSA under which they share information on financial institutions and findings of inspections. If necessary, both have powers to initiate proceedings within each other's organisation. The agreement specifies the scope and forms of exchange and is reviewed annually. Representatives of the HFSA are invited to NBH board meetings, if there are agenda items related to the HFSA's responsibilities. A number of regular meetings take place between the staff of the two institutions and the annual schedule of on-site supervision is mutually agreed. In addition, the NBH holds seats on the Boards of the National Deposit Insurance Fund, the Investor Compensation Fund, the Council of the Budapest Stock Exchange, the Budapest Commodity Exchange, and the GIRO Ltd (the operator of the Hungarian interbank clearing system).

Data collection/exchange: a common reporting scheme was introduced in 1998 which both the NBH and the prudential supervisors use for their own purposes. Both agencies may conduct inspections in relation to their own spheres of competence, and share the results with each other as well as with the management of the institution inspected. The NBH is empowered to request data directly from financial institutions and, in relation to foreign exchange transactions, may request data from any relevant institution.

Crisis management: the division of crisis management responsibilities are outlined by the law and also by less formal agreement. The NBH focuses on preventative measures and systemic situations. The supervisory agency takes the primary role in the resolution of individual problems but the NBH may act as lender of last resort to provide emergency liquidity assistance. The NBH may also extend emergency credit to potentially insolvent institutions if deemed to be systemic. The extension of such credits would be made with the support of the government and dependent on certain supervisory measures and adequate collateral and/or a government guarantee.

---

are dominated by a few institutions, in some cases state owned or recently privatised. Some wield significant economic and political power and have close relationships with the government. In such an environment a strong centralised regulatory agency would be most likely to provide a counter-weight to the power of these institutions.

These considerations do not unambiguously point to the establishment of an integrated supervisory body outside the central bank. Regulation could be consolidated inside the central bank (as in Singapore). This option might seem particularly attractive if the central bank has a high reputation and therefore a comparative advantage in attracting good staff. Usually, the financial sectors of transition economies are dominated by banks and the establishment of an integrated supervisory agency outside the central bank may carry a risk of a loss of banking supervisory staff. However, the government may feel uncomfortable with concentrating power over both monetary policy and regulation of the whole financial industry within one institution, particularly if the financial system is still dominated by state-owned institutions (see Table 2.6 for central bank 'independence' scores).

DEVELOPING ECONOMIES

In most of the developing economies shown on Table 2.5, the central bank is responsible for the regulation and supervision of deposit-taking institutions, and in some cases of other financial intermediaries as well (India, Malaysia, Malawi, Malta, Sri Lanka and Uganda). Only three central banks, those of *Chile, Mexico* and *Peru*, do not perform the primary prudential regulator and supervisor role; and they never have done. In these three countries, the supervisory agencies have a long history.

Peru appears to assign the narrowest financial stability role to its central bank: it has no direct responsibilities for the development or implementation of the regulatory or supervisory environment. However, the central bank consults with the supervisory agencies and may, for example, offer views on prospective new entrants to the Peruvian financial system. The Chilean central bank has certain powers specified in the law and retains responsibility for the regulation and supervision of the foreign exchange market under the Central Bank Organic Law. The central bank may also give its views to the supervisor on new entrants and closures, with respect to the stability of the financial system. The Banco de Mexico's role in the regulation and supervision of financial markets is wider. Under its law, the central bank may issue regulations to credit institutions with respect to credits, loans and repos, and operations in foreign exchange and precious metals. Off-site supervision of these activities is carried out by the central bank. However, capital and other prudential regulation and supervision of credit institutions, including on-site supervision, is carried out by the National Banking and Securities Commission and the Ministry of Finance and Public Credit.

Among the developing countries we surveyed, several mentioned plans (Indonesia) or the possibility (Brazil, Malta, South Africa) of integrating financial supervision outside the central bank. In some countries the growth of financial conglomerates is prompting a review (Brazil, Malta and South Africa). Many of the same issues that apply to transition economies also apply to developing economies: can a change of institutional arrangements generate economies of scale and consistency of regulation, what will be the balance of power among financial sector players, will an integrated approach reflect the integration in the financial sector, etc.?

In some countries the central bank has expanded its supervisory role as new financial intermediaries have developed and pressures to regulate and supervise them have grown (India – see Box 2.5, Malaysia and Malawi). Broadening the central bank's supervisory role beyond banks has enabled countries to respond to gradual changes in the financial sector without incurring the costs of a review and the implementation of a change in institutional responsibilities.

Table 2.6 Survey countries – central bank independence and supervision

Country	Central Bank Act	Central Bank as supervisor – past, present and future†	Independence score*
Industrial economies			
Australia	Reserve Bank Act, 1959 (plus Ministerial Statement by the Treasurer, 2 September 1997 and the Statement on the Conduct of Monetary Policy, 1996)	In 1998 supervisory responsibilities were consolidated within two new separate supervisory agencies. The Australian Securities and Investments Commission was created to cover the conduct of business. Separately, the Australian Prudential Regulation Authority (APRA) was established through the amalgamation of the insurance supervisor and the banking supervision responsibilities previously carried out by the RBA. In 1999 the remaining deposit-taking institutions in Australia were also amalgamated into APRA.	73
Canada	Bank of Canada Act, 1934 (plus subsequent amendments)	Regulation and supervision of financial institutions has never been within the central bank. Supervision is carried out at the federal and provincial levels. The Department of Finance has broad responsibility for policy and the Office of the Superintendent of Financial Institutions is the primary supervisor of banks and other federally incorporated financial institutions (established in 1987 through the amalgamation of the banking and insurance supervisors). See Box 2.1.	91
Denmark	Nationalbank Act, 1936	Regulation and supervision of financial institutions has never been within the central bank. A consolidated supervisory agency which covers the whole of Denmark's financial sector was established in 1988 through the amalgamation of the banking and insurance supervisory agencies.	88
Finland	Act on the Bank of Finland (Revised), 1999	Regulation and supervision of financial institutions has never been within the central bank. The Financial Supervision Authority (FSA) was established in 1993 when the former Banking Supervision Office was abolished and its activities were linked with the Bank of Finland. The FSA is connected administratively with the Bank of Finland, but is independent in its decision	91

Country	Act	Description	
		making. In addition, a separate body, the Insurance Supervision Authority, is responsible for the supervision of insurance companies. It was established in 1999 and functions under the Ministry of Social Affairs and Health.	
Hong Kong	Exchange Fund (Amendment) Ordinance, 1993	Regulation and supervision of deposit-taking institutions within the Hong Kong Monetary Authority. There are separate supervisory agencies for the insurance and securities sectors.	74
Ireland	Central Bank Acts, 1971–98	Regulation and supervision of deposit-taking institutions within the Central Bank of Ireland since 1971. In 1989 gained responsibility for building societies, futures exchanges, securities firms, investment schemes and money brokers. In 1995 these responsibilities were expanded to cover stock exchanges and their member firms and investment firms. In 1998 the Government decided to establish a single regulatory authority to cover banking, securities and insurance sectors but the timing and location of the new authority has yet to be decided. In addition, responsibility for insurance intermediaries transfers to the central bank from April 2001, leaving only insurance companies supervised by a body other than the central bank (insurance companies remain with the government Department of Enterprise, Trade and Employment).	87
Korea, South	Bank of Korea Act (Revised), 1997	In 1998 a consolidated supervisory agency, the Financial Supervisory Commission, was created by amalgamating the supervisory bodies for the securities, insurance and credit management sectors and the banking supervision function (which was transferred out of the BOK).	73
Netherlands	De Nederlandsche Bank Act, 1998	Regulation and supervision of banks, investment funds and exchange offices within the central bank. There are separate supervisory agencies for the securities and insurance sectors. In July 1999 the Council of Financial Supervisors was established as a co-ordinating body on cross-sector policy issues (such as consumer protecting codes of conduct and advising the Minister of Finance on legislation regarding supervision of financial conglomerates), which consists of executive directors of all three supervisory bodies.	91

Table 2.6 Continued

Country	Central Bank Act	Central Bank as supervisor – past, present and future†	Independence score*
New Zealand	Reserve Bank of New Zealand Act, 1989	Regulation and supervision of banks within the RBNZ, but since 1996 the RBNZ has operated a supervisory system which emphasises the responsibility of the individual Directors of institutions to comply with regulations (and to disclose compliance) and reduces direct prudential supervision by the RBNZ.	89
Norway	Act No. 28, 1985 (Norges Bank Act)	Regulation and supervision have never been within the Norges Bank (except for the foreign exchange market under the Norwegian Currency Control Act). In 1986 a consolidated separate supervisory agency, the Kredittilsynet, was established by amalgamating the Banking and Insurance Inspectorates. Previously responsibilities for banking supervision had been gradually consolidated in the Banking Inspectorate including some of the functions of the securities bureau of the Ministry of Finance in 1983. The only part of the Norwegian financial sector that is not currently covered by the Kredittilsynet is the responsibility for supervising the Oslo Stock Exchange, but this function will soon be transferred to it from the Ministry of Finance.	57
Singapore	Monetary Authority of Singapore Act, 1970	Regulation and supervision of all financial institutions within the MAS. Prior to the establishment of the MAS, the regulation and supervision of depositories was distributed among several government agencies. Responsibility for depositories was given to MAS from the outset and in 1984 MAS gained responsibility for insurance and securities from the relevant government agencies.	90
Sweden	The Sveriges Riksbank Act, 1988	Regulation and supervision of financial institutions has never been within the Riksbank. A consolidated separate Financial Supervisory Authority was established in 1991. Previously, banks were covered by a government controlled Bank Inspection Board and there were separate agencies supervising the insurance and securities sectors.	97

UK	Bank of England Act, 1998	In 1998 a consolidated supervisory agency, the Financial Services Authority, was created by amalgamating the supervisory bodies for all financial services sectors and the banking supervision function previously carried out by the BoE.	77

Transition economies

Bulgaria	Law on the Bulgarian National Bank, 1997	Regulation and supervision of banks within the BNB. There is a separate securities supervisory agency and a two-level state insurance supervisory structure consisting of the Insurance Supervision Directorate at the Ministry of Finance and the National Insurance Council.	79
Czech Republic	Act of the Czech National Council No. 6, 1993	Regulation and supervision of banks within the Czech National Bank. There is a separate securities supervisory agency.	98
Estonia	Law on the Central Bank of the Republic of Estonia, 1993. Amendments 1994, 1998	Regulation and supervision of banks currently within Eesti Pank but there is agreement to form a consolidated supervisory agency outside of the central bank in the next few years. A law has been drafted which, if implemented, will establish such an agency by 1 January 2002. Currently there are also agencies for each of the insurance and securities sectors.	85
Hungary	Act on the National Bank of Hungary, 1991	Regulation and supervision within NBH is limited to legal regulations specified in the Central Bank Act and NBH decrees on money circulation, foreign exchange, data supply and minimum reserves. Capital and other prudential regulation and supervision has always been carried out by a separate supervisory agency, although the NBH is involved in the issuance and withdrawal of licences (from April 2000 the Hungarian Banking and Capital Market Supervision agency merged with the insurance supervisory agency and the State Private Fund Supervision to create the Hungarian Financial Supervisory Authority). (See Box 2.4 on Hungary.)	86
Latvia	Republic of Latvia Law on the Bank of Latvia, 1992	Regulation and supervision of banks currently within BoL and there are also currently separate agencies for each of the insurance and securities sectors. However, a new law was passed on 1 June 2000 which set out a Financial and Capital Markets Commission which should start functioning on 1 July 2001. This Commission will be an independent supervisory authority covering banking, capital markets and insurance.	98

Table 2.6 Continued

Country	Central Bank Act	Central Bank as supervisor – past, present and future†	Independence score*
Poland	Act on National Bank of Poland, 1997	Regulation and supervision of banks situated in the NBP, carried out by the General Inspectorate of Banking. Since 1998 these functions have been under the direction of an independent Commission for Banking Supervision. There are separate supervisory agencies for the insurance and securities sectors. A draft law has been prepared which will transfer the licensing power of the Ministry of Finance to the insurance supervisory body and this body will be governed by representatives of the other financial regulatory and supervisory bodies (including the NBP).	86
Russia	Federal Law on the Central Bank of the Russian Federation (Bank of Russia), 1990	Regulation and supervision of credit institutions within BoR. There are also currently separate agencies for each of the insurance and securities sectors.	76
Slovenia	Law on the Bank of Slovenia, 1991	Regulation and supervision of credit institutions within BoS but the possibility of a separate consolidated supervisory agency has been raised. There are also currently separate agencies for each of the insurance and securities sectors.	86
Developing economies			
Argentina	Law on the Central Bank of the Argentine Republic, 1992	Regulation and supervision of all deposit-taking institutions carried out by administratively separate Superintendence of Financial and Foreign Exchange Institutions, which reports directly to the Governor of the central bank. There is a separate insurance regulator and securities regulator. In 1999 a Permanent Committee was set up as a co-ordinating body with representatives of the Insurance Company Superintendence, Pension Funds Superintendence, National Security Commission and Ministry of Economy and the central bank.	79

Country	Legislation	Description	
Brazil	Law No. 4.595, 1964	Regulation and supervision of banks (and Consortium Management Companies) within Banco Central do Brazil but the possibility of a separate consolidated supervisory agency is under discussion in Congress. (Banco Central do Brazil is an executive arm of the National Monetary Council.) There are currently separate supervisory agencies for the insurance and securities sectors.	N/A
Chile	Central Bank's Organic Law, Law No. 18.840, 1989	Prudential regulation and supervision has never been within the Banco Central de Chile. However, BCdC has power to regulate and supervise the foreign exchange market. A separate prudential supervisory agency, the Superintendency of Banks and Financial Institutions, was established in 1926.	93
Cyprus	Central Bank of Cyprus Law, 1963	Regulation and supervision of banks within the CboC – prior to independence in 1960 the Treasurer was the controller of banks, mainly for licensing purposes. Co-operative societies supervised by their own Commissioner. Plus separate regulators for insurance and securities.	77
India	Reserve Bank of India Act, 1934	Regulation and supervision of banks, development financial institutions and non-bank financial institutions within the RBI, under a Board for Financial Supervision. There are separate insurance and securities regulatory agencies.	83
Indonesia	Bank Indonesia Act, 1999	Regulation and supervision of banks within central bank. However, these responsibilities will be transferred to a separate supervisory board of financial services sector no later than the end of 2002. There is also currently a securities regulator.	66
Malaysia	Central Bank of Malaysia Act, 1958 (revised 1994)	Regulation and supervision of depositories within CBoM. These responsibilities were extended to include the insurance industry in 1988, and to include finance and credit institutions in 1989.	75
Malawi	Reserve Bank of Malawi Act, 1989	Regulation and supervision of banks and other financial institutions is within the RboM. Gained responsibility as Registrar of Insurance from Ministry of Finance and supervision of insurance companies and building societies. There is no other supervisory body in Malawi.	N/A

Table 2.6 Continued

Country	Central Bank Act	Central Bank as supervisor – past, present and future†	Independence score*
Malta	Central Bank of Malta Act, 1967 (plus amendments)	Regulation and supervision of banks is the responsibility of the central bank as the Competent Authority appointed by the Minister of Finance under the Banking and Financial Institutions Acts of 1994 (previously the central bank was nominated as the banking supervisor under the Banking Act of 1970). The central bank also supervises the Malta Stock Exchange. There is a possibility that the supervisory function of the central bank will be transferred to the Malta Financial Services Centre (established 1994 and covers insurance companies, investment firms and four offshore banks).	83
Mexico	Law on Banco de Mexico, 1995	Regulation and supervision within the Banco de Mexico is limited to financial market activity. Capital and other prudential regulation and supervision has never been within the central bank and is currently carried out by the National Banking and Securities Commission and the Ministry of Finance and Public Credit. There is a separate insurance regulator.	82
Peru	Central Reserve Bank of Peru Act, 1993	Regulation and supervision have never been within the central bank. A separate agency, The Superintendency of Banking and Insurance, was established in 1931. There is also a separate securities regulator.	89
South Africa	South African Reserve Bank Act, 1989	Responsibility for regulation and supervision of banks passed from the Ministry of Finance to the SARB in 1987 while the responsibility for non-bank financial institutions and markets was assigned to the Financial Services Board (insurance and securities regulator). In 1993 the Policy Board for Financial Services and Regulation and the Financial Markets Advisory Board were established to oversee the implementation of appropriate regulatory policy in South Africa. A separate consolidated supervisory agency is a possibility but not imminent.	85

Sri Lanka	Monetary Law Act, 1949	Regulation and supervision of commercial banks within the Central Bank of Sri Lanka, expanded to include finance companies in the early 1980s, offshore foreign currency banking units and Licensed Specialised Banks in mid-1990s. There are separate insurance and securities regulatory bodies.	54
Thailand	Bank of Thailand Act, 1942	Regulation and supervision of banks within the BoT. Under current legislation extensive powers lie with the Ministry of Finance. A new Financial Institutions Act is scheduled to enhance the independence and supervisory power of the BoT.	82
Uganda	Bank of Uganda Act, 1993	Regulation and supervision of all financial institutions, insurance companies and pension funds within the BoU.	81
Zimbabwe	Reserve Bank of Zimbabwe Act, (revised 1999)	Regulation and supervision of banks within the Reserve Bank (although applications for licences and the closure of an institution have to be made to the Registrar of Banks, located within the Ministry of Finance). Responsibility for non-bank financial institutions is shared between the Registrar's office and other government agencies, such as the Commissioner of Insurance and Pension Funds.	N/A

† Sources: websites, survey responses, Coutis (1999)
* Score for independence derived by Fry *et al.* (2000)
N/A – Not available as they were not part of the Fry *et al.* survey sample.

Box 2.5: India – institutional responsibility for financial stability

Who is involved: there are a number of public sector agencies involved in financial stability in India. The Securities and Exchange Board of India (SEBI), the Insurance Regulatory Authority (IRA) within the Ministry of Finance, the National Bank for Agricultural and Rural Development (NABARD), the National Housing Bank (NBH), the Reserve Bank of India (RBI), and the Ministry of Finance which has a overarching interest in the promotion of financial stability.

Reserve Bank of India's role: the preamble to the Reserve Bank of India Act, 1934 sets out the objectives of the RBI as 'to regulate the issue of Bank notes and the keeping of reserves with a view to securing monetary stability in India and generally to operate the currency and credit system of the country to its advantage'. With specific respect to the promotion of financial stability the RBI is entrusted with the sole responsible body for the regulation and supervision of banks under the Banking Regulation Act, 1949. The RBI also contributes to financial stability by:

* promoting the development of the financial system; and
* maintaining orderly conditions in financial markets;

via the promotion of prudent regulation, the development and adoption of new technology, prudential documentation and a robust legal framework.

In its supervisory role the RBI carries out both on-site and off-site surveillance and is gradually moving to a risk-based supervisory framework. In 1994 a Board for Financial Supervision was constituted under the aegis of the RBI. The RBI's supervisory responsibilities were expanded in 1995 to include development financial institutions and in 1997 to include non-bank financial companies. The Board for Financial Supervision ensures an integrated approach to the regulation and supervision of banks, development financial institutions and non-bank financial institutions (see organisation chart below for the current arrangement).

Relationships between agencies: there are no formal arrangements. However, the various supervisory agencies meet regularly to discuss relevant issues of concern. For example, a high level committee, consisting of the RBI Governor, the SEBI Chairman and the Finance Secretary of Central Government, has been convened to discuss developments in, and proposals to strengthen, the functioning of the capital markets.

Data collection/exchange: these informal arrangements also cover the exchange of data. The RBI has powers to require information from a banking company under Section 27 of the Banking Regulation Act and under the provisions of the RBI Act from non-bank financial institutions.

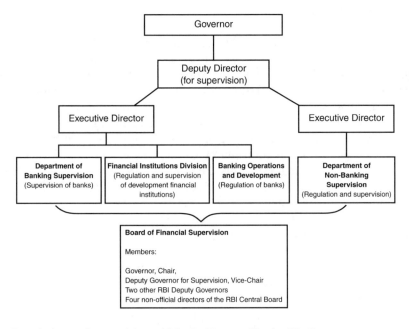

Regulation and supervision within the Reserve Bank of India

Crisis management: arrangements for managing a crisis are not formalised. Each regulator would tend to focus on their areas within their jurisdiction and responsibility for crisis management would be shared jointly with the Government (via the Ministry of Finance). At present a large part of the banking system is Government owned.

2.4   Monetary policy independence and central bank responsibility for prudential regulation and supervision – conflict or synergy?

As noted earlier, there is a strong inter-relationship between monetary and financial stability. Central banks need information about the financial system to make the best possible judgements about monetary policy in order to achieve their monetary policy objectives. There are a number of sources for that information: aggregate monetary and credit data, financial market data, anecdotal market intelligence and supervisory data of individual institutions, among others. This section addresses briefly the principal arguments about whether a central bank should carry out regulation and supervision in addition to its monetary policy responsibilities. We also look briefly at whether there is a correlation between the degree to which a central bank may be 'independent' and whether it has responsibility for prudential regulation and supervision.

So what are the implications for monetary policy of removing financial regulation and supervision from the central bank?

Central bankers who have responsibility for financial regulation and supervision tend to argue that there are important synergies between this function and their responsibilities for monetary policy. For example, the US Federal Reserve has strongly defended this position, on the grounds that it facilitates the timely access to relevant data and that the experience and understanding gained from the involvement of Fed staff in supervisory activities is an important contribution to their understanding of the financial system.[30] Consistent with this, Peek *et al.* (1999) show that banking supervisory data could be used to improve the Federal Reserve's forecasts of both unemployment and inflation.

On the other side of the argument, many commentators, primarily outside central banks, point to the possible temptation of central bankers responsible for the regulation and supervision of individual institutions to compromise their monetary policy objectives for financial stability reasons. This possible conflict is often quoted as one of the reasons why central banks should not have supervisory responsibilities. However, many central bankers have pointed out that this tension potentially exists whether supervision is inside or outside the central bank, and that the central bank would still have to assess the extent to which monetary policy should take account of financial system weakness.[31] Certainly, this potential conflict does not appear to have been an important consideration in changing either the UK or Australian institutional frameworks. Furthermore, the Bundesbank, which has, in the past, placed great weight on this issue in public, nevertheless liaises closely with the banking supervisory agency and undertakes some banking supervision itself.

Was there evidence of a conflict between monetary and financial stability objectives amongst our survey central banks? Among the thirty-seven survey countries a majority had experienced periods of financial sector distress over the last twenty years. Most respondents recognised the interdependence between financial and monetary stability. Asked to what extent financial stability concerns had influenced monetary policy decisions, many countries could identify instances where financial stability concerns were considered in formulating monetary policy but there were few examples where it was clear that monetary policy had been compromised.

In some cases central banks made adjustments in their key monetary policy instruments in response to a financial crisis that threatened the overall economy, for example, by lowering reserve requirements or adjusting central bank targets for short-term interest rates. Making the distinction between 'emergency lending' and an easing in monetary policy is not easy since the instruments used may be the same in both cases. The key

issue is the motivation for the operation. In principle, emergency assistance to the market is an abnormal and temporary measure designed to
relieve market pressure following some adverse exogenous shock, whereas
changes in monetary policy are directed at maintaining longer-term price
stability. However, because in practice financial stability concerns may
affect the monetary outlook, changes in policy may be for both financial
stability and monetary stability purposes. Most of the examples given by
the survey participants fell into this category. In other cases the monetary
implications were negated as central banks that had provided liquidity to
financial institutions in difficulty neutralised the impact on overall market
liquidity.[32]

That said, there were a few instances where central banks felt that monetary policy objectives had been compromised. For example, in Bulgaria
during 1991–7, there was considerable tension between money growth
targets and banking sector stability. While monetary management generally prevailed there were periods of giving priority to the stability of the
banking sector by providing support to weak banks and failing to fully
neutralise such liquidity injections. Considerable tension was also evident
in Thailand in the mid-1990s, to the extent that part of the reason why
their pegged exchange rate regime was finally abandoned in July 1997 was
the failure to defend the currency by tightening liquidity – instead, the
authorities injected large amounts of liquidity into financial institutions. In
both these examples it is a matter of speculation whether the official
response to such tensions would have been significantly different if the
central bank were not the banking supervisor, given the depth of the crisis
and the strength of external pressures. New Zealand gave a more marginal
example. In 1985, just ahead of the float of the exchange rate, a modest
run on reserves led to bank holdings of liquidity assets being extremely
low. Demand to cover those positions drove short-term interest rates
extremely high. Although normal monetary policy considerations would
have eventually driven the authorities to restore normal liquidity levels,
the threat to the soundness of financial institutions if short-term monetary
rates were allowed to remain at abnormal levels for long, and the threat
posed to the access of other parties to credit was, at the margin, a
consideration in prompting quicker action to reinject liquidity.

So how important did the central banks in the survey feel that supervisory data were in the early identification of financial stability concerns?
We asked countries which had experienced periods of financial instability
over the last twenty years to identify which data source first raised financial stability concerns (thirty-one countries). In descending order of popularity: there were fifteen votes for supervisory data, twelve votes for
financial market data, twelve votes for aggregate monetary and credit
data, six votes for anecdotal market intelligence and three other varied
data sources were identified. Of these countries, sixteen felt that supervisory data had been *very important* in assessing the extent of the problem,

ten said the data were *important*, two that the data were *helpful but not essential* and the remaining three pointed out that the relevance varied from case to case. Clearly the experiences of the majority of central banks over the last twenty years supports the view that prompt access to supervisory data is crucial in identifying and/or assessing the extent of a financial stability problem.

There are other arguments for separating monetary policy from banking supervision. Separation reduces the risk of a crisis distracting senior management from their monetary policy tasks, and it reduces the possibility of a banking failure damaging the central bank's reputation, and thereby the credibility of monetary policy.

The significance of these arguments will vary according to each country's institutional framework and context. The precise trade-off between the benefits and the costs depends on what measures can be implemented to reduce the costs and increase the benefits. In general, the following will be key issues: arrangements for exchanging and sharing information relevant for monetary policy; transparency of responsibility, particularly in crisis management, will impact on damage to credibility from financial failures; and accountability will affect the incentives for individuals and organisations to remain focused and perform well. However, the precise design of effective measures to maximise the benefits and minimise the costs will vary across countries.

Finally, governments may consider it unwise to concentrate power beyond certain limits within an unelected body. Goodhart (1996) said that 'a central bank which is both independent in its conduct of monetary policy and responsible for banking supervision may be perceived as too powerful and separate an entity in the otherwise democratic body politic'. In the 1990s, there has been a marked trend of central banks being granted independence to formulate and implement monetary policy. This is highlighted in a survey of ninety-four central banks by Fry *et al.* (2000) which shows that two-thirds were granted independence over monetary policy with little or no qualification. This has given those central banks more power and influence over the economy. As central banks have gained power in one realm, it is likely that policy-makers feel it is unwise to increase the central bank's supervisory role and they may even wish to reduce it. In the case of the UK, Goodhart *et al.* (1998) believe that the Bank of England gaining monetary policy independence in 1997 and the announcement just two weeks later that it would lose responsibility for banking supervision was no coincidence.

So has the move towards more independent central banks been accompanied by a withdrawal from prudential regulation and supervision? We have taken the survey group of countries to see if we could identify a relationship between the responsibility for prudential supervision and independence. The chart shown below uses a score for monetary policy independence derived by Fry *et al.* (2000) for eighty-three countries (i.e.

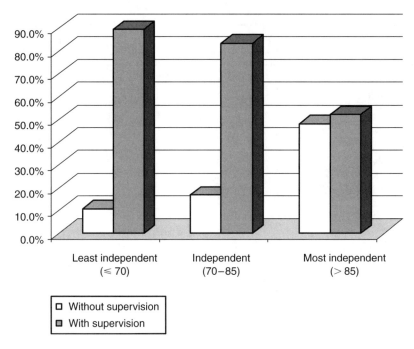

Chart 2.2 Central bank independence in monetary policy and financial supervision

those countries surveyed by Fry *et al.* for which we could ascertain whether the central bank did or did not have responsibility for prudential supervision. (See Table 2.7 for a list of the sample countries and their independence scores.) The approach adopted by Fry *et al.* follows that of Cukieman (1992) and Grilli, Masciandaro and Tabellini (1991). The overall measure of independence is defined over a range of characteristics covering legal objectives, goals, instruments, finance of the government deficit and term of office of the Governor (see pages 64–9 of *Monetary Frameworks in a Global Context*). The sample is broken down into three groups according to their independence rating.

A regression over the whole sample gave a statistically significant response with a negative correlation between independence and supervision, i.e. the more monetary policy independence a central bank has, the less likely it is to also carry out prudential regulation and supervision. The results are affected by the sample, which represents roughly half the world's central banks, and the 'independence' scores are notoriously sensitive to different measurement specifications.[33] Looking at the sample by type of economy shows that for the industrial and transition countries the correlation actually goes the other way – non-supervisory central banks have an unweighted mean independence score of eighty-two compared

Table 2.7   Independence scores and supervisory role of eighty-three countries
included in regression sample (see Chart 2.2 in Section 2.4)

Country	Central bank is the prudential banking supervisor = 1	Independence score*
Albania	1	66
Argentina	1	79
Armenia	1	76
Australia	0	73
Bahamas	1	39
Bahrain	1	54
Bangladcsh	1	56
Barbados	1	24
Belgium	1	77
Bosnia	0	81
Botswana	1	65
Bulgaria	1	79
Canada	0	91
Chile	0	93
China	1	68
Croatia	1	79
Cyprus	1	77
Czech Republic	1	98
Denmark	0	88
Ecuador	0	93
Egypt	1	53
Estonia	1	85
Fiji	1	73
Finland	0	91
France	0	90
Georgia	1	80
Germany	0	96
Ghana	1	60
Greece	1	86
Guyana	1	65
Hong Kong	1	74
Hungary	0	86
Iceland	0	59
India	1	83
Indonesia	1	66
Ireland	1	87
Israel	1	66
Italy	1	88
Jamaica	1	39
Japan	0	93
Jordan	1	74
Kazakhstan	1	76
Kenya	1	66
Korea, South	0	73
Kuwait	1	63
Latvia	1	98
Lithuania	1	89

Country	Central bank is the prudential banking supervisor = 1	Independence score*
Macedonia	1	80
Malaysia	1	75
Malta	1	83
Mauritius	1	70
Mexico	0	82
Mongolia	1	70
Mozambique	1	71
Netherlands	1	91
New Zealand	1	89
Nigeria	1	42
Norway	0	57
Peru	0	89
Poland	1	86
Portugal	1	85
Romania	1	77
Russia	1	76
Sierra Leone	1	62
Singapore	1	90
Slovakia	1	90
Slovenia	1	86
South Africa	1	85
Spain	1	80
Sri Lanka	1	54
Sweden	0	97
Switzerland	0	90
Taiwan	1	85
Tanzania	1	60
Thailand	1	82
Tonga	1	52
Turkey	0	70
Uganda	1	81
UK	0	77
Ukraine	1	63
Uruguay	1	70
USA	1	92
Zambia	1	66

* Derived by Fry *et al.* (2000)

with eighty-six for those that supervise (see Table 2.7 above). This difference is modest and too much should not be read into it. However, it highlights that it is the fact that developing countries exhibit lower independence and more widespread supervisory responsibilities that drives the negative association overall.

2.5   Key issues in establishing an effective regulatory institutional structure

As financial systems become increasingly integrated, pressure for integrated financial regulation and supervision will grow, both at a domestic and an international level. There does not appear to be a single optimal model and the precise institutional arrangements chosen by any country will need to reflect many country-specific factors.[34] In the end, institutional arrangements are largely a political decision and out of the hands of central banks. However, based on the experiences of our survey countries, there appear to be certain features that are important in devising an appropriate and effective institutional structure:

- the supervisor needs a good reputation in order to attract staff and the resources to train staff and maintain an effective supervisory regime (while the skill sets needed to focus on consumer protection versus systemic stability are different – a factor which supports the separation of these functions – one concern is that consumer protection may come to dominate separate supervisory agencies, leaving systemic stability, which has greater effects on the economy, to suffer (see Chapter 3 of this volume for a discussion of these issues);
- the central bank needs timely access to supervisory information in order to perform its monetary policy responsibilities and its lender of last resort function;
- the responsibilities of, and the division of responsibilities between, the central bank, regulatory authorities and the government should be clear and public – the more accountability there is the greater the incentives to perform. Therefore, each institution should have few objectives and multiple objectives should be prioritised and any trade-offs between objectives recognised. (For example, the UK's FSA has four objectives under the Financial Services and Markets Act 2000: maintaining market confidence; promoting public understanding of the financial system; the protection of consumers; and fighting financial crime.) There is a competition versus safety trade-off between maintaining market confidence (by maintaining efficient and orderly financial markets) and the protection of consumers. However, the trade-off is not explicit and different stakeholders may have different views about the optimal balance between the two objectives); and
- even where current relationships between agencies work well, there should be formal arrangements in place that support a cooperative approach, if necessary enshrined in law (e.g. Memorandum of Understanding, exchange of staff, joint examinations, formal committees, mutual board membership, information gateways). This is particularly important for surveillance of risks and crisis management. If a number of agencies are involved: a shared philosophy/approach is essential;

clarity about roles reduces the risk of disagreements or lengthy negotiations; and good existing relationships promote trust.

2.6   Conclusions

Central bank involvement in financial stability has a long and interesting history. Today there are more central banks than ever before and they have wide-ranging and extensive powers. However, the scope of their roles varies considerably. In particular, whether central banks carry out prudential regulation and supervision or not, they will nearly always have a role in 1) promoting a sound infrastructure, 2) surveillance and 3) crisis management. Certainly, all but one of our survey central banks considered the promotion of 'systemic stability' and the stability of payment and settlement systems as part of their core mandate. It is also notable that whatever the formal powers or tools allocated to a central bank it is its influence that counts – and this can be very hard to measure.

The survey results indicate that central banks tend to exercise a larger range of functions in *smaller* and *poorer* economies. The five out of the thirteen industrial countries that have regulatory and supervisory responsibilities include the three smallest by population (Singapore, Ireland and New Zealand). By contrast, twenty of the twenty-four transition and developing countries' central banks perform regulatory and supervisory duties. In the four that do not, Chile, Hungary, Mexico and Peru, GDP per head is somewhat above average for their groups. It would appear that broader central bank responsibilities go hand in hand, in the main, with lower total GDP and also with lower GDP per head.[35] This is not surprising. In less advanced economies, banks tend to be less complex institutions and financial markets are typically simpler. Financial sector policy is dominated to a greater degree by the need to build capacity for growth and to a lesser degree by consumer protection issues. Given the absence of private sector skills and finance, governments and their agents perform a wider range of functions.

The institutional structure of regulation and supervision has recently become an issue of public policy debate in a number of countries, largely as a result of changes in the structure of financial systems. Given the range of responses by authorities, there does not appear to be a universal ideal model. Also, not all of the movement is in the direction of integrating supervision outside the central bank. In some countries supervision is being/has been integrated within the central bank. There is also a question for central banks who lose their macroeconomic role – what is their function if they do not retain other responsibilities, the most obvious being prudential supervision? Concerns for survival may lead to some strengthening of central banks' supervisory role. For example, in Germany, where the Bundesbank currently cooperates with the supervisory agency, the German Government is considering transferring banking supervision completely to the Bundesbank.

While we have made some preliminary observations in the previous section with respect to devising an appropriate and effective institutional structure, each country will have to consider their own set of relevant factors. More analysis should be possible over time as alternative models, both older and newer (such as the arrangements adopted by Australia, Korea, Japan and the UK), are tested by a financial crisis or severe instability. However, any expectations of being able to adopt an 'ideal' model for any country have to be tempered by the reality that these decisions are largely in political hands – some compromise is likely.

And while institutional structure is important, it does not guarantee effective and efficient regulation and supervision. Changing the structure of regulatory and supervisory institutions is not a panacea.

Notes

1 The author is heavily indebted to the central banks who contributed to the survey upon which this chapter is based. The author would also like to thank Bill Allen, Glenn Hoggarth, Lavan Mahadeva, Chang Shu, Peter Sinclair, Paul Tucker and many of the central bank survey contacts for their helpful comments. Also, grateful thanks go to Chang Shu, Lucy Clary, Tony Ison, Carron Robson and Lorraine Yuille for their assistance. The opinions in this chapter are those of the author and not necessarily those of the Bank of England or those of any other contributing central bank.

2 However, any errors, either factual or interpretation, are solely the responsibility of the author.

3 The sample needed to be large enough to enable useful comparisons but small enough to ensure that the workload was manageable. The countries were chosen to provide a mix of industrial, transitional and developing countries, and a large number of countries which had experienced a crisis in the last twenty years. The sample also includes most of the countries where the central bank is not the banking supervisor. A few countries chose not to complete the questionnaire. However, of these, both the USA and Japan provided source references. See Boxes 2.2 and 2.3 which describe their practices.

4 The description here is necessarily brief. For a more comprehensive description of the development of central banking, refer to *The Future of Central Banking* by Capie, Goodhart, Fischer and Schnadt 1994.

5 The range of frameworks adopted by countries and recent developments were explored by Fry *et al.* (2000) in *Monetary Policy Frameworks in a Global Context*, edited by Mahadeva and Sterne.

6 Also, in some cases, for example the UK, the central bank's own credit exposures.

7 But not without reference to costs – both the central bank's costs and the costs borne by financial institutions.

8 All of these countries also carry out broader financial stability surveillance. In particular Denmark, Finland, Norway, Sweden and the UK regularly publish macro prudential analyses.

9 The exception is Peru, where the central bank is only concerned with monetary stability, and responsibility for financial stability is shared between the Treasury (as lender of last resort) and the regulatory and supervisory agency.

10 Of course these central banks continue to act as a settlement bank to the banking system as the provider of the ultimate settlement assets.

11 A recent example is the development of CLSB (Continuous Linked Settlement Bank). With the cooperation of the key central banks and under the licensing authority of the US Federal Reserve, a group of private sector banks are in the process of establishing a cross-border multi-currency simultaneous settlement mechanism.

12 For example, the Norges Bank Act allows the central bank, in special circumstances, to make loans and extend other forms of credit to non-bank entities. Similarly, the Bank of Korea Act stipulates that the BOK may offer credit to non-bank financial institutions in periods of severe monetary and credit contraction when banking institutions call outstanding loans and refrain from entertaining new ones.

13 In principle, ELA is available to any institution supervised by APRA, provided that the institution is solvent and failure to make its payments poses a threat to the stability of the financial system, and there is a need to act expeditiously.

14 See Chapter 5 of this volume. See also Saapar and Soussa (2000).

15 For an examination of how different design features affect deposit interest rates and market discipline, see Demirgüç-Kunt and Huizinga (2000). Also, at the time of writing, the Financial Stability Forum had issued an interim report, 'International Guidance on Deposit Insurance' with a view to developing practical guidance on deposit insurance issues for countries considering the adoption of a deposit insurance system.

16 For a comprehensive examination of deposit insurance around the world see 'Deposit Insurance: A Survey of Actual and Best Practices', Gillian Garcia, IMF Working Paper, April 1999.

17 In all countries the government is the body responsible for implementing changes to the law.

18 For example, Australia has adopted a 'twin peaks' approach whereby prudential supervision and conduct of business regulation are carried out by separate agencies. In Canada, some firms are federally chartered and others are provincially incorporated, which means that not all banking and securities firms are regulated and supervised by the same agency (see Box 2.1).

19 The nearest any of the central banks came to being responsible for regulation and supervision were two Norwegian proposals, one in 1974 for the merger of the bank inspectorate with the central bank and one in 1992 for the integrated supervisory body to merge with the central bank – both proposals were defeated in parliament.

20 The existence of compulsory private sector pension schemes may make a fully-integrated approach to regulation inappropriate for Finland. See Taylor and Fleming (1999).

21 By 1997 it was estimated by the Reserve Bank of Austrialia that financial conglomerates held around 80 per cent of Australia's financial system assets.

22 The three-peaked system built on the existing structure, with the Bank of England responsible for banking groups and the wholesale market, the Securities and Investment Board for investment firms and investment and derivative exchanges, and an insurance agency for insurance companies.

23 See Box 2.3 for a description of Japan's institutional responsibilities for financial stability. Japan did not participate in the survey and is therefore not included in Tables 2.3–2.5.

24 However, under the Bank of Korea Act, the BOK may, when the Monetary Policy Committee deems it necessary for the implementation of its monetary and credit policies, require the Financial Supervisory Service to examine

banking institutions and, when necessary, to accept BOK staff as participants in the examination of banking institutions.

25 For example, see *One Money, Many Countries*, CEPR, January 2000.
26 The USA did not participate in the survey and is therefore not included in Tables 2.3–2.5.
27 14 January 2000, remarks made before a National Bureau of Economic Research Conference.
28 See remarks by Governor Meyer on 15 December 1999, before the Symposium on Financial Modernisation Legislation.
29 Exceptions are: agriculture, forestry and fisheries which are jointly supervised with MAFF; labour credits unions which are jointly supervised with the Ministry of Labour; the Postal Savings and Postal Life Insurance which are supervised by MPTT; and government financial institutions which are supervised by MoF.
30 See, for example, statements by E. Gerald Corrigan (1990, 1991).
31 There is a considerable amount of economic literature which stresses that, via the bank lending channel, the output costs of any monetary policy action depends on financial stability.
32 Emerging countries may face different challenges compared with a typical G-10 country in the face of a systemic liquidity problem. If there is strong demand for foreign assets and low demand for domestic assets the key issue will not be the ability to provide liquidity in local currency but access to a credible foreign currency like US dollars. See Powell (2000).
33 As Cukieman said, 'Actual, as opposed to formal, central bank independence depends on the degree of independence conferred on the bank by law, but also on a myriad of less structured factors such as informal arrangements between the bank and other parts of the government, the quality of the bank's research department, and the personalities of key individuals in the bank and other policymaking organs like the Treasury' (1992: 369). See a special issue of *Oxford Economic Papers* in July 1998 that includes eleven articles on many of the issues.
34 Hawkesby (2000) sets out a general framework for addressing this issue and Taylor and Fleming (1999) investigate lessons from the Scandinavian experience. See also Chapter 3 of this volume and Briault (1999).
35 This result might be less obvious if the sample of industrial countries were widened, for example, to include more of the EU member states.

3 The organisational structure of banking supervision

Professor Charles Goodhart[1]

3.1 Introduction

In 1997 the newly-elected Labour Government in the United Kingdom transferred responsibility for the prudential supervision of commercial banks from the Bank of England to a newly-established body, the Financial Services Authority (FSA). The FSA was to take on responsibility for, and combine, both the prudential and the conduct of business supervision for virtually all financial institutions (banks of all kinds, finance houses, mutual savings institutions, insurance companies, etc.), and financial markets. So, during the course of 1998 most of the banking supervisors who had been working together in a designated section of the Bank moved together, *en bloc*, to the new headquarters of the FSA at Canary Wharf, a few miles further east.

The same people continued to do the same job. What then had changed?[2] Moreover, the commercial confidentiality of their work had meant that their offices in the Bank had previously been sealed off internally from the rest of the Bank (Chinese Walls!). Given the increasing ease of long-distance communication (by e-mail as well as telephone and fax), would channels of information really be that much changed by the physical move?

One possible answer could be that both the physical location and the organisational structure of the financial supervision of banks is, indeed, a second-order problem. It is not the purpose, or intention, of this chapter to argue whether, and if so exactly how, financial institutions need to be supervised. On the maintained assumption that some such supervision will continue to be needed, the banking/financial supervisors will *have to* work closely with the central bank, and vice versa, whatever the organisational structure.

However much the central bank is focused on macroeconomic issues of monetary and price stability, the achievement of such macro objectives rests on the basis of maintaining micro-level financial stability, in the payments system, in the banking system and the smooth working of the financial system more broadly. So the central bank will have an on-going concern for financial stability and financial regulation; a central bank will feel that it needs to be in close and continuous contact with the supervisory body, however that may be organised. By the same token, the health and profitability of the financial system depend on the macro-conjuncture; the supervisory authorities will want to learn from the central bank what may be expected on this front.

No-one particularly likes having an older relative looking over their shoulder, and an independent supervisory body may be jealous of its own independence. Indeed, such *amour propre* may be one of the obstacles to a full and satisfactory flow of information. Nevertheless a sensible supervisory authority would realise both that the central bank should act as a partner in any proposed change in the regulatory structure, and that, as a supervisory body, it has no ability on its own to provide financing (to lend or to create money) to financial institutions needing some financial injection. Again, it is not the purpose of this paper to argue whether, when and how lender of last resort functions should be carried out. But, should the supervisory body want to propose the injection of extra funding into the financial system, it needs to obtain the approval of the central bank (and nowadays in most cases also of the Ministry of Finance) to do so. In the first instance, and normally, LOLR functions would be carried out by the central bank. It is certainly possible to conceive of a banking supervisor approaching its own Ministry of Finance directly in order to use taxpayers' funds to obtain resources for such a financial injection. But if that were done behind the back, or against the professional wishes, of that country's central bank, it would surely trigger the resignation of that Bank's Governor and a (constitutional) crisis within, and amongst, the monetary authorities. Perhaps the resignation of Miguel Mancera from the Central Bank of Mexico in 1982, when there was an over-riding political imperative to bail out banks using public money, could be cited as a possible example.

So, whatever the details and form of organisational structure, those in charge of banking supervision and those in the central bank most concerned with financial stability are, perforce, going to have to work together. If so, it could be argued that the precise details of the organisational structure are, at most, of second order importance, and that the scale of attention given to this issue in practice is an indication of the incidence of 'turf wars' rather than of matters of real substance.

In support of this proposition, one can adduce the fact that the organisational relationship between banking supervision and central banks has been established in many separate ways in different countries (see Goodhart and Schoenmaker 1995; Goodhart, Hartmann *et al.* 1998). There are undoubtedly some changing factors that shift the balance towards a preference for one, or other, institutional structure – and these will be discussed further below – as well as changing fashions of viewpoint in this field. Nevertheless the fact that organisational diversity has been so prevalent indicates that it may not have an over-riding influence on outcomes. Despite some studies claiming to find significant differences on a variety of outcomes dependent on the organisational structure adopted (see, for example, Heller 1991; Briault 1997; Di Noia and Di Giorgio 1999), the practical implication of the observed diversity could be that it is not a matter of first moment. Indeed, the problem of trying to assess the best organisational structure is not made easier by the propensity of all institutions, notably including central banks, to argue, and with great cogency, that, whatever their present structure may be, it is *optimal*, or at least would be if some slight additional extra funding and powers could be made available to it!

If we accept, as a maintained hypothesis, that banking supervisors and the central bank should work closely together whatever the organisational structure, why should that structure matter? There are numerous reasons, most of which will be outlined and discussed subsequently. One of the main reasons for concern about such differences is that organisational structure may have some influence on the type of people involved in the exercise of banking supervision, their calibre and professional skills, and the ethos and culture of the organisation in which they work.[3] At the outset of Section 3.1, we saw that most of the same individual banking supervisors who had worked at the Bank of England are still working at the FSA.[4] But in five or ten years time will the skill-structure, outlook and incentives of those working in this capacity at the FSA be the same as if responsibility for this function had remained with the Bank? And will the Bank also retain its skills to handle crises (see Ferguson 2000; Greenspan 1994)? One of the features of this chapter is that we shall emphasise the issue of the influence of organisational structure on the personnel involved, particularly with respect to emerging and transitional countries.

In so far as the maintained assumption that banking supervisors and the central bank must continue to work closely together, hand in glove, remains, then the obvious (default) solution would seem to be to keep banking supervision within the central bank. Information flows must surely be enhanced; differences of view patched up, and decision-making expedited and facilitated by such internalisation. The fact that price stability and financial stability go hand-in-hand, and have historically always been seen as doing so, would seem to provide a strong *a priori* argument in favour of keeping them organisationally unified within the central bank[5] (see Volcker 1984), though, perhaps, in a semi-detached manner, as has been achieved in recent decades in their various ways in both France and Germany.[6]

Roger Ferguson Jr, a Governor of the Federal Reserve Board, in a 1998 Conference speech (published 2000), covered much the same ground as this chapter. He was clearly making the case for the Fed maintaining a significant role in banking supervision, a case that the Federal Reserve

Board has argued cogently in recent decades (e.g. Volcker 1984 and Greenspan and FRB 1994). He argued that

> In the last analysis, there simply is no substitute for understanding the links among supervision, regulation, market behavior, risk taking, prudential standards, and – let us not lose sight – macro stability. The intelligence and know-how that come from our examination and regulatory responsibilities play an important – at times, critical – role in our monetary policy-making. No less relevant, our economic stabilization responsibilities contribute to our supervisory policies. Observers and supervisors from single-purpose agencies often lose sight of how too rigorous or too lenient a supervisory stance – or a change in stance – can have serious and significant macro-economic implications, the consideration of which is likely to modify the supervisory policy.
>
> In short, I think the Fed's monetary policy is better because of its supervisory responsibilities, and its supervision and regulation are better because of its stabilization responsibilities.
>
> (2000: 301)

And yet, as was highlighted by the survey evidence presented in Chapter 2, it is clear that the current tide is running now quite strongly in the opposite direction.[7] The Wallis Report in Australia, the establishment of the FSA in the UK, much of the advice of the IMF to its member countries[8] (whether developed, or not), recent developments in Korea and Japan,[9] and proposals in South Africa and India, all have moved towards the separation of financial supervision from central banks.[10] In the Eurozone a separation between monetary policy (at the federal level) and banking supervision (at the national level) has occurred *de facto*, though many commentators are unhappy with this separation, (see Dubouchet 2000; Goodhart 2000). Such separation has already been established in most Scandinavian countries (Denmark, Iceland, Norway and Sweden).[11] Indeed, there are cogent reasons advanced for advocating such a separation, and the grounds for this shift have become stronger in the light of current developments. Partly because we have started, in this Introduction, by setting out the historical, *a priori* case for internalising banking supervision within the central bank, we shall move on next in Section 3.2 to outlining the reasons advanced for *separation*. We shall do so first within the context of more developed countries. Then, in Section 3.3, we shall return to arguments in favour of *combination*, again sticking primarily to the case as seen amongst developed countries. In Section 3.4 we shall move on to review some of the additional issues relevant particularly to *developing* and emerging countries. Section 3.5 concludes, and contains some suggestions for future research.

3.2 Arguments for separation

3.2.1 The changing structure of the financial system

Initially in the course of development, commercial banks have provided most of the services of financial intermediation. When, thereafter, a variety of other financial intermediary services developed, e.g. investment banking, insurance, fund management, and so on, it so happened historically (notably between 1930 and 1970) that macroeconomic developments and the fashion of policy led to the enforcement of strict demarcation lines between the various financial intermediaries and their functions, e.g. the Glass–Steagall Act in the USA. Moreover, for much of this period (1930–70) and in many of the countries, there were direct controls on competition between such intermediaries, and on the quantities, and pricing, of the business that they could do. The *quid pro quo* for the existing intermediaries was control over new entry and the establishment of controlled prices/interest rates at levels that ensured a comfortable franchise value. The result, in many cases, was the establishment of cartelised clubs of semi-specialised intermediaries, for whom the oligopolistic structure, and with official encouragement, led to the establishment of largely self-regulating clubs with agreed rules of conduct.

This oligopolistic structure, with limited competition and guaranteed franchise value, reduced the likelihood of financial failure; following the recovery from the great depression in the 1930s until the 1970s, the incidence of financial failure and crises plummeted, partly because of international stability achieved by the Bretton Woods arrangements. This reduced, indeed almost obviated, the need for hands-on banking, and financial, supervision. Until the Fringe Banking Crisis in 1974/75, the Bank of England restricted their direct supervision to a small number of Merchant Banks (the Accepting Houses) and to the Discount Market, stemming from the Bank's own credit exposures. The supervisory function was carried out by one single senior official, the Principal of the Discount Office, with a handful of staff! So, historically, the conduct of banking supervision did *not*, in practice, play a really large, or central, role in central bank activities,[12] because the structure both reduced the need for such an exercise and allowed it to be largely achieved through self-regulation (though this may have been particularly so in the UK, and less representative of other countries). In the USA, the Fed only really became a major player in banking regulation and supervision with the enactment of the Bank Holding Act in 1956, which gave it authority over Bank Holding Companies (BHCs).[13]

Limitation of competition and oligopoly hindered competition, efficiency and innovation. The protected and regulated financial system that emerged after the end of the Second World War eventually gave way under the assault of international competition (mostly emanating from the USA); technological innovation (mostly in information technology); a drive for greater efficiency and improved services for customers; and a return to enthusiasm for liberal, market-based, ideology. The greater competition placed downwards pressure on profitability, capital ratios and franchise values. Financial instability and failures became more prevalent. Central banks found themselves increasingly involved in supervisory activities. Some would add that poorly-designed regulation and safety nets then became a further cause of bank failures.

These same forces, however, were blurring the previously clear boundaries between categories of financial intermediaries. Universal banking became more popular and commonplace. Banking became mingled with insurance, bank assurance, and both undertook fund management. Eventually that meant that the attempt to supervise separately by *function*, e.g. commercial banking, investment banking, fund management, etc., would involve a multiplicity of separate supervisors, all crawling over parts of the same single institution. This was hardly efficient, or cost effective.

The boundaries between financial intermediaries had become thoroughly blurred.[14] Borio and Filosa (1994) were, perhaps, the first to explore the consequences of this for the structure of financial supervision (see also Abrams and Taylor (forthcoming)). So one obvious conclusion that was reached was equivalently to place responsibility for the supervision of all financial intermediaries in one institution. But this naturally caused a problem for central banks, should they wish to maintain internal control of banking supervision. The logic of placing all supervision under one roof would then require the central bank to take responsibility for supervision over activities which lay outside its historical sphere of expertise and responsibility. An even more serious problem than already exists would arise of how to demarcate the boundaries between those sub-set of depositors/institutions which would be covered by the 'safety net' (explicit or implicit), deposit insurance, lender of last resort facilities, etc., and those not so covered. Would the central bank really want to take under its wing the responsibility for customer protection in fund management? In practice, much of staff time, even in banking supervision, is taken up with customer protection issues (other than deposit insurance). Would a central bank really want to extend its operational remit to dealing with financial markets and institutions where issues relating to systemic stability were limited, and consumer protection of much greater importance (e.g. the pension mis-selling scandal in the UK?). So if efficiency and cost saving implied the unification of financial supervision, this suggested placing such a unified body outside the central bank (see, for an excellent exposition, Briault 1999).

But did it necessarily imply such unification? One alternative proposal was to divide the structure of supervision not by market function, e.g. banking, insurance, fund management, but by the *purpose* of supervision. Here the suggestion was that supervision should be organised around the two purposes of *systemic stability* (prudential supervision) on the one hand

and *customer protection* (conduct of business supervision) on the other; this was the Twin Peaks proposal, pushed in the UK primarily in the work of Michael Taylor (1995, 1996). The supervisory body charged with customer protection would naturally take the lead in some areas, markets and institutions. *Per contra*, the body charged with responsibility for systemic stability would take the lead in dealing with the payments system, and with certain aspects of banking and, perhaps, other financial markets. Even so, there would remain considerable overlaps and duplication.

There are residual vestiges of the Twin Peaks concept in the more unified systems adopted, e.g. in Australia and the UK. The central bank usually maintains control of overseeing the payments mechanisms, and will have a much closer involvement in those aspects of supervision potentially raising systemic concerns. Nevertheless the Twin Peaks concept has, so far, not found favour in practice, though, in a slightly inchoate manner, the US system has evolved in a way that approximates to it, with the FRB coming close to a systemic stability (prudential) supervisor, and the SEC undertaking the conduct of business role.

It is not clear, to me at least, quite why this has been so. There would, undoubtedly, have been room for overlap and friction between the two bodies involved; and having to deal with two sets of supervisors would raise the cost to the supervised entities. On the other hand, there would have been some merit in focusing each of the bodies on one particular purpose. A concern that some have is that customer protection is almost certain to take up the greater bulk of the staff's work-load within a unified supervisory body. Might then the requirements of maintaining systemic stability, which has larger effects on real incomes and national wealth in the longer run, come to play second fiddle to a culture and ethos concentrating on customer protection? Pauli (2000) comments that, 'The different focus as between investor protection and systemic stability is however so pronounced that there are good arguments for having the primary responsibilities for these two functions divided between separate bodies.'[15]

If the Twin Peaks concept had been adopted, it would have been odd if the systemic stability group of supervisors had *not* been kept within – or under the umbrella of – the central bank. One reason for moving to a unified system may, indeed, have been to extract supervisory responsibilities altogether from the central bank. We shall come to reasons for advocating this shortly.

In practice, however, (a) to a large extent a 'systemic stability' regulator and a 'customer protection' regulator would approach the regulation of a large bank in exactly the same way (so there would be considerable duplication and overlap), and (b) as with the FSA and its multiple statutory objectives, there is no reason why a single regulator should not combine a number of objectives and fine-tune its regulatory approach accordingly.[16]

A somewhat different distinction, than between systemic stability and customer protection issues, is that between top-down (macro) and bottom-up (micro) approaches towards these same issues. Most consumer protection issues are micro, whereas some prudential, stability issues are macro, with some micro. It can be, and has been, argued that dividing the systemic stability issues between top-down macro, kept with the central bank (e.g. in the UK and in Australia), and bottom-up micro, all with an independent agency (or agencies), reinforces clarity and responsibility.

For example, in its Annual Report, June 2000, the BIS is concerned that a purely micro-level concern with the treatment of risk could have unforeseen, and unintended, effects at the aggregate level.[17] This might be dealt with best by interacting the top-down expertise of the central bank with the bottom-up approach of the supervisor. If both approaches were subsumed within the central bank, one or other might be suppressed or overlooked.

3.2.2   *International issues*

First, however, we should also note that amongst the boundaries that have been crumbling are the geographical limitations of the financial activities of commercial institutions to their own nation state. The largest financial entities are now multinational. The contrast between such multinational commercial activities and the inevitable reliance of regulators and supervisors on *national* laws (since regulation depends on law, and law-making is in the domain of the sovereign state), produces many strains, see for example the G-30 paper *on Global Institutions, National Supervision and Systemic Risk* (1997). It is, however, far less clear whether, and why, such commercial multinationalism would influence the choice of national structure.

In so far as (most of) the major banks in any one country have their headquarters, and site of consolidated supervisory oversight, in another country, that would imply that the (smaller) country dominated by foreign banks might take a somewhat more relaxed view of banking supervision (e.g. New Zealand). But such a possible relaxation could occur whatever the domestic structure. Such multinational commercial activity places greater emphasis on cross-country cooperation amongst regulators and supervisors; for example, who provides the financial support and who takes on the fiscal loss in the case of the collapse of an international bank? Central banks have been renowned for their collegial approach, fostered by the good offices of the BIS. But international cooperation on such issues is hardly going to be damaged if each country should now send two representatives (i.e. from its central bank and its separate supervisory body) to the Basel meetings of supervisors.[18]

It is sometimes suggested that the multinational operations of major banks, and other financial entities, may reduce the ability of domestic central banks to control macro-economic monetary policy within their own country. But so long as the central bank maintains a floating exchange rate regime, its capacity to control its own short-term interest rate, and growth rate for the monetary aggregates, are not impaired by the global spread of business. The central bank will maintain as much concern for price stability, and with that for financial stability, in a world of international commercial entities, as it had when its financial firms were overwhelmingly national in coverage.

The assessment of the situation changes, however, when the central bank switches from a floating exchange rate to a fixed rate. The extent of fixity can vary from an irrevocably unified exchange rate, as in the Euro area, through dollarisation, as in Panama and now in Ecuador, through to a Currency Board regime, as in Argentina, Bulgaria, Estonia and Hong Kong. In each case the central bank loses the power to control macro-economic monetary policy. That consideration tells both ways. On the one hand, if central banks are to lose their macro-economic role, what is to be their function, their *raison d'être*, if they do not hold on to their other responsibilities, notably for supervision? Indeed, a radical might ask whether, without some supervisory function, they will really be needed at all in future; perhaps just an historical (and expensive) monument. Concerns for institutional survival will cause central banks, when stripped of their macroeconomic role, to argue more strenuously for retention of their other activities, notably banking supervision.

But by the same token, central banks in such a subsidiary state (subsidiary to a hegemonic central bank, e.g. the ECB or Fed), have less ability to create money (and perhaps undertake LOLR functions, but that issue remains moot for the NCBs in the ESCB) on their own. They have less independent power to maintain financial stability. Indeed, the ability of the monetary authorities in some such circumstances to intervene may depend more on the fiscal ability of the Ministry of Finance to make euros/dollars available for financial intervention than on the capacity of the central bank to take loans on to its own balance sheet. In such circumstances LOLR becomes even more directly a fiscal measure than a monetary action. So the question of the role of the central bank will depend largely on its relationship with the relevant fiscal authorities in the pursuit of financial stability.

Nevertheless, the multinational coverage of the major financial intermediaries means that supervisors and regulators in any one country have a concern with the standards and competence of such supervision/regulation in other countries, especially where such intermediaries may have their headquarters. Such concern can be met (minimally) by the agreement of codes, or principles, of good conduct in these fields. Such codes have proliferated in recent years, multiplying at an almost exponential rate. Beyond codes, there can be agreements on minimum standards, either at a regional level, as in the European Community Directives, or globally as in the Basel Accords on Capital Adequacy.

It is relatively simple to agree on codes, on what represents good behaviour. It is more difficult to monitor and to apply sanctions for infringement. But international sanctions do exist. Publicity, or 'naming and shaming', is an important instrument, e.g. as used by the Financial Stability Forum to grade the relative status of supervision among off-shore centres.[19] Beyond publicity, the possibility of excluding intermediaries in the offending countries from financial markets elsewhere would represent a strong, and quite credible, potential punishment.

Perhaps as difficult and important as sanctions is the problem of how to monitor (bank) supervision and regulation elsewhere, an issue of importance in so far as a financial crisis in one country might have contagious spill-over effects on other countries. Suggestions have been made that such international monitoring could be done by one, or other, or a combination of international financial agencies, e.g. BIS, IBRD, IMF, or, perhaps, by a 'college' of national regulators, i.e. self-regulation for the regulators. But, at the time of writing not much practical advance had been made, and the question 'Quis custodiet ipsos custodes?' remained largely unanswered.

One argument *against* a unified supervisor that is occasionally heard is that this would prevent any competition *between* supervisory methods. Greenspan (1994) and the accompanying memorandum from the Board of Governors (1994) argued that a single micro-level regulator, without macro-economic responsibilities, would be more likely to over-regulate and to stifle innovation and risk-taking. But the form of supervisory divisions normally envisaged in most countries would still leave the various supervisors as monopolists in their own areas of responsibility. Moreover, in all smaller, open economies, i.e. virtually everywhere except the USA[20] and, perhaps Japan, the relevant competition with respect to supervisory procedures is *international*. This is, moreover, measurable, up to a point, by the evidence, and threat, of the regulated to relocate activities to another country/financial centre. On that view any tendency, so far rather notable for its absence, to introduce international harmonisation of legal regulation and supervisory procedures could be seen as a dangerous threat to competition in supervisory practices, not a benefit.

3.2.3   *The balance of power*

As earlier noted, one reason for leaving supervision of the payments and banking system to a subsidiary central bank is what else is going to occupy its President and staff? By the same token, part of the case for *removing* supervision from an independent central bank is that it, an unelected body, would otherwise become too powerful. The trend towards giving operational independence to central banks has coincided with a trend towards shifting responsibility for (banking) supervision to a separate, specialist and unified, supervisory body. Is this coincidence causal, or accidental?

Democratically-elected governments are sovereign. An element of such a sovereign, say the Minister of Finance, is unlikely to want to delegate so much power to another body (the central bank) that it might be seen as a separate (and competing?) centre of influence. Nor would it be thought right within a democratic country to cede so much power to a non-elected body.[21] It may, however, be remarked that such an argument raises some difficult issues in Europe, where the European Commission and its President are also not directly elected.

Whether, and how far, a Parliament may feel that there are limits to the powers that should be delegated to an (independent and unelected) central bank, i.e. a pure power play, is uncertain. An alternative, and perhaps better based, reason for the coincidence of enhanced responsibility among central banks for operational independence in macro-monetary policy with reduced responsibility for supervisory responsibility is that there could be *conflicts of interest* between the two functions.

3.2.4   *Conflicts of interest*

In the Introduction, and subsequently, the maintained assumption was that the achievement of monetary and price stability on the one hand, and of financial stability on the other, were natural complements, went hand-in-hand. So the natural implication was that these objectives should be jointly internalised within a single institution, i.e. the central bank. The main challenge to that viewpoint comes from those who perceive the ability to conduct good stabilising monetary policy as conflicting with having a simultaneous responsibility for supervision. There are several facets of this argument about conflicts of interest.

The first, and simplest, is that managerial time is limited. Supervisory issues are time-consuming, and in the midst of a financial crisis can distract attention from virtually anything else. Decisions on macro-monetary policy are sufficiently important to want the Governor to concentrate on that, if he/she has operational responsibility for monetary policy. Each job, i.e. monetary decisions and supervisory decisions, is important and separable; a single focus will mean that each will be done better. Complementarities can be handled by consultation and cooperation.

Another aspect of this argument over conflicts is that the conduct of supervision is a thankless task which is all too likely to tarnish the reputation of the supervisor. Academic analysis of monetary operations stresses the importance of being able to influence expectations, and central bank practitioners emphasise the importance of credibility. The objectives of macro-monetary policy can, and increasingly are, being set in terms of quantified objectives for inflation targets. This means that the success/failure of such policy is reasonably transparent. Such quantification and transparency is much more difficult in the case of supervision. Supervision is primarily concerned with the prevention of undesirable events, of systemic instability, of financial failures and of malpractice with respect to rip-offs. The best that a supervisor can expect is that nothing untoward happens. A supervisor is only noticed when either he/she angers the regulated by some restrictive or intrusive action, or when supervision 'fails' in the sense that a financial institution collapses or a customer gets ripped-off. One can talk oneself blue in the face about the desirability of allowing some freedom for banks or other financial institutions to fail, etc., but supervisors will always tend to get a bad press when that does happen, come what may. If an independent central bank feels the need to achieve credibility and a good reputation, then being yoked with simultaneous responsibility for banking supervision may not be advisable.[22] Separation may lead to an impression of an Olympian body (i.e. the central bank) coming in to pick up the pieces of the failure of more mundane supervisory glitches by the financial supervisory authority.

Beyond the conflicts that may arise from the diversion of scarce managerial attention, and of the danger of association with a body whose failures are obvious (and whose successes have often to remain cloaked in commercial confidentiality), there is the stronger accusation that the internalisation of supervisory concerns may lead to worse, wrong, monetary decisions. This is an argument that gets quite a lot of air-time from some economists,[23] but not one that I find appealing. On this, see Bruni (1997), especially Section 3, pp. 350–4, and the comments of his discussant, Briault. The Shadow Financial Regulatory Committee in the USA is amongst those that believe such conflicts do occur on occasions and may be serious. Thus their Statement No. 153, issued on 7 December 1998, states that:

> Indeed, it is the Committee's view that the Fed should not retain responsibility for both monetary policy and the prudential regulation of banks or bank holding companies.
>
> There is at times a clear conflict of interest inherent in the Fed's carrying on roles as both a promoter of stability in the domestic and international financial markets and as a supervisor of banking organizations. This year, as in past years, the Fed has both complained about the relaxation of bank lending standards and encouraged banks to lend to or in foreign countries that were experiencing financial difficulties.

The claim has been made that this conflict becomes particularly apparent in periods that require more restrictive monetary policy but when large banks are undercapitalised and weak.[24] It is argued that the Fed unduly delayed tightening for this reason. I cannot easily assess the validity of that interpretation.

The historical evidence instead suggests that periods of financial instability, and of major, continuing failures among banks are those where monetary policy has been too tight, e.g. Japan since 1991, USA between 1930 and 1939. Declines in the monetary aggregates occur at times of bank failures. *Per contra*, rapid credit expansion is simultaneously a danger signal for macro monetary policy and for supervisory concern at the micro level of the individual bank. It would seem to be natural for the micro concerns of supervisors and the macro concerns of the monetary authorities to reflect and complement each other, rather than conflict.

One condition where there could be such conflict is where the prime concern of the monetary authorities is with external objectives, i.e. with the exchange rate. It is certainly the case, as was seen in the attempts to hold the ERM in 1992–93 and again in the Asian crisis in 1997–98, that the interest rate deemed necessary to achieve maintenance of the exchange rate could endanger internal financial stability. Perhaps this conflict between internal and external objectives might be influenced somewhat by the direct involvement of the central bank with supervisory responsibilities, probably tending to having a central bank with such supervisory responsibilities giving a greater weight to domestic considerations. But would that necessarily be such a bad outcome?

This argument about potential conflicts of interest has been around for a long time, and I have never found it convincing. But when allied with the issue of how to supervise effectively in a world without boundaries either between different kinds of financial activity or between countries, and concerns about the possibly excessive power of an (operationally) independent central bank, the arguments for removing (banking) supervision to a separate unified agency, outside the central bank, have become stronger and more persuasive in recent years.

3.3 Arguments for unification

3.3.1 *Can systemic risk be resolved by committee?*

Because the (high-powered) reserves of the banking system become centralised in the central bank (through the competitive processes of the banking system, see Laidler 1988), commercial banks which find themselves facing liquidity problems have historically gone to the central bank for lender of last resort assistance.[25] In dealing with such requests, particularly under time pressure, and in conditions when temporary illiquidity is often hard to disentangle from more permanent insolvency, the central bank has to weigh the dangers of moral hazard on the one hand from those of systemic instability on the other.

We all have prior judgements about the likely incidence and severity of these two forces, i.e. moral hazard and systemic instability. Those who see moral hazard as an ever-present serious threat, and doubt the prevalence and importance of systemic instability (Benston and Kaufman 1995; Schwartz 1995; G. Kaufman 1996) would seek to restrict LOLR actions severely, e.g. by setting penal rates. Indeed, there are some who argue that, in the absence of the distortions caused by (explicit or implicit) deposit insurance, the banking system need have no special public sector oversight.

Be that as it may, the central bank in virtually all countries has an LOLR function, and is charged with responsibility for so regulating banks that systemic stability is maintained in the payment and banking systems. How can it possibly discharge these functions adequately unless it has sufficient good information? Would not the transmission of information be most enhanced by locating the banking supervisors within – or under the umbrella of – the central bank?

Probably the answer to this latter question is 'Yes', but that simply leads on to the next, and much more difficult, issue, of how much information flow may be lost when the banking supervisors are separated from the central bank. There have been anecdotes, in several countries, that separation does lead to frictions, to barriers, in the free flow of information. But it is extraordinarily difficult to test or to quantify that. Moreover, the behaviour of the newly unified supervisory bodies in their first few years of operation may not prove an accurate indication of their longer-term methods of working.

At a minimum, separation means that information flows are more at risk from the accidents of personality, since it becomes harder for the Governor of the central bank to bang the heads of the separate Divisions together. Internal control mechanisms give way to Memoranda of Understandings (MOU), and internal meetings give way to inter-agency committee meetings.

Once upon a time, the handling of a financial crisis was concentrated within the central bank. But the central bank never had the capital base, or resources, necessary to undertake any large rescues on its own. So, the central bank used to turn to the rest of the country's private sector banking system for financial support and other assistance in crisis management. Because of the cartelised, oligopolistic, protected nature of national financial systems, the domestic banks had both the ability and the incentive to comply with such requests. Again, however, such an account may be more representative of the UK (Barings 1890, the Fringe Bank Crisis 1974–5) than of other countries.

The central bank's ability to call on the private banking sector for (financial) assistance has, however, become more difficult, almost impossible, with the advent of the more competitive, multinational system already described in the previous Section. The multinational banks will claim that home-country forces, whether shareholders, regulators, or their own domestic law, prevent them from risking their own capital in any co-ordinated rescue exercise in another country. If the multinationals will not play, then competition will prevent the domestically headquartered banks from doing so either.

That has forced, and will continue to force, central banks to turn to their own Ministries of Finance for (taxpayers') funds in order to handle all but the smallest (*de minimis*) of failures and crises within the banking system. So crisis management, at least in most countries, has already gone beyond the capacity of the central bank to handle on its own. The days when the Governor could subsequently inform the Minister of how the central bank had sought to resolve the crisis are history.[26]

So crisis management already involves joint cooperation, assessment and agreement between central banks and Ministries of Finance. Does it then matter so much if the Committee becomes tripartite, involving the specialist supervisor, central bank and Ministry of Finance?[27] The prospective Committee structure in the Euro-zone, with a multiplicity of Finance Ministries, with a federal European system of central banks, and a variety of national supervisory bodies, becomes even more complex (see Louis 1995; Goodhart 2000). The administrative mechanisms for handling financial crises are becoming increasingly complex. Does that matter? Is it possible to handle financial crises by Committee? How much, if at all, have recent problems with resolving financial crises (e.g. in Japan) been due to such organisational problems?

Although there will be understandable reluctance to embark on contingency planning in this respect between Bank of England, FSA and Treasury, the relative inexperience of the Treasury at such crisis decision taking (meetings through weekends, market-critical announcements and deadlines that do not obligingly fit Parliamentary announcement timescales, etc.) does at least justify indicating this as a potentially major (both logistically and substantive) issue for the future.

Even if such organisational problems do exist, the main stumbling blocks to quick, correct and decisive action may arise primarily from other factors (e.g. the need of the politicians to generate public consensus for any action) than from the separation of banking supervision from the central bank. Is this latter a relatively minor, or a major issue? Since it may well depend on accidents of personality and the evolving culture of the supervisory body, how could anyone generalise, at least for many years to come?

3.3.2 Information and the conduct of monetary policy

The transmission mechanism of monetary policy, whereby the effects of changes in the central bank's instruments, e.g. short-term interest rates, eventually affect nominal incomes and inflation, largely flow through the intermediation of the banking system. An understanding of how the commercial banks may react to changes in interest rates, and in reserve availability, in their own decisions on lending and credit creation can be crucial in getting the money-macro policy decision right in the first place.

Under normal circumstances, when commercial banks are earning reasonably healthy profits and have adequately comfortable capital, worries about the effect of bank intermediation on the transmission mechanism will, as a rule, play second fiddle to other more direct concerns about inflationary pressures, e.g. wage/cost pressure, the output gap, demand pressures, etc. (though even then the growth rate of the monetary and credit aggregates will be valuable information variables).[28]

Nevertheless, and especially in countries where the banking system has proved fragile, there is some evidence that direct evidence from supervisory data can improve economic forecasting and analysis.[29] The more troubled the banking system, the more essential such micro supervisory information may well be in order to reach correct macro decisions.[30]

This point, that micro-level supervisory information may be a valuable input into macro-level monetary decisions, certainly during periods of financial instability, should not be novel, or contentious. But, the question then remains how much information, if any, would be lost, or corrupted, by the physical separation of banking supervision from the central bank to a separate, unified institution. Is that question answerable? If so, how might one try to proceed to answer it?

It is, perhaps, not just, or not so much, the *willingness* of the separate supervisory body to supply information, relatively freely, to the central bank that is at question,[31] but rather biases to the kind of information that a supervisory body might seek on its own to obtain, dependent on whether it is inside, or separate from, a central bank. With the greater part of a unified supervisory authority working on consumer protection issues, and with the professional skill base coming primarily from lawyers (in place of the central bank emphasis on systemic stability and a skill base of economics), will the banking supervisors in a unified supervisory agency lose sight of the wider macro issues? This is not to suggest that the supervisory authority would fail to be cooperative in providing such data as the central bank might request. Moreover, the shock of separation may force the central bank to think more carefully and more rigorously about exactly what micro-level data are actually needed. More care about detail and allocation of responsibility might emerge from separation. I have heard anecdotes to this effect in the Australian case.

Again, in the case of a large financial conglomerate, the central bank (and the Ministry of Finance) might have much better and more rapid access to information on the position of the group as a whole from a single integrated financial services regulator, than would be available in a world in which the conglomerate was overseen by multiple regulators (even if one of these regulators was located within the central bank).[32]

But what would be the priorities? And would the supervisor catch the early-warning signals of prospective systemic difficulties? If the central bank is bereft of its own micro-level information system, would it actually get to know what to ask for in the shape of data from the separate agency until any such problems had already appeared? And by then it might be too late. Or are such concerns purely fanciful?

Ferguson (*op. cit.*: 300) puts these points vividly:

> A Central Bank that always must be ready to manage financial crises has to know – at a practical, institutional level – not only how financial markets and institutions operate but also how they are changing and how they are managed. I would even add that such a Central Bank needs to know which people make the management decisions and how their control and management information systems work. We do not need to supervise all institutions to accomplish this end. But we do need to be involved directly with a sufficient number to know how institutions in various size classes will respond to stress. I shudder to think about crisis management with staff without such knowledge and experience and without the international contacts with other Central Banks.

There is also the question whether, having lost regular supervisory contact with the (main) banks, a central bank might become less capable of interpreting properly the information that it is given. The Fed has argued that they would need to remain familiar with such large systemic banks, e.g. by supervising them, in order to stay fully effective as a crisis manager. Be that as it may, I rather doubt whether those central banks without supervisory responsibility would take kindly to the suggestion that they could be losing their capacity to interpret supervisory information adequately. As so often in this field, the observer is struck by the ability of the participants to argue in favour of the current status quo, whatever that may be.

3.3.3 The payment system

Alongside responsibility for macro-monetary price stability, and for maintaining systemic stability in the banking system (and to a lesser extent in the broader financial system), central banks have responsibility for ensuring the smooth working of the various payment systems in the economy. For example, the ECB was charged, in the Maastricht Treaty, Article 105.2, with the task 'to promote the smooth operation of payment systems'. Sometimes they run these themselves, e.g. Fedwire, Target; sometimes they are just major participants. In all cases they have direct concern to see that they operate smoothly without gridlock, hitches or stoppages. The closure, or collapse, of such central infrastructure would be devastating.

How far can central banks accept responsibility for payment systems unless they have direct access to micro-level direct information on the viability of the other participants? Some structural changes, such as the adoption of RTGS (Real-Time Gross Payments Systems), of the Lamfalussy rules for net payments systems, of clearing houses interposing themselves between counterparties, e.g. the CLS bank in the foreign exchange market, and of PvP (Payment versus Payment) and PvD (Payment versus Delivery) can, and have, serve(d) to reduce risk in such systems.

Even so, there will remain, at least in some such systems, some residual risk. Information will be needed to assess that risk. Again the question remains whether the central bank needs direct access to its own sources of information on micro-level risk, or whether it can rely on a separate supervisory agency to supply it with timely and appropriate data.

The same argument also runs in the opposite direction. If the central bank does manage the payment systems, then that could bring with it information of importance to the bank supervisors. If the supervisors are separated from the central bank, they in turn could find it more difficult to access relevant data. Pauli (2000: 19) puts the point as follows:

> Typically problems first show up in a bank's payment traffic and its position vs the central bank. By managing banks' reserve and settlement accounts, the central bank automatically monitors continuously in real time the liquidity positions of individual banks. Furthermore, being active in the money market, the central bank receives first hand information on how each bank is perceived by the other market participant.

3.3.4   *Information, information, information*

Prime Minister Blair is reported to have stated that the three main priorities for the UK were 'Education, Education, Education'. In the conduct of its various responsibilities for macro-monetary policy, systemic stability and the smooth working of the payments system, a central bank needs adequate micro-level information on the structural state of the major banks in its country in order to fulfil its duties adequately.

The question then arises of whether the transfer of banking supervision to a separate (unified) authority outside of the banking system might potentially impair such information flows. But even if the answer is 'maybe', how does one balance such a consideration against the efficiency gain of having a unified supervisory authority within a unified financial system, and the various issues relating to bureaucratic power and 'turf' and possible conflicts of interest already identified in the previous Section?

The evidence appears to be that the weight of argument is moving towards the adoption of a separate unified supervisory body within more developed economies. But does that same balance hold for emerging and transitional countries? It is to this issue that we turn next.

3.4   Are the issues the same in emerging countries?

The simple answer to the above question is 'no', though this needs to be qualified by the realisation that there is no clear dividing line between 'emerging' and developed countries; rather, there is a continuum. Moreover, emerging countries are becoming increasingly developed. For example, the presence of financial conglomerates may differ markedly amongst them. Thus for countries such as Hungary or South Africa the arguments in the first three Sections may be more germane.

There are four main reasons for this generally negative answer in ascending order of importance.[33] The first, and perhaps least important, is that the legal system may impact co-ordination between banking supervision and the central bank, and their ability to use MOUs as a means to institutionalise the flow of information and/or to co-ordinate decisions when there is an overlap in legal powers. Civil code systems tend to spell out in a very detailed way what each specific government agency may and may not do, while common law systems are more flexible in allowing institutions to adapt to changing economic and financial conditions. Most developing and transitional economies have civil code systems while developed countries, especially those that are at the forefront of modern prudential financial supervision, operate within common law legal systems. Legal systems also shape institutional culture, and civil code systems certainly tend to make inter-agency co-ordination more difficult. This is an argument in favour of having simpler, leaner institutional frameworks in developing and transitional countries. I am grateful to Ruth Krivoy for making this point to me in private correspondence.

The second is that the financial structure in developing and transitional countries tends to be less complex, with more reliance on standard commercial banking (i.e. without the frills of other functions), than in developed economies. It is that complexity, and the blurring of boundaries, that forces either (i) central banking supervisors to extend far more widely beyond traditional limits, or (ii) a multiplicity (two or more) of supervisors, or (iii) a unified supervisory body outside the central bank. This problem is not so stark in developing countries. In such countries separate supervisors for the banking system, insurance companies and, perhaps, the Stock Exchange can coexist without much friction or overlap. The arguments, in terms of efficiency, for a unified financial supervisory authority are not so strong at the earlier stages of development.

The third reason is that emerging countries have been more prone to systemic disturbances, especially in the aftermath of an initial liberalisation of the banking system. So the main focus of bank supervision in such countries has, perforce, been on systemic stability rather than on consumer protection and conduct of business issues. So the connections between supervision and monetary policy, including LOLR operations, are more frequent and evident than in developed countries.

But the fourth and main difference in the case of emerging countries probably relates instead to the personnel and status of the supervisors themselves. In discussion of this issue amongst OECD countries, the main concern was whether separation of banking supervision from the central bank would adversely affect information flows to the latter. Even here, there was some attention paid to the question of whether the focus of a unified, separate financial authority would switch towards customer protection, rather than systemic stability, and whether its skill base would shift towards lawyers, as contrasted with economists.

Otherwise, however, it was (implicitly) assumed that within developed countries the organisational structure of (banking) supervision would *not* affect the overall financing, ability to hire the necessary skilled staff, or the independence from (political and commercial) pressures (i.e. the ability to resist corruption) of the supervisors themselves. This assumption, that organisational structure will not affect staffing, cannot be made in many developing countries.

Central banks in developing countries tend to have more independence from political and commercial pressures than most other organisations, and also tend to be better financed. This is in some large part because governments need central banks to act on their behalf as specialist experts in international financial dealings. If such central bankers are not both expert and able to provide a source of independent advice, they would not be credible and effective in such a context, especially in the collegial, and quite frequent, gatherings of international central bankers. The informal club of central banks has influence. Again, the ability of the domestic government to prevent financial instability, and a flight from its currency both internally and externally, will depend in part on the perceived expertise, independence and credibility of the central bank and its Governor. Moreover, as the initial recipient of seigniorage, sometimes the most reliable source of government funding during troubled times, the central bank is comparatively well placed in developing countries to achieve and to maintain adequate funding.

The central bank is, therefore, an institution which can often provide satisfactory levels of expertise, independence and funding in a country where these may be in short supply.[34] If banking supervisors come under the umbrella of the central bank they are more likely to share in the good fortune of better, and more independent, staff and stronger funding.

A dramatic case of such matters is provided by Ruth de Krivoy in her recent book, *Collapse: The Venezuelan Banking Crisis of 1994*. Let me first provide three examples, relating to Venezuela, from Chapter 1.

First, outside the central bank, there will be political interference with supervisors:

> All financial sector regulatory authorities reported to the minister of finance. The minister, appointed by the President, had tremendous personal power in deciding how banks would be treated. The superintendent of banks, who reported to him, was in charge of regulating, supervising and sanctioning banks. Yet he lacked the power to take key actions, such as intervening in ailing financial institutions, autho-

rizing the establishment of new ones and approving changes in a bank's capital base. The superintendent could not authorize the sale, merger or dissolution of a financial institution, or suspend or revoke its operating license. The minister of finance had control over these areas, and highly discretionary powers. That meant a bank depended directly on the will of a minister for its survival. Thus, the most important rules could be, and often were, managed on a political basis.

(2000: 24)

Second, outside the central bank, there is a greater likelihood of corruption, and inefficiency:

Accounting rules and prudential norms, covering areas such as loan classification, asset valuation, provisioning, income accounting and lending to affiliated parties, were also inadequate. The Office of the Superintendent of Banks received mountains of data, undertook ritualistic scrutiny of financial statements and remained largely in the dark. The longstanding requirement that banks publish their monthly balance sheets and half-yearly income statements in newspapers was also inconsequential. Instead of providing real information, these statements were often riddled with window dressing and misleading creative accounting. Because the regulations themselves were meaningless, bank supervision became generally lax and ineffective in practice. Additionally, the Office of the Superintendent of Banks carried the stigma of corruption (Oscar Garcia Mendoza, *Crónica involuntaria de una crisis inconclusa* (Caracas: Editorial Planeta de Venezuela, 1995), p. 194). Bluntly put, supervision had become a meaningless ritual, no matter who held the job. There may have been formal monitoring of compliance, but there was no ongoing analysis of the solvency of Venezuela's financial institutions. As a result, bank assets were simply not what they appeared to be.

ibid.

Third, outside a central bank, funding for bank supervision is less likely to be adequate:

Technological, financial and personnel resources with which the government could have implemented supervision dwindled with the deterioration of public finances, reaching record lows after 1989. Neither the government nor most legislators cared. Banking supervision was simply not a political priority. On the eve of the 1994 banking crisis, the Office of the Superintendent of Banks had a staff of 60 to supervise more than 150 financial institutions. While the banking system's technological capabilities were state-of-the-art, the Office of the Superintendent of Banks had virtually no data processing capability.

Banking law required supervisors to conduct an on-site inspection of each bank at least once a year. Yet the superintendent's annual budget had dwindled to about $8,000 per financial institution – less than the annual salary of a mid-level clerk. On-site inspections – when conducted – were largely ceremonial, hand-shaking affairs. Many banks were not inspected for years.

(2000: 26)

Not surprisingly, therefore, one of her main conclusions is that the central bank should 'Play a role in banking supervision, since the central bank is the lender of last resort' (2000: 203). She emphasises three requirements, as follows:

The institutional framework will best serve to promote stable money and sound and safe banking if it:

- rests upon politically independent institutions,
- allows proper coordination between monetary policy and banking regulation and supervision, and
- enables officials to anticipate systemic risk and to react to it in a timely and efficient manner.

Giving supervisory powers to an independent central bank is especially advantageous if public institutions are weak, coordination between different public sector agencies is troublesome, or skilled human resources are scarce. Central banks are usually a country's most prestigious and well-equipped institution, and are in a good position to hire, motivate and keep skilled staff.

(*op. cit.*: 203–4)

However pointed, this is but one single example. Yet in the Central Bank Governors' Symposium on Financial Stability held at the Bank of England, on Friday, 2 June 2000, a summary of the debate for which is presented in the Appendix to this volume, many of the same points were made by the participating Governors. Thus Mr Venner of the Eastern Caribbean Central Bank noted that 'no one else [except the central bank] was there in a disinterested way', e.g. to mediate between foreign and domestic banks, and that the central bank was best placed to maintain auditing standards. Dr Marion Williams of the Central Bank of Barbados stated that, 'If the central bank has to pick up the pieces, it should have charge of preventative measures', a point echoed by Mr Alweenoo of the Bank of Namibia. Mr Joseph Yam of Hong Kong emphasised 'The crucial importance of a high degree of cooperation and information sharing'. Mr Hamad Al Sayri argued that it was important not 'to spread the know-how too thin'. Many similar points were made.[35]

One of the purposes of the survey being undertaken by Schoenmaker and myself is to try to throw some light on the relative skill base of supervisors, both by organisational structural form (e.g. within or outside central banks) and by stage of development. It is uncertain whether any such qualitative exercise can provide any clear, quantitative results. Nevertheless a combination of anecdote and experience (admittedly mostly observed through a central banking prism) does suggest that banking supervision in developing countries has been rather better done if taken under the wing of a central bank.

Even if that were so in the past, i.e. that banking supervision in developing countries is done generally better under the aegis of a central bank, this will not necessarily hold in future. The weaknesses of national supervisory bodies have come under the international spotlight as a consequence of recent financial crises, e.g. in Asia. It is possible that international pressures, for example, through the IMF, will interact with domestic forces to lead towards better funded, more skilled and more independent supervisory bodies irrespective of how these are structurally organised.

If so, then structure may come *not* to be an important issue for the conduct of banking supervision. Perhaps, but for the time being the balance of argument would suggest that in less developed and transitional economies it would be safer and better to integrate banking supervision into the ambit of the central bank.[36]

3.5 Conclusions

The arguments for separating banking supervision from central banks, and placing this within a unified financial supervisory agency, have become increasingly powerful in recent years, more particularly in developed countries with complex financial systems. The blurring of functional boundaries has led to a seamless financial system; so efficiency suggests that a unified financial supervisor should mark that system. Add in perennial concerns about putative conflicts of interest, and a worry whether an (operationally) independent central bank with added supervisory functions might become too powerful within a democratic context, and the result is a potent cocktail of reasons for such a change.

The counter-argument rests on fears whether the information base needed by a central bank to carry out its various essential functions might be less good if it did not have direct control of banking supervision in-house. While there are some reasons adduced for such concerns within developed countries, they are, as yet, somewhat speculative. Why can information flows not be almost as good between agencies, as when they are internalised within the same institution? If so, the above arguments for a unified financial supervisory authority tend to become dominant.

It is, however, the thesis of Section 3.4 above that there are much stronger reasons to believe that the conduct of banking supervision will be better done under the wing of the central bank in less developed countries. Within a central bank, supervisors in such countries are, I claim, likely to be better funded, more independent and hence more expert and reliable.

Apart from case studies, experience and anecdote there is not much hard evidence to go on, especially on this latter subject.

Notes

1 My thanks are due to P. Armendariz, C. Briault, G. Caprio, T. Dubouchet, P. Jackson, G. Kaufman, R. Krivoy, D. Llewellyn, G. Schinasi, D. Schoenmaker, M. Taylor, P. Tucker, D. Walker, W. White, and participants at a BIS seminar for helpful comments. Responsibility for all views and remaining errors remains with me.
2 The FSA would, I believe, argue that what has changed is that it can take advantage of the efficiency benefits of a unified supervisor, to be discussed later in this chapter, by putting greater emphasis on the integrated supervision of financial groups, and, more generally, put the regulation of banks on a basis that is more closely correlated with the regulation of other parts of the financial services industry, see *A New Regulator for the New Millennium*, FSA (2000).
3 Schoenmaker and I, with the assistance of some research assistants, are analysing the results of a survey of supervisory bodies on these issues. Unfortunately the results are unlikely to be available until some time in the future.
4 A study, in a couple of years time perhaps, of who stayed and who left, and why, might be interesting, but is beyond the scope of this chapter.
5 Pauli (2000: 25) concludes that

> legal stipulations, appropriateness and strong complementary links form the basis for the central bank's three basic functions: controller of the money supply, settlement agent, and macroprudential supervisor/payment system overseer. Together these constitute an integrated whole. It would not be possible to leave out one of the functions without seriously hampering the conduct to the other two.

See also H. Kaufman (2000: 219) as follows:

> As I see it, the proper responsibility of the central bank – assuring the financial well-being of society – requires an intimate involvement in financial supervision and regulation. In fact, I have long believed that it is only the central bank – among the various regulatory agencies that share responsibility in this area – that can represent the perspective of the financial system as a whole. This should be the central organizing principle behind any comprehensive reform of financial regulation and supervision in the United States.

6 One needs to be careful about interpretation, as David Llewellyn (personal correspondence) has reminded me. What happens in practice is often quite different from what appears to be the case simply by observing the formality of institutional structure. The central bank often has a significant role in supervision even when it is not formally the agency responsible. Practice is seldom as clear-cut as formality.
7 See Tuya and Zamalloa (1994).
8 Several Fund officials have, however, written to me personally to say that the Fund is *not* an unquestioning enthusiast for unification, and prefers a country-by-country (case-by-case) approach.

9 Although Japan has now established a single regulator (very similar to the FSA in the UK), the Bank of Japan still undertakes on-site inspections of major banks, i.e. those which are its counterparties in the payments system.

10 On this, see Table 2.6 in Chapter 2 of this volume. Also Briault (1999), especially Section 2 on 'Developments in Other Countries'. Others, however, would contend that the momentum towards separation is not that strong. One central bank regulator has written to me (personal correspondence) as follows:

> You may have overstated the 'trend' towards separation of banking supervision from central banks, at least in the developed world. When we looked at the Basel Committee members, we found that only one – UK – had taken away banking supervision from its central bank since the Committee was founded. There were a number of other countries where the central bank was not the main banking supervisory agency, but these were very long standing arrangements.

11 See Freshfields (1999), and Taylor and Fleming (1999).

12 My colleague Dirk Schoenmaker reminds me that banking supervision started seriously rather earlier in some continental European countries, Germany with the Reich Banking Law of 1934, and the Netherlands with its Banking Law of 1948.

13 I am indebted to G. Kaufman for this information.

14 Even so, regulation – and some economies of specialisation? – sought to maintain boundaries between financial and non-financial businesses, with only limited success in some notorious cases, e.g. Russia.

15 Ferguson *op cit.*: 299, similarly argues as follows:

> But, I would also note that the argument for a single supervisory authority for all financial institutions contains a real risk – the risk of extending supervision and regulation because the agency with the single mission tends to forget or pay less attention to other purposes, such as the effects of its actions on the economy.

16 Clive Briault, *op. cit.*, writes:

> [T]he distinction between prudential and conduct of business regulation is not in practice as neat and simple as Taylor's twin peaks model might imply. Even without the emergence of financial conglomerates, a large number of financial services firms would need to be regulated by both of his proposed Commissions because their business would require both prudential and conduct of business regulation. This would certainly include life insurance companies, securities firms and institutional fund managers, and in practice would also include the many banks and building societies who combine deposit-taking with various forms of investment business. This in turn would generate inefficiencies (firms having to be authorised and supervised by more than one regulator) and the possibility of the communication, co-operation and consistency problems discussed earlier.
>
> Moreover, there is a considerable overlap – both conceptually and in practice – between prudential and conduct of business regulation. Both have a close and legitimate interest in the senior management of any financial institution subject to both of these types of regulation, in particular because of the crucial roles of senior management in setting the 'compliance culture' of a firm, in ensuring that management responsibilities are properly allocated and cover comprehensively the business of the firm, and in ensuring that other internal systems and controls are in place. The detail of some of these systems and controls may indeed be specific to either prudential or conduct of business considerations, but many of them will be more general.

17 BIS, *op. cit.*: 149:

>   [M]uch more attention should be paid by the public sector to monitoring developments and to developing analytical procedures for evaluating the risk of systemic problems. Indeed, using stress tests as a corollary to such forecasts also has a lot to recommend it. Whether analyses of this sort should be done primarily by supervisors or by other bodies (commonly central banks) charged with overall responsibility for systemic stability, or by both, needs to be clarified to ensure that this important function does not simply fall between the cracks. One argument for involving central banks is that there may be a useful complementarity between their 'top down' approach and the 'bottom up' approach more commonly followed by the supervisory community. It is a simple but important insight that many recommendations supporting prudent behaviour at the level of a single firm can have undesirable effects if a large number of firms have simultaneously to alter their behaviour in the same way. Fallacies of composition of this kind are well known in the macroeconomic literature.

18 Ferguson, however, argues that the longer-standing, and possibly better, international linkages of central banks provides yet another argument for keeping banking supervision in central banks. Thus he writes that

>   Globalization of financial markets means that crises in any financial market have significant effects in other nations' markets – in fact, there is increasingly only one global financial market with the interbank connections occurring in both credit and payments flows. The institutions best able to coordinate and address these problems are the world's central banks (2000: 300).

19 Such gradings provoked much concern, in some cases fury, amongst the authorities in some centres who felt that they had been judged without due process, without being able to give evidence in rebuttal, and without the possibility of redress. Perhaps, but they could always choose to invite outside observers to attest to their good offices. Moreover, the strength of reaction was testimony to the efficacy of the instrument.

20 The Shadow Financial Regulatory Committee in the USA issued a Statement on 'The Proposed Federal Banking Commission', No. 100, December 1993, which stated, *inter alia*, that,

>   A potential objection to the Administration's consolidation proposal is that it may harm consumers of financial services in the long run by limiting the regulatory choice that banks have historically had. In the past this choice has often enhanced market competition and facilitated innovation. While this Committee has been receptive to this view in the past, market evolution has lessened the need for regulatory competition in the banking industry. Today, intense competition between banks and nonbank financial institutions provides ample opportunity for consumers of financial services to reap the full benefits of competition and financial innovation.

21 But has the move to a single mega-regulator not also concentrated power, though of a somewhat different form, in a non-elected body? Would one argue in the UK, for instance, that the shift from the Bank to the FSA has increased or weakened the concentration of power? One could argue that creating a single regulator has increased the concentration of power though in a different way. I am grateful to David Llewellyn for such thoughts.

22 Some well-placed commentators in the UK give considerable weight to this argument. One of them has written to me, as follows:

>   [T]he recent effort to make the Bank's commitment and effectiveness in promoting monetary stability more credible has not been distracted or eroded by retention of a parallel responsibility for financial supervision and cus-

tomer protection. The fact that there have been no large incidences of failure since the transfer of power is irrelevant: the risk of some failure at some stage remain quite high and one only has to recall the damage done to the Bank's credibility on monetary policy matters in, for example, the late 1980s after the JMB affair, to sense the Bank's vulnerability in a future financial institution or market crisis if it had retained direct supervisory responsibility. I would give rather greater weight to this factor in the paper.

23 There is some inverse correlation between central banks having supervisory responsibility and their inflation records; see Briault (1997). But this may be due to those central banks granted (operational) independence also being stripped of supervisory responsibilities on 'balance of power' grounds. See also the discussion on this in Chapter 2.

24 Also see Louis (1995); Haubrich (1996); Di Noia and Di Giorgio (1999); Lannoo (1999).

25 Indeed it was the failure of the National Banking System in the USA to provide such an 'elastic currency' that led to the foundation of the Federal Reserve System in 1913.

26 A well-placed commentator, in personal and confidential, correspondence with me, observed that:

> [C]entral banks have become much less capable of exercising the LOLR function independently of the fiscal authorities, i.e. central government. The two principal reasons are that the amounts likely to be required are larger than the capacity of the central banks' balance sheets (to which the democratic accountability consideration is obviously closely linked) and the ability to bring in foreign banks (despite their significance in the market place) is limited and diminishing. While this reduces the centrality of the role of the central bank in any LOLR process and thus reduces the significance of the transfer of supervisory powers, it does highlight the potential importance of crisis dialogue with the Treasury/Ministry of Finance, for which there has been no real precedent in the UK (nor possibly elsewhere).

27 Following the Memorandum of Understanding in the UK between the Bank, FSA and Treasury, such a tripartite Standing Committee has regular monthly meetings, and would meet as frequently as required were a crisis to arise.

28 In my own three years on the Monetary Policy Committee, worries about the effects of structural developments in banking, as a potential factor to influence our own decisions, only surfaced briefly for a few months in the autumn of 1998 when fears arose of a potential credit crunch in the USA, and (even less likely) in the UK; in the event this danger passed.

29 See, for example, Peek, Rosengren and Tootell (1998, 1999).

30 Professor Ueda of the Monetary Policy Committee of the Bank of Japan has told me in personal discussion of the considerable importance that he places on such information.

   On the other hand, Alan Blinder (like me) is more sceptical. In his speech at the ECB Conference on 3/4 December 1999, reprinted in *Monetary Policy-Making Under Uncertainty* (ECB 2000), he stated:

> My personal view is that the Fed has taken a grain of truth and greatly exaggerated its importance. Proprietary information that the central bank receives in bank examinations is of some, limited use in formulating monetary policy – and is on rare occasions very important. So, on balance, it is probably better to have it than not. On the other hand, a bank supervisor may sometimes have to be a protector of banks and sometimes a stern disciplinarian – and either stance may conflict with monetary policy.

31 Certainly in cases when the macro-level monetary decisions might be significantly dependent on the state of the financial sector, then the FSA would contribute directly to the MPC's deliberations.

32 I am grateful to Clive Briault for this latter thought.

33 An additional reason why the separation model may not be such a good one for developing countries, as for developed, is that the quality of published information in developing countries is very poor. Thus, if we acknowledge that separation does lead to some deterioration in the flow of relevant information to the central bank, this leaves developing country central banks in a very difficult position. I am grateful to Patricia Jackson for this thought.

34 In countries with a small, quite weak, financial sector, the alternative option of an industry-funded supervisory body is hardly available, and would anyhow be more subject to 'capture'. So, the main alternative to a central bank supervisory body is one run by government. A major concern with government funding of regulation is that budgetary pressures can lead to arbitrary cuts in the regulation budget; examples from developed, as well as developing, countries are, alas, only too common.

35 Cynics will say that central banks were just seeking to protect their own turf. But many of the arguments set out here for separating supervision from central banking were also raised, e.g. the diversion of executive time (Dr Fraga of Brazil and Mr Gunnarson of Iceland), and the legal problems of being a supervisor and having to intervene in the governance of commercial banks (Mr Massad of Banco Central de Chile). When Mr Yong Guan Koh of the Monetary Authority of Singapore argued that the integration of supervision with a broader Monetary Authority facilitated career planning (as well as promoting a quicker response to arising problems), Mr George of the Bank of England replied that this was dubious since many of the analytical skills required in supervision (e.g. accountancy, customer relations) were less in need in other areas of a central bank.

36 One cynic even suggested that encouragement from the IMF for the adoption of supervisory agencies independent of the central bank was because these would be more malleable and amenable to IMF guidance, than if under the wing of the national central bank.

4 Alternative approaches to regulation and corporate governance in financial firms

David T. Llewellyn[1]

4.1 Introduction and issues

The objective of this chapter is to draw lessons from recent banking sector crises, most especially with respect to the design of an optimum 'regulatory regime'. Just as the causes of banking crises are multi-dimensional, so the principles of an effective *regulatory regime* also need to incorporate a wider range of issues than externally imposed rules on bank behaviour. This suggests that strategies to avoid future crises also need to be multi-dimensional, involving macro policy, the conduct of regulation and supervision, the creation of appropriate incentive structures, the development of market discipline, and the internal governance and management of financial institutions.

In this context, the chapter considers alternative approaches to achieving the objective of financial stability. A maintained theme is that what are often defined as alternatives are in fact complements within an overall regulatory strategy. The discussion is set within the context of what will be termed a *regulatory regime* which is wider than the rules and monitoring conducted by regulatory agencies. In essence, the focus is on how the components of a regulatory regime are to be combined to produce an optimum regulatory strategy. This follows on the tradition of Lindgren *et al.* (1996), who emphasise the three key strands of governance: internal to the firm; the discipline of the market; and regulation and supervision by official agencies. However, the chapter takes their paradigm further and discusses alternative approaches to regulation and supervision.

When a particular regulatory problem emerges, the instinct of a regulator is often to respond by creating new rules. This implies an *incremental approach* to regulation by focusing upon the rules component of the *regulatory regime*. The chapter argues that there are potentially serious problems with such an incremental rules approach in that it may blunt the power of the other mechanisms in the regime and may, in the process, reduce the overall effectiveness of the regime.

Bank failures can be very costly. In the case of Indonesia, Malaysia, South Korea and Thailand, non-performing loans of banks recently amounted to around 30 per cent of total assets. In around 25 per cent of cases, the cost has exceeded 10 per cent of GNP (e.g. in Spain, Venezuela, Bulgaria, Mexico, Argentina, Hungary). Evans (2000) suggests that the costs of crises amounted to 45 per cent of GDP in the case of Indonesia, 15 per cent in the case of Korea and 40 per cent in the case of Thailand. These figures include the costs of meeting obligations to depositors under the blanket guarantees that the authorities introduced to handle systemic crises, and public sector payments to finance the recapitalisation of insolvent banks. Barth *et al.* (2000) also note that the costs of recent bank crises in Chile, Argentina, Korea and Indonesia are estimated at 41 per cent, 55 per cent, 60 per cent, and 80 per cent of GDP respectively.

As bank failures clearly involve avoidable costs that may be significant, there is a welfare benefit to be derived from lowering the probability of bank failures, and reducing the cost of bank failures that do occur. In what follows these are the twin objectives of the regulatory regime. The objective of the chapter is to suggest a wider paradigm for ensuring financial stability, i.e., reducing the probability of bank failures and the costs of those that do occur.

The general economic rationale for financial regulation (in terms of externalities, market imperfections, economies of scale in monitoring, grid-lock problems, and moral hazard associated with safety nets) has been outlined elsewhere (Llewellyn 1999). For the purposes of the present chapter, the economic rationale for regulation is taken as given.

While this ground will not be repeated, two observations are entered at the outset. First, the presence of an economic rationale for regulation, and a consumer demand for it, does not justify everything that a regulator does. Second, the case for regulation does not exclude a powerful role for other mechanisms to achieve the objectives of systemic stability and legitimate (but limited) consumer protection. On the contrary, the central theme of the chapter is to emphasise that the various components of the regulatory regime need to be combined in an overall *regulatory strategy*, and that while all are necessary, none are sufficient. There is always a potential danger that the regulation component, if pressed too far, will blunt other mechanisms and, in the process, compromise the overall impact.

The structure of the chapter is as follows. The main themes are summarised in the remainder of this Section. Section 2 offers a brief overview of recent banking crises as a context for the main themes of the chapter. Section 3 establishes the concept of the regulatory regime and the trade-offs that can exist between its components. This is followed, in Section 4, by a more detailed discussion of each of the seven components of the regime. Section 5 reviews how the optimum structure of a regulatory regime will vary for different countries and will change over time. Section 6 suggests a series of desirable shifts within the regulatory regime and offers a brief assessment of the recently-issued Basel Committee consultative paper on capital adequacy. A brief overall assessment is offered in Section 7.

The main themes of the chapter are summarised below.

1   Debate about regulation is often excessively polarised with too many dichotomies. What are often posed as alternative approaches are, in truth, complementary mechanisms. It is emphasised that the skill in formulating regulatory strategy is not so much in choosing between the various options, but in the way the seven components of the regulatory regime are combined.

2   Regulation needs to be viewed and analysed not solely in the narrow terms of the rules and edicts of regulatory agencies, but in the wider context of a *regulatory regime* which has seven core components:

- the *rules* established by regulatory agencies (the regulation component);
- *monitoring and supervision* by official agencies;
- the *incentive structures* faced by regulatory agencies, consumers and, most especially, banks;
- the role of *market discipline and monitoring*;
- *intervention arrangements* in the event of compliance failures of one sort or another;
- the role of internal *corporate governance* arrangements within financial firms; and
- the *disciplining and accountability* arrangements applied to regulatory agencies.

3   Regulatory strategy is not to be viewed solely in terms of the rules and supervision applied by regulatory agencies. The debate about regulation is often too narrow because it focuses almost exclusively on the first component of the regime, namely rules imposed by the regulator. The debate should rather be about how to optimise the combination of the seven components of the regime. Strategy should focus on optimising the overall regulatory regime rather than any one component. This is a difficult and demanding mandate, and to the regulator the more effective approach in the short-run might appear to be imposing more rules. The danger is of thinking in terms of incremental change to regulation, rather than strategically with respect to the overall regime. The objective is to move towards an optimum mix of the components, combined with careful choice of the various regulatory instruments within each. Thus, it is not a question of choosing between *either* regulation *or* market disciplines.

4   A key issue for the regulator is how its actions can not only contribute directly to the objectives of regulation, but how they impact on the other components of the regime. Most important is the issue of how regulation

affects incentive structures within firms, and the role played by market discipline and monitoring.

5   The optimising strategy needs to be set in the context of trade-offs between the various components of the regime. In some circumstances the more emphasis that is given to one of the components (e.g. regulation) the less powerful becomes one or more of the others (e.g. market discipline on financial firms) and to an extent that may reduce the overall effectiveness and efficiency of the regime.

6   The optimum mix of the components of the regulatory regime will vary between countries, over time for all countries, and between banks.

7   The optimum mix of the components of the regime changes over time as market conditions and compliance culture change. It is argued that, in current conditions, there needs to be a shift within the regime in five dimensions: less reliance placed on detailed and prescriptive rules; more emphasis given to official supervision; a greater focus on incentive structures; an enhanced and strengthened role for market discipline and monitoring; and a more central role for corporate governance arrangements within banks.

8   As financial firms and different types of financial business are not homogeneous, the optimum regulatory approach will be different for different banks and businesses. This has been recognised by the regulatory authorities in the UK with more emphasis being given to a risk-based approach. However, there should be yet more differentiation. The skill lies in making sufficient differentiations to reflect the heterogeneous nature of regulated firms, while not unduly complicating the regulatory process to an extent that can cause unwarranted inequality of treatment.

This all amounts to emphasising an overall 'regulatory strategy' rather than focusing on regulation *per se*. A central theme is that regulation is an important, but only one, component of a regulatory regime designed to achieve the objectives of systemic stability and consumer protection. Giving too much emphasis to regulation *per se* has the danger that the importance of the other components are down-played, or even marginalised.

Regulation is about changing the behaviour of regulated institutions on the grounds that unconstrained market behaviour tends to produce socially sub-optimum outcomes. A key question is the extent to which behaviour is to be altered by way of externally imposed *rules*, or through creating *incentives* for firms to behave in a particular way.

4.2 The experience of banking crises

The vast majority of banking crises are a complex and interactive mix of economic, financial and structural weaknesses. For an excellent survey of the two-way link between banking systems and macro policy, see Lindgren *et al.* (1996). The trigger for many crises has been macro-economic in origin and often associated with a sudden withdrawal of liquid external capital from a country. As noted by Brownbridge and Kirkpatrick (2000), financial crises have often involved triple crises of currencies, financial sectors, and corporate sectors. Similarly, it has been argued that East Asian countries were vulnerable to a financial crisis because of 'reinforcing dynamics between capital flows, macro-policies, and weak financial and corporate sector institutions' (Alba *et al.* 1998). The link between balance of payments and banking crises is certainly not a recent phenomenon and has been extensively studied (e.g. Sachs *et al.* 1996; Godlayn and Valdes 1997; Kaminsky and Reinhart 1998). The close parallels between banking and currency crises is emphasised by Kaufman (2000). There is a further discussion of banking crises in Chapter 7 of this volume, and Chapter 5 considers the causes and consequences of banking crises.

In most (but not all) cases, systemic crises (as opposed to the failure of individual banks within a stable system) are preceded by major macroeconomic adjustment, which often leads to the economy moving into recession after a previous strong cyclical upswing (Llewellyn 2000). While financial crises have often been preceded by sharp fluctuations in the macro economy and asset prices, it would be a mistake to seek the origin of such crises and financial instability exclusively in macroeconomic instability. While macro instability may often be the proximate cause, banking crises usually emerge because instability in the macro economy reveals existing weaknesses within the banking system. It is usually the case that the seeds of a problem (e.g. over-lending, weak risk analysis and control, etc.) are sown in the earlier upswing of the cycle. The downswing phase reveals previous errors and over-optimism. Mistakes made in the upswing emerge in the downswing. In South East Asia, for instance, a decade of substantial economic growth up to 1997 concealed the effects of questionable bank lending policies.

Analyses of recent financial crises, in both developed and less-developed countries (see, for instance, Lindgren *et al.* 1996; Corsetti *et al.* 1998; Brealey 1999; Llewellyn 2000) indicate that 'regulatory failures' are not exclusively (or even mainly) a problem of the rules being wrong. Five common characteristics have been weak internal risk analysis; management and control systems within banks; inadequate official supervision; weak (or even perverse) incentives within the financial system generally and financial institutions in particular; inadequate information disclosure; and inadequate corporate governance arrangements both within banks and their large corporate customers.

While, as already noted, banking crises can be triggered by developments in the macro economy, an unstable or unpredictable macro-economic environment is neither a necessary nor sufficient condition for banking crises to emerge. The fault also lies internally within banks, and with failures of regulation, supervision, and market discipline on banks. This reinforces the concept of a regulatory regime and the potential trade-offs between its components.

Banks can fail, and bank insolvencies can be concealed, within a reasonably stable macro-economic environment if, for instance, internal risk analysis and management systems are weak, incentive structures are perverse, regulation and supervision are inadequate, market discipline is weak, and corporate governance arrangements are not well developed. Equally, if these are in place, banks can avoid insolvency even within a volatile economic environment.

4.3   The regulatory regime

The concept of a regulatory regime is wider than the prevailing set of prudential and conduct of business rules established by regulatory agencies. External regulation has a positive role in fostering a safe and sound financial system and consumer protection. However, this role, while important, is limited, and insufficient in itself. Equally, and increasingly important, are the other components of the regime and most especially the incentive structures faced by financial firms, and the efficiency of the necessary monitoring and supervision by official agencies and the market.

There are several reasons why emphasis is given to the overall regulatory regime rather than myopically to regulation:

- prescriptive regulation is not invariably effective in achieving the twin components of financial stability: reducing the probability of bank failures and the costs of those that do occur;
- regulation may not be the most effective way of securing these objectives;
- regulation is itself costly both in terms of its direct costs and unwarranted distortions that may arise (e.g. via inaccurate risk weights applied in capital adequacy arrangements) when regulation is inefficiently constructed;
- regulation may not be the most efficient mechanism for achieving financial stability objectives in that alternative routes may achieve the same degree of effectiveness at lower cost;
- regulation tends to be inflexible and insufficiently differentiated;
- there are always potential dangers arising from a monopolist regulator;
- regulation may impair the effectiveness and efficiency of other mechanisms for achieving the objective of financial stability.

A sustained theme is that a regulatory regime needs to be viewed more widely than externally-imposed regulation on financial institutions. In current conditions it would be a mistake to rely wholly, or even predominantly, on external regulation, monitoring and supervision by the 'official sector'. The world of banking and finance is too complex and volatile to warrant dependence on a simple set of prescriptive rules for prudent behaviour. The central role of incentive structures is constantly emphasised. There are many reasons (market imperfections and failures, externalities, 'grid lock' problems, and moral hazards associated with safety net arrangements) why incentive structures within financial firms may not be aligned with regulatory objectives (Llewellyn 1999).

How the regulator's rules affect regulated firms' incentive structures, whether perversely or to reinforce them, is critical. Incentive structures are central to all aspects of regulation: if these are wrong it is unlikely that the other mechanisms in the regime will achieve the regulatory objectives. It is necessary to consider not only how the various components of the regime impact directly on regulatory objectives, but also how they operate indirectly by affecting the incentives of regulated firms and others. Incentive structures are at the heart of the regulatory process. Consultation between regulators and regulated institutions should ensure consistency between external regulation and internal risk procedures.

4.3.1   *Trade-offs within the regime*

Within the regulatory regime trade-offs emerge at two levels. In terms of regulatory strategy, a choice has to be made about the balance of the various components and the relative weight to be assigned to each. For instance, a powerful role for official regulation with little weight assigned to market discipline might be chosen, or alternatively a relatively light touch of regulation but with heavy reliance on the other components. A given degree of effectiveness can be provided by different combinations of rules, supervision, market discipline, etc. and with various degrees of discretion applied by the regulator.

The second form of trade-off relates to how the components of the regime may be causally related. In some circumstances the more emphasis that is given to one of the components (e.g. regulation), the less powerful becomes one or more of the others (e.g. market discipline on banks) and, to an extent, that may reduce the overall impact. Thus, while regulation may be viewed as a response to market failures, weak market discipline, and inadequate corporate governance arrangements, causation may also operate in the other direction with regulation weakening these other mechanisms. For instance, the more emphasis that is given to detailed, extensive and prescriptive rules, the weaker might be the role of incentive structures, market discipline and corporate governance arrangements within financial firms. An excessive reliance on detailed and prescriptive rules may weaken incentive structures and market discipline.

Similarly, an excessive focus on detailed and prescriptive rules may weaken corporate governance mechanisms within financial firms, and may blunt the incentive of others to monitor and control the behaviour of banks. Weakness in corporate governance mechanisms may also be a reflection of banks being monitored, regulated and supervised by official agencies. The way intervention is conducted in the event of bank distress (e.g. whether forbearance is practised) may also have adverse incentive effects on the behaviour of banks and the willingness of markets to monitor and control banks' risk-taking.

An empirical study of regulation in the United States by Billett *et al.* (1998) suggests that some types of regulation may undermine market discipline. They examine the costs of market discipline and regulation and show that, as a bank's risk increases, the cost of uninsured deposits rises and the bank switches to insured deposits. This is because changes in regulatory costs are less sensitive to changes in risk than are market costs. They also show that when rating agencies down-grade a bank, the bank tends to increase its use of insured deposits. The authors conclude: 'The disparate costs of insured deposits and uninsured liabilities, combined with the ability and willingness of banks to alter their exposure to each, challenge the notion that market discipline can be an effective deterrent against excessive risk taking.'

The public policy objective is to optimise the outcome of a regulatory strategy in terms of mixing the components of the regime, bearing in mind the possibility of negative trade-offs. The key to optimising overall effectiveness is the mix of the seven core components. All are necessary but none alone are sufficient. The skill of the regulator in devising a regulatory strategy lies in how the various components in the regime are combined.

4.4   Components of a regulatory regime

Having established the overall framework and the nature of the regulatory regime this Section considers some of the key issues related to each of the seven components with particular reference to regulatory strategy designed to optimise the overall effect of the regime as a whole rather than any of the components.

4.4.1   *Regulation*

Five particular issues arise with respect to the regulation part of the regime: the type of rules established; the weight to be given to formal and prescriptive rules of behaviour; the form of the rules that are established; the impact that rules may have on the other components of the regulatory regime; and the extent to which regulation and supervision differentiate between different banks.

4.4.1.1 Type of rules

Four types of rules can be identified: (1) rules with respect to allowable business (e.g. the extent to which banks are allowed to conduct securities and insurance business); (2) with respect to the prudential management of banks and other financial firms (e.g. capital adequacy rules, large exposure limitations, rules on inter-connected lending, etc.); (3) with respect to conduct of business (e.g. how financial firms conduct business with their customers, disclosure requirements, etc.); and (4) rules with respect to ownership, i.e. who is allowed to own banks. A detailed consideration of these different types of rules goes beyond the scope of this chapter. Nevertheless, Barth *et al.* (2000), in an extension of the model of Demirgüç-Kunt and Detragiache (1998), find some evidence that regulatory restrictions on activities and ownership increase the probability of bank crises.

4.4.1.2 Prescriptive rules

A former US regulator has noted that: 'Financial services regulation has traditionally tended towards a style that is command-and-control, dictating precisely what a regulated entity can do and how it should do it . . . generally, they focus on the specific steps needed to accomplish a certain regulatory task and specify with detail the actions to be taken by the regulated firm' (Wallman 1999). This experience of the US also suggests that the interaction of the interests of the regulator and the regulated may tend towards a high degree of prescription in the regulatory process. Regulators tend to look for standards they can easily monitor and enforce, while the regulated seek standards they can comply with. The result is that regulators seek precision and detail in their requirements, while the regulated look for certainty and firm guidance on what they are to do. Wallman suggests that: 'The result is specific and detailed guidance, not the kind of pronouncements that reflect fundamental concepts and allow the market to develop on its own.'

Although precise rules have their attractions for both regulators and regulated firms, several problems emerge with a highly prescriptive approach to regulation:

- An excessive degree of prescription may bring regulation into disrepute if it is perceived by the industry as being excessive, with many redundant rules.
- Risks are often too complex to be covered by simple rules.
- Balance sheet rules reflect the position of an institution only at a particular point in time, and its position can change substantially within a short period.
- An inflexible approach based on a detailed rule book has the effect of

impeding firms from choosing their own least-cost way of meeting regulatory objectives.

- Detailed and extensive rules may stifle innovation.
- A prescriptive regime tends to focus upon firms' processes rather than outcomes and the ultimate objectives of regulation. The rules may become the focus of compliance rather than the objectives they are designed to achieve. In this regard, it can give rise to a perverse culture of 'box ticking' by regulated firms. The letter of the regulation may be obeyed but not the spirit or intention.
- A prescriptive approach is inclined towards 'rules escalation' whereby rules are added over time, but few are withdrawn.
- A highly prescriptive approach may create a confrontational relationship between the regulator and regulated firms, or alternatively cause firms to over-react and engage in excessive efforts at internal compliance out of fear of being challenged by the regulator. In this sense, regulation may become more prescriptive and detailed than is intended by the regulator because of the culture that a rules-based approach generates.
- In the interests of 'competitive neutrality', rules may be applied equally to all firms, although they may be sufficiently heterogeneous to warrant different approaches. A highly prescriptive approach to regulation reduces the scope for legitimate differentiations. Treating as equal firms that in practice are not equal is not competitive neutrality.
- A prescriptive rules approach may, in practice, prove to be inflexible and not sufficiently responsive to market conditions.
- A potential moral hazard arises in that firms may assume that, if something is not explicitly covered in regulations, there is no regulatory dimension to the issue.
- Detailed rules may also have perverse effects if they are regarded as actual standards to be adopted rather than minimum standards with the result that, in some cases, actual behaviour of regulated firms may be of a lower standard than without rules. This is most especially the case if each firm assumes its competitors will adopt the minimum regulatory standard.

4.4.1.3   Form of rules

A second issue relates to the type of rules chosen by the regulator. Black (1994) distinguishes different types of rules along three dimensions: precision (how much is prescribed and covered in the rule), simplicity (the degree to which the rule may be easily applied to concrete situations), and clarity. The more precise is the rule, the easier it is to enforce. On the other hand, precise rules are less flexible within the overall regime.

4.4.1.4   Impact of rules

A third issue is whether the degree of precision in rules has a positive or negative impact on compliance, and the other components of the regime. For reasons already suggested, precision and detail may have a negative effect on compliance and compliance culture: if something is not explicitly disallowed it is presumed to be allowed. Conversely, a regime based more on broad principles than detailed and extensive rules has certain advantages: principles are easily understood and remembered, they apply to all behaviour, and they are more likely to have a positive impact on overall compliance culture. It might also be the case (as suggested by Black 1994) that principles are more likely to become board issues with the board of financial firms adopting compliance with principles as a high level policy issue, rather than a culture of 'leaving it to the compliance department'. As put by Black, 'it helps chief executives to see the moral wood for the technical trees'.

4.4.1.5   Differentiation

A central issue in regulation for financial stability is the extent to which it differentiates between different banks according to their risk characteristics and their risk analysis, management and control systems. Most especially when supervisory resources are scarce, but also in the interests of efficiency in the banking system, supervision needs to be more detailed and extensive with those banks deemed to be riskier than others. The objective of 'competitive neutrality' in regulation does not mean that all banks are to be treated in the same way if their risk characteristics are different. Reflecting the practice in the UK, Richardson and Stephenson (2000) argue that the Financial Services Authority (and formerly the Bank of England) treats the requirements of the Basel Accord as minima and requires individual banks to hold more capital than the minima dependent upon their risk exposure. Capital requirements are set individually for each bank. The authors list the major factors that are taken into account when setting an individual bank's capital requirements: experience and quality of the bank's management; the bank's risk appetite; the quality of risk analysis, management and control systems; the nature of the markets in which it operates; the quality, reliability and volatility of earnings; the quality of the bank's capital and access to new capital; the degree of diversification; exposure concentrations; the complexity of a bank's legal and organisational structure; the support and control provided by shareholders; and the degree to which a bank is supervised by other jurisdictions. As the authors note: 'these considerations imply that the appropriate margin above the minimum regulatory capital requirements will differ across banks.'

4.4.2   Monitoring and supervision

Because of the nature of financial contracts between financial firms and their customers, continuous monitoring of the behaviour of financial firms is needed. The question is who is to undertake the necessary monitoring: customers, shareholders, rating agencies, etc. In practice, there can be only a limited monitoring role for retail depositors due to major information asymmetries which cannot easily be rectified, and because depositors face the less costly option of withdrawal of deposits. Saunders and Wilson (1996) review the empirical evidence on the role of informed depositors. The funding structure of a bank may also militate against effective monitoring in that, unlike with non-financial companies, creditors tend to be numerous with a small stake for each.

As most (especially retail) customers cannot in practice undertake monitoring, and in the presence of deposit insurance they may have no incentive to do so, an important role of regulatory agencies is to monitor the behaviour of banks on behalf of consumers. In effect, consumers delegate the task of monitoring to a regulatory agency. There are strong efficiency reasons for consumers to delegate monitoring and supervision to a specialist agency to act on their behalf as the transactions costs for the consumer are lowered by such delegation (Llewellyn 1999). However, this is not to argue that a regulatory agency should become a monopolist monitor and supervisor of financial firms.

4.4.3   Incentive structures

The maintained theme is that the incentive structures and moral hazards faced by decision-makers (bank owners and managers, lenders to banks, borrowers and regulators) are major parts of the regulatory regime. The overall issue is two-fold: there need to be appropriate internal incentives for management to behave in appropriate ways, and the regulator has a role in ensuring internal incentives are compatible with regulatory objectives. Overall, we need to know more about incentive structures within financial firms and whether, for instance, incentive structures align with compliance. Research is also needed into how regulation impacts positively and negatively on incentives within regulated firms. We have already alluded to the possibility that detailed rules may have the negative effect of blunting compliance incentives.

Within the *regulatory regime* paradigm, a central role for regulation is to create appropriate incentives within regulated firms so that the incentives faced by decision-makers are consistent with financial stability. At the same time, regulation needs to avoid the danger of blunting the incentives of other agents (e.g. rating agencies, depositors, shareholders, debtholders) that have a disciplining role with banks. The position has been put well by Schinasi *et al.* (1999): 'Policy makers are therefore faced with the difficult challenge of balancing efforts to manage systemic risk against efforts to ensure that market participants bear the costs of imprudent risk taking and have incentives to behave prudently.' They argue that banks have complex incentive structures. There are internal incentives that motivate key decision-makers involved with risk, corporate governance mechanisms (such as accountability to shareholders), an external market in corporate control, market disciplines which may affect the cost of capital and deposits, and accountability to bank supervisors. The presence of regulation and official supervision overlays the structure of incentives faced by bank decision-makers.

The key is to align incentives of the various stake-holders in the decision-making process. The alignment of incentive structures has three dimensions: between the objectives set by regulators and supervisors and those of the bank; between the overall business objectives of the bank and those of actual decision-makers in the management structure, and between managers and owners of banks. Conflicts can arise at each level, making incentive structures within banks particularly complex.

If incentive structures are hazardous, regulation will always face formidable obstacles. There are several dimensions to this in the case of banks: the extent to which reward structures are based on the volume of business undertaken; the extent to which the risk characteristics of decisions are incorporated into reward structures; the nature of internal control systems within banks; internal monitoring of the decision-making of loan officers; the nature of profit-sharing schemes and the extent to which decision-makers also share in losses, etc. Reward systems based on short-term profits can also be hazardous as they may induce managers to pay less attention to the longer-term risk characteristics of their decisions. High staff turnover, and the speed with which officers are moved within the bank, may also create incentives for excessive risk-taking. A similar effect can arise through the herd behaviour that is common in banking. In the case of the Barings collapse, managers who were supposedly monitoring the trading activity of Leeson also benefited through bonuses derived from the profits he was making for the bank. Dale (1996) suggests that profit-related bonuses were an important feature in the Barings collapse.

It is clear that some incentive structures may lead to dysfunctional behaviour (Pendergast 1993). This may often emerge when incentives within regulated firms relate to volume and create a clear bias towards writing business. Bank managers may be rewarded by the volume of loans, not by their risk-adjusted profitability. Many cases of bank distress have been associated with inappropriate incentive structures creating a bias in favour of balance sheet growth, and with moral hazard created by anticipated lender of last resort actions (Llewellyn 2000).

Laws, regulations and supervisory actions provide incentives for regulated firms to adjust their actions and behaviour, and to control their own risks internally. In this regard, they can be viewed as *incentive contracts*. Within this general framework, regulation involves a process of creating incentive compatible contracts so that regulated firms have an incentive to act consistently with the objectives of financial stability. Well-designed incentive contracts induce appropriate behaviour by regulated firms. Conversely, if they are badly constructed and improperly designed, they might fail to reduce systemic risk (and other hazards regulation is designed to avoid) or have undesirable side-effects on the process of financial intermediation (e.g. impose high costs). At centre stage is the issue of whether all parties have the right incentives to act in a way that satisfies the objectives of regulation.

Given that incentives for managers can never be fully aligned with the objectives of the bank, there need to be external pressures on them to encourage adequate internal control systems to be established. Several procedures, processes and structures can, for instance, reinforce internal risk control mechanisms. These include internal auditors, internal audit committees, procedures for reporting to senior management (and perhaps to the supervisors), and making a named board member of financial firms responsible for compliance and risk analysis and management systems. In some countries the incentive on bank managers has been strengthened by a policy of increased personal liability for bank directors, and bank directors are personally liable in cases involving disclosure of incomplete or erroneous information. The Financial Services Authority in the UK has also proposed that individual directors and senior managers of financial firms should, under some circumstances, be made personally liable for compliance failures.

The form and intensity of supervision can differentiate between regulated institutions according to their relative risk and the efficiency of their internal control mechanisms (Goodhart *et al.* 1998). Supervisors can strengthen incentives by, for instance, relating the frequency and intensity of their supervision and inspection visits (and possibly rules) to the perceived adequacy of the internal risk control procedures, and compliance arrangements. In addition, regulators can create appropriate incentives by calibrating the external burden of regulation (e.g. number of inspection visits, allowable business, etc.) to the quality of management and the efficiency of internal incentives. Evans (2000) suggests several routes through which incentive structures can be improved: greater disclosure by financial institutions; subjecting local banks to more foreign competition; ensuring a closer alignment of regulatory and economic capital; greater use of risk-based incentives by supervisors, and lower capital adequacy requirements for banks headquartered in jurisdictions which comply with the BIS's core principles of supervision.

With respect to prudential issues, capital requirements should be structured so as to create incentives for the correct pricing of absolute and relative risk. In this area in particular, the potential for regulation to create perverse incentives and moral hazard is well established. The basic problem is that if regulatory capital requirements do not accurately map risk then banks are encouraged to engage in regulatory arbitrage. For instance, if differential capital requirements are set against different types of assets (e.g. through applying differential risk weights) the rules should be based on calculations of true relative risk. If risk weights are incorrectly specified, perverse incentives may be created for banks because the implied capital requirements are either more or less than justified by true relative risk calculations. A critique of the current Basel capital arrangements is that risk weights bear little relation to the relative risk characteristics of different assets, and the loan book largely carries a uniform risk weight even though the risk characteristics of different loans within a bank's portfolio vary considerably. The current BIS consultation paper seeks to address this issue.

The moral hazard associated with perceived safety-net arrangements have been extensively analysed in the literature. Garcia (1999b) in particular analyses the trade-off between systemic stability and moral hazard. Three possible hazards are associated with deposit insurance: banks may be induced to take excessive risk as they are not required to pay the risk premium on insured deposits; there are particular incentives for excessive risk-taking when a bank's capital ratio falls to a low level; and depositors may also be induced to seek high-risk banks due to the one-way-option bet.

Deposit insurance has two opposing impacts on systemic risk. By reducing the rationality of bank runs (though this is dependent on the extent and coverage of the deposit insurance scheme and the extent of any co-insurance) it lowers the potential for financial instability. On the other hand, the moral hazard effects of deposit insurance may increase risk in the system. Given that there is little firm empirical evidence for bank runs in systems without deposit insurance (including in the US prior to deposit insurance), the second factor probably outweighs the first. There is a trade-off in this: the stronger is the deposit protection scheme, the smaller is the probability of bank runs and systemic instability, but the greater is the moral hazard. This reinforces the case for accompanying deposit insurance by regulation to contain risk-taking by banks subject to deposit insurance. Reviewing the experience of bank crises in various countries, Demirgüç-Kunt and Datragiache (1998) argue, on the basis of their sample of countries: 'Our evidence suggests that, in the period under consideration, moral hazard played a significant role in bringing about systemic banking problems, perhaps because countries with deposit insurance schemes were not generally successful at implementing appropriate prudential regulation and supervision, or because the deposit insurance schemes were not properly designed.' However, this conclusion cannot be generalised everywhere. European Union countries have deposit protection schemes, but have not experienced banking distress: properly constructed deposit insurance may work.

Bhattacharya *et al.* (1998) consider various schemes to attenuate moral hazards associated with deposit insurance. These include cash-reserve requirements, risk-sensitive capital requirements and deposit insurance premia, partial deposit insurance, bank closure policy, and bank charter value.

There is a particular issue with respect to the incentive structure of state-owned, or state-controlled, banks as their incentives may be ill-defined, if not hazardous. Such banks are not subject to the normal disciplining pressures of the market, their 'owners' do not systematically monitor their behaviour, and there is no disciplining effect from the market in corporate control. Managers of such banks may face incentives and pressure to make loans for public policy reasons. Political interference in such banks, and the unwitting encouragement of bad banking practices, can itself become a powerful ingredient in bank distress. Lindgren *et al.* (1996) found, for instance, that banks that were, or had recently been, state-owned or controlled were a factor in most of the instances of unsoundness in their sample of banking crises.

Several adverse incentive structures can be identified in many of the countries that have recently experienced distressed banking systems:

- The expectation that government commitment to the exchange rate was absolute induced imprudent and unhedged foreign currency borrowing both by banks and companies.
- Expectations of bail-outs or support for industrial companies (which had at various times been in receipt of government support) meant that the bankruptcy threat was weak. This may also have affected foreign creditors.
- A belief in the role of the lender of last resort and expectations that banks would not be allowed to fail. The IMF notes that the perception of implicit guarantees was probably strengthened by the bailouts in the resolution of earlier banking crises in Thailand (1983–7), Malaysia (1985–8) and Indonesia (1994).
- The effect of close relationships between banks, the government, other official agencies and industrial corporations which often meant that lending relationships that would normally be conducted at arms-length became intertwined in a complex structure of economic and financial linkages within sometimes opaque corporate structures. This also meant that corporate governance arrangements, both within banks and their borrowing customers, were often weak and ill-defined.

4.4.4   Market discipline

The fourth component of the regulatory regime relates to the arrangements for market discipline on banks. The central theme is that regulation can never be an alternative to market discipline. On the contrary, market discipline needs to be reinforced within the regime. In fact, market discipline is one of the three pillars in the proposed new Basel Capital Adequacy Accord. A starting point is that, as noted by Lang and Robertson (2000), the existence of deposit insurance creates a large class of debt-holders who have no incentive to engage in costly monitoring of banks.

Monitoring is not only conducted by official agencies whose specialist task it is. In well-developed regimes, the market has incentives to monitor the behaviour of financial firms. The disciplines imposed by the market can be as powerful as any sanctions imposed by official agencies. The disciplining role of the markets (including the inter-bank market) was weak in the crisis countries of South East Asia in the 1990s. This was due predominantly to the lack of disclosure and transparency of banks, and to the fact that little reliance could be placed on the quality of accountancy data provided in bank accounts. In many cases standard accountancy and auditing procedures were not applied rigorously, and in some cases there was wilful misrepresentation of the financial position of banks and non-financial companies. This is not an issue for less developed countries alone. For instance, Nakaso *et al.* (2000) argue that market discipline did not operate efficiently in Japan due largely to insufficient financial infrastructure (weak accountancy rules, inadequate disclosure, etc.).

Market discipline only works well with full and accurate information disclosure and transparency. Good quality, timely and relevant information is needed by all market participants and regulators so that asset quality, creditworthiness and condition of financial institutions can be adequately assessed. So disclosure requirements can enhance the role of market discipline.

A potentially powerful disciplining power of markets derives from the market in corporate control which, through the threat of removing control from incumbent management, is a discipline on managers to be efficient and not endanger the solvency of their banks. As put in a recent IMF study: 'An open and competitive banking market exerts its own form of discipline against weak banks while encouraging well-managed banks' (Lindgren *et al.* 1996).

Several parties are potentially able to monitor the management of banks and other financial firms: owners, bank depositors and customers, rating agencies, official agencies (e.g. the central bank or other regulatory body), and other banks in the market. In practice, excessive emphasis has been given to official agencies. The danger in this is that a monopoly monitor is established with many of the standard problems associated with monopoly power. There may even be adverse incentive effects in that, given that regulatory agencies conduct monitoring and supervision on a delegated basis, the incentive for others to conduct monitoring may be weakened.

In the interests of an effective and efficient regulatory regime, the role of all potential monitors (and notably the market) needs to be strengthened, with greater incentives for other parties to monitor financial firms in parallel with official agencies. An advantage of having agents other than official supervisory bodies monitor banks is that it removes the inherent danger of having monitoring and supervision conducted by a monopolist with less than perfect and complete information, with the result that inevitably mistakes will be made. A monopolist supervisor may also have a different agenda than purely the maintenance of financial stability. It has been noted that 'Broader approaches to bank supervision reach beyond the issues of defining capital and accounting standards, and envisage co-opting other market participants by giving them a greater stake in bank survival. This approach increases the likelihood that problems will be detected earlier ... [it involves] broadening the number of those who are directly concerned about keeping the banks safe and sound' (Caprio and Honahan 1998).

Given how the business of banking has evolved, and the nature of the market environment in which banks now operate, market discipline needs to be strengthened. The issue is not about market *versus* agency discipline, but the mix of all aspects of monitoring, supervision and discipline. In its recent consultation document on capital adequacy, the Basel Committee (1999a) recognised that supervisors have a strong interest in facilitating effective market discipline as a lever to strengthen the safety and soundness of the banking system. It argues: 'market discipline has the potential to reinforce capital regulation and other supervisory efforts to promote safety and soundness in banks and financial systems. Market discipline imposes strong incentives on banks to conduct their business in a safe, sound and efficient manner.'

Some analysts (e.g. Calomiris 1997) are sceptical about the power of official supervisory agencies to identify the risk characteristics of banks compared with the power and incentives of markets. Along with others (including Evanoff and Wall 2000, who present a detailed set of proposals for the implementation of a subordinated debt rule), he has advocated banks being required to issue a minimum amount of subordinated and uninsured debt as part of the capital base. Holders of subordinated debt have an incentive to monitor the risk-taking of banks. As noted by Lang and Robertson (2000), discipline can be imposed through three routes: the cost of raising funds, market signals as expressed in risk premia implicit in the price of subordinated debt, and through supervisors themselves responding to market signals. Discipline would be applied by the market as its assessment of risk would be reflected in the risk premium in the price of traded debt. In particular, because of the nature of the debt contract, holders of a bank's subordinated debt do not share in the potential upside gain through the bank's risk-taking, but stand to lose if the bank fails. They therefore have a particular incentive to monitor the bank's risk profile compared with shareholders who, under some circumstances, have an incentive to support a high-risk profile. This is particularly the case when a 'gamble for resurrection' strategy becomes optimal for shareholders. In this respect, there is a degree of symmetry between the reward structures faced by equity and subordinated debt holders, in that equity holders have the prospect of unlimited upside gain while losses are restricted to the value of their holding, while debt holders do not share in any excess rewards (in the absence of default, their rewards are fixed) but face the prospect of total loss in the event of default. For such a scheme to work, however, it must be well established that holders of such subordinated debt will never be rescued in the event of the bank failing.

The impact of an increase in the debt-equity ratio (arising through substituting subordinated debt for equity) on the incentives for risk-taking by banks is ambiguous. On the one hand, a rise in the ratio raises the proportion of liability holders who have an incentive to monitor risk. This might be expected to lower the risk-appetite of banks. On the other hand, a decline in the equity ratio may raise the risk-appetite of equity holders as they have less to lose and may face a rational gamble-for-resurrection option. A decline in the equity ratio also has the disadvantage of increasing the probability of insolvency. It is also the case that the market disciplining role of subordinated debt may be limited because, in practice, such debt will always be a small proportion of a bank's total liabilities. The most powerful route is likely to be through market signals and how these induce supervisors to respond.

A scheme along these lines has been introduced in Argentina whereby holders of subordinated debt must be entities of substance which are independent of a bank's shareholders, and banks are required to issue debt in relatively lumpy amounts on a regular basis (Calomiris 1997). However, while there is a potentially powerful role for market discipline to operate through the pricing of subordinated debt, the interests of holders of such debt do not necessarily precisely coincide with those of depositors or the public interest more generally (Dewatripont and Tirole 1994). It is not, therefore, a substitute for official monitoring. It is intended as an extension of the role of market monitoring.

A further example of market discipline could be to link deposit insurance premia paid by banks to the implied risk of the bank as incorporated in subordinated debt yields or classifications of rating agencies.

The merit of increasing the role of market discipline is that large, well-informed creditors (including other banks) have the resources, expertise, market knowledge, and incentives to conduct monitoring and to impose market discipline. For instance, the hazardous state of BCCI was reflected in market prices and inter-bank interest rates before the Bank of England closed the bank. Market reports also indicate that some money brokers in London had ceased to deal with BCCI in advance of it being closed.

Leaving aside the merits and drawbacks of particular mechanisms that might be proposed, the overall assessment is that regulation needs to reinforce, not replace, market discipline. The regulatory regime needs to be structured so as to provide greater incentives than exist at present for markets to monitor banks and other financial firms.

In addition, there is considerable advantage in regulators utilising market data in their supervisory procedures whenever possible. Evidence indicates that markets give signals about the credit-standing of financial firms which, when combined with inside information gained by supervisory procedures, can increase the efficiency of the overall supervisory process. Flannery (1998) suggests that market information may improve two features of the overall process: (1) regulators can identify developing problems more promptly, and (2) regulators have the incentive and justification to take action more quickly once problems have been identified. He concludes that market information should be incorporated into the process of identifying and correcting problems.

If financial markets are able to assess a bank's market value as reflected in the market price, an asset-pricing model can, in principle, be used to infer the risk of insolvency that the market has assigned to each bank. Such a model has been applied to UK banks by Hall and Miles (1990). Similar analysis for countries which had recently liberalised their financial systems has been applied by Fischer and Gueyie (1995). On the other hand, there are clear limitations to such an approach (see Simons and Cross 1991) and hence it would be hazardous to rely exclusively on it. For instance, it assumes that markets have sufficient data upon which to make accurate assessments of banks, and it equally assumes that the market is able to efficiently assess the available information and incorporate it into an efficient pricing of bank securities.

An additional route is to develop the role of rating agencies in the oversight role. Rating agencies have considerable resources and expertise in monitoring banks and making assessments of risk. It could be made a requirement, as in Argentina, for all banks to have a rating which would be made public.

While market discipline is potentially powerful, it has its limitations, and Bliss and Flannery (2000) argue that there is no strong evidence that equity and debt holders do in fact affect managerial decisions. This means that, in practice, it is unlikely to be an effective complete alternative to the role of official regulatory and supervisory agencies:

- Markets are concerned with the private costs of a bank failure and reflect the risk of this in market prices. The social cost of bank failures, on the other hand, may exceed the private cost (Llewellyn 1999) and hence the total cost of a bank failure may not be fully reflected in market prices.
- The cost of private monitoring and information collection may exceed the benefits.
- Market disciplines are not effective in monitoring and disciplining public sector banks.

- 'Free-rider' problems may emerge.
- In many countries, there are limits imposed on the extent to which the market in corporate control (the take-over market) is allowed to operate. In particular, there are often limits, if not bars, on the extent to which foreign institutions are able to take control of banks, even though they may offer a solution to under-capitalised institutions.
- The market is able to efficiently price bank securities and inter-bank loans only to the extent that relevant information is available, and in many cases the necessary information is not available. Disclosure requirements are, therefore, an integral part of the market disciplining process.
- It is not self-evident that market participants always have the necessary expertise to make risk assessment of complex, and sometimes opaque, banks. In addition, there are some areas within a bank (e.g. its risk analysis and control systems) where disclosure is not feasible.
- In some countries, the market in debt of all kinds (including securities and debt issued by banks) is limited, inefficient and cartelised, although market discipline can also operate through inter-bank and swaps markets.
- When debt issues are very small it is not always economic for rating agencies to conduct a full credit rating on a bank.

While there are clear limitations to the role of market discipline (discussed further in Lane 1993) the global trend is in the direction of placing more emphasis on market data in the supervisory process. The theme being developed is not that market monitoring and discipline can effectively replace official supervision, but that it has a powerful role which should be strengthened within the overall regulatory regime. In addition, Caprio (1997) argues that broadening the number of those who are directly concerned about the safety and soundness of banks reduces the extent to which insider political pressure can be brought to bear on bank regulation and supervision. In fact, the recent consultative document issued by the Basel Committee on Banking Supervision (Basel Committee 1999a) incorporates the role of market discipline as one of the three pillars of a proposed new approach to banking supervision. The Committee emphasises that its approach 'will encourage high disclosure standards and enhance the role of market participants in encouraging banks to hold adequate capital'.

As neither the market nor regulatory agencies are perfect, the obvious solution is to utilise both with neither having a monopoly of wisdom and judgement. The conclusion is that more systematic research is needed into the predictive power of market data, and how market information can usefully be incorporated into the supervisory process both by regulators and the markets.

This Section should not conclude without reference to competition.

However well intentioned, regulation has the potential to compromise competition and to condone, if not in some cases endorse, unwarranted entry barriers, restrictive practices, and other anti-competitive mechanisms. Historically regulation in finance has often been anti-competitive in nature. But this is not an inherent property of regulation. The purpose of regulation is not to displace competitive pressures or market mechanisms, but to correct for market imperfections and failures. As there are clear consumer benefits and efficiency gains to be secured through competition, regulation should not be constructed in a way that impairs it. Regulation and competition need not be in conflict: on the contrary, properly constructed they are complementary. Regulation can also make competition more effective in the market place by, for instance, requiring the disclosure of relevant information that can aid market participants to make informed choices.

Discipline can also be exerted by competition. Opening domestic financial markets to external competition can contribute to the promotion of market discipline. There are many benefits to be derived from foreign institutions entering a country. They bring expertise and experience and, because they themselves are diversified throughout the world, what is a macro shock to a particular country becomes a regional shock, and hence they are more able to sustain purely national shocks which domestic institutions are less able to do. It is generally the case that competition that develops from outside a system tends to have a greater impact on competition and efficiency than internal competition. Foreign institutions tend to be less subject to domestic political pressures in the conduct of their business, and are also less susceptible to local euphoria which, at times, leads to excessive lending and over-optimistic expectations

4.4.5   *Intervention*

A key component of the regulatory regime is the nature, timing and form of intervention by regulatory agencies in the event of either some form of compliance failure within a regulated firm, or when financial distress occurs with banks. While not downgrading the significance of the former, in the interest of brevity we reserve discussion of this issue to the question of intervention in the event of bank distress.

The closure of an insolvent or, under a Structured Early Intervention and Resolution (SEIR) regime, a near-insolvent bank, can impose a powerful discipline on the future behaviour of banks. Such 'creative destruction' has benefits. 'Closure' also needs to be defined. It need not mean that depositors lose, even in the absence of deposit insurance, depositors lose. Nor do bank–customer relationships and information sharing have to be destroyed. As with the bankruptcy of any company, there is always some residual value within an insolvent bank. Bank closure may simply mean a change in ownership of a bank and the imposition of losses on equity holders. In most countries, 'bank closure' has not meant the destruction of the bank. Thus, Barings was purchased by ING Bank. In many instances, regulatory authorities have brokered a change in ownership of insolvent banks while imposing losses on shareholders. The skill in intervention that leads to the 'closure' of an institution lies in ensuring that what remains of value is maintained.

Intervention arrangements are important not least because they have incentive and moral hazard effects which potentially influence future behaviour by banks and their customers. These arrangements may also have important implications for the total cost of intervention (e.g. initial forbearance often has the effect of raising the eventual cost of subsequent intervention), and the distribution of those costs between taxpayers and other agents. Different intervention arrangements also have implications for the future efficiency of the financial system in that, for instance, forbearance may have the effect of sustaining inefficient banks and excess capacity in the banking sector.

The issue focuses on when intervention is to be made. The experience of banking crises in both developed and developing countries indicates that a well-defined strategy for responding to the possible insolvency of financial institutions is needed. A response strategy in the event of bank distress has three key components:

- taking prompt corrective action to address financial problems before they reach critical proportions;
- being prepared to close insolvent financial institutions while nevertheless not destroying what value remains;
- closing unviable institutions, and vigorously monitoring weak and/or restructured institutions.

A key issue relates to rules *versus* discretion in the event of bank distress: the extent to which intervention should be circumscribed by clearly-defined rules (so that intervention agencies have no discretion about whether, how and when to act), or whether there should always be discretion simply because relevant circumstances cannot be set out in advance. The obvious *prima facie* advantage for allowing discretion is that it is impossible to foresee all future circumstances and conditions for when a bank might become distressed and close to (or actually) insolvent. It might be judged that it is not always the right policy to close a bank in such circumstances.

However, there are strong arguments against allowing such discretion and in favour of a rules approach to intervention. First, it enhances the credibility of the intervention agency in that market participants, including banks, have a high degree of certainty that action will be taken. Second, allowing discretion may increase the probability of forbearance which usually eventually leads to higher costs when intervention is finally made. Kane (2000), for instance, argues that officials may forbear because they face different incentives from those of the market: their own welfare, the interests of the agency they represent, political interests, reputation, future employment prospects, etc. Perhaps less plausibly, he also argues that, under some circumstances, the present generation of taxpayers may believe they can shift the cost of resolution to future generations. Third, and this was relevant in some countries which recently experienced banking distress, it removes the danger of undue political interference in the disciplining of banks and regulated firms. Experience in many countries indicates that supervisory authorities face substantial pressure to delay action and intervention. Fourth, and related to the first, a rules approach to intervention is likely to have a beneficial impact on *ex ante* behaviour of financial firms.

A rules-based approach, by removing any prospect that a hazardous bank might be treated leniently, has the advantage of enhancing the incentives for bank managers to manage their banks prudently so as to reduce the probability of insolvency (Glaessner and Mas 1995). It also enhances the credibility of the regulator's threat to close institutions. Finally, it guards against hazards associated with risk-averse regulators who themselves might be disinclined to take action for fear that it will be interpreted as a regulatory failure, and the temptation to allow a firm to trade-out of its difficulty. This amounts to the regulator also 'gambling for resurrection'. In this sense, a rules approach may be of assistance to the intervention agency as its hands are tied, and it is forced to do what it believes to be the right thing.

Put another way, time-inconsistency and credibility problems should be addressed through pre-commitments and graduated responses with the possibility of over-rides. Many analysts have advocated various forms of pre-determined intervention through a general policy of Structured Early Intervention and Resolution. There is a case for a graduated-response approach since, for example, there is no magical capital ratio below which an institution is in danger and above which it is safe. Other things equal, potential danger gradually increases as the capital ratio declines. This, in itself, suggests that there should be a graduated series of responses from the regulator as capital diminishes. No single dividing line should trigger action, but there should be a series of such trigger points with the effect of going through any one of them being relatively minor, but the cumulative effect being large. Goldstein and Turner (1996) argue that SEIR is designed to imitate the remedial action which private bond holders would impose on banks in the absence of government insurance or guarantees. In this sense it is a mimic of market solutions to troubled banks. An example of the rules-based approach is to be found in the Prompt Corrective Action (PCA) rules in the US. These specify graduated intervention by the regulators with pre-determined responses triggered by capital thresholds. In fact, several countries have such rules of intervention (Basel Committee 1999a). SEIR strategies can, therefore, act as a powerful incentive for prudent behaviour.

Although a policy of 'constructive ambiguity' has merits, the need to maintain the credibility of supervisory agencies creates a strong case against forbearance. The overall conclusion is that there should be a clear bias (though not a bar) against forbearance when a bank is in difficulty. While there should be a strong presumption against forbearance, and that this is best secured through having clearly-defined rules, there will always be exceptional circumstances when it might be warranted in the interests of systemic stability. However, when forbearance is exercised the regulatory agency should, in some way or another, be made accountable for its actions.

A useful case study is to be found in the example of Finland where strict conditions were imposed in the support programme. These are summarised by Konskenkyla (2000) as:

- support was to be transparent and public;
- the attractiveness of public funding of the programme was to be minimised;
- the owners of supported banks were, where possible, to be held financially responsible;
- the terms of the programme were to support the efficiency of the banking system and the promotion of necessary structural adjustments within the system;
- the potential impact on competitive distortions were to be minimised;
- banks receiving support were to be publicly monitored;
- the employment terms of bank directors were to be reasonable and possible inequities removed.

It is also the case that some bank directors and managers in Finland have been held financially liable for hazardous behaviour (see Halme 2000).

4.4.6   Corporate governance

The focus of corporate governance is the principal–agent relationship that exists between managers and shareholders (owners) of companies. The owners (principals) delegate the task of management to professional managers (agents) who, in theory, act in the interests of the shareholders. In practice, managers have information advantages over shareholders and also have their own interests which may not coincide with those of the owners. Differences may emerge between the owners and managers with respect to their appetite for risk. For instance, managers may at times have a greater appetite for risk than do shareholders because they do not stand to lose if the risk fails. On the other hand, at other times (e.g. when capital in the bank is low) shareholders may have a strong appetite for risk in a gamble for resurrection strategy.

In the final analysis, all aspects of the management of financial firms (including compliance) are ultimately corporate governance issues. This means that, while shareholders may at times have an incentive to take high risks, if a financial firm behaves hazardously it is, to some extent, a symptom of weak corporate governance. This may include, for instance, a hazardous corporate structure for the financial firm; inter-connected lending within a closely-related group of companies; lack of internal control systems; weak surveillance by (especially non-executive) directors, and ineffective internal audit arrangements which often includes serious under-reporting of problem loans. Corporate governance arrangements were evidently weak and under-developed in banks in many of the countries that have recently experienced bank distress.

A particular feature of corporate governance relates to cross-share-holdings and inter-connected lending within a group (Falkena and Llewellyn 2000). With respect to Japan, Nakaso *et al.* (2000) note that such cross-share-holdings, which have long been a feature of Japanese corporate structures, increased during the 'bubble era' that preceded the banking crisis. In some cases, banks sold capital to companies (in order to raise their capital-asset ratios) and at the same time purchased stock in the companies. Several problems arise in cross-share-holding arrangements: credit assessment may be weak; the mix of debt and equity contracts held by banks may create conflicts of interest; when equity prices fall banks simultaneously face credit and market risk; and banks often counted un-realised gains as capital even when, in practice, they could not be realised.

There are several reasons why corporate governance arrangements operate differently with banks than with other types of firms. First, banks are subject to regulation which adds an additional dimension to corporate governance arrangements. Second, banks are also subject to continuous supervision and monitoring by official agencies. This has two immediate implications for private corporate governance: shareholders and official agencies are to some extent duplicating monitoring activity, and the actions of official agencies may have an impact on the incentives faced by other monitors, such as shareholders and even depositors. However, official and market monitoring are not perfectly substitutable. Third, banks have a fiduciary relationship with their customers (e.g. they are holding the wealth of depositors) which is rare with other types of firm. This creates additional principal–agent relationships (and potentially agency costs) with banks that generally do not exist with non-financial firms.

A fourth reason why corporate governance mechanisms are different in banks is that there is a systemic dimension to banks. Because in some circumstances (e.g. presence of externalities) the social cost of a bank failure may exceed the private costs, there is a systemic concern with the behaviour of banks that does not exist with other companies. Fifth, banks are subject to safety net arrangements that are not available to other companies. This has implications for incentive structures faced by owners, managers, depositors and the market with respect to monitoring and control.

All these considerations have an impact on the two general mechanisms for exercising discipline on the management of firms: internal corporate governance and the market in corporate control. While there are significant differences between banks and other firms, corporate governance issues in banks have received remarkably little attention. A key issue noted by Flannery (1998) is that little is known about how the two governance systems (regulation and private) interact with each other and, in particular, the extent to which they are complementary or offsetting.

A key issue in the management of banks is the extent to which corporate governance arrangements are suitable and efficient for the management and control of risks. In the UK, the FSA has argued as follows: 'Senior management set the business strategy, regulatory climate, and ethical standards of the firm ... Effective management of these activities will benefit firms and contribute to the delivery of the FSA's statutory objectives.' Corporate governance arrangements include issues of corporate structure, the power of shareholders to exercise accountability of managers, the transparency of corporate structures, the authority and power of directors, internal audit arrangements, and lines of accountability of managers. In the final analysis, shareholders are the ultimate risk-takers and agency problems may induce managers to take more risks with the bank than the owners would wish. This in turn raises issues about what information shareholders have about the actions of the managers to which they delegate decision-making powers, the extent to which shareholders are represented on the board of directors of the bank, and the extent to which shareholders have power to discipline managers.

Corporate governance arrangements need to provide for effective monitoring and supervision of the risk-taking profile of banks. These arrangements need to provide for, *inter alia*, a management structure with clear lines of accountability; independent non-executive directors on the board; an independent audit committee; the four-eyes principle for important decisions involving the risk profile of the bank; a transparent ownership structure; internal structures that enable the risk profile of the firm to be clear, transparent and managed; and the creation and monitoring of risk analysis and management systems. There would also be advantage in having a board director being responsible for the bank's risk analysis, management and control systems. Some bank ownership structures also produce ineffective corporate governance. Particular corporate structures (e.g. when banks are part of larger conglomerates) may encourage connected lending and weak risk analysis of borrowers. This was the case in a significant number of bank failures in the countries of South East Asia and Latin America. Some corporate structures also make it comparatively easy for banks to conceal their losses and unsound financial position.

The Basel Committee has appropriately argued that effective oversight by a bank's board of directors and senior management is critical. It suggests that the board should approve overall policies of the bank and its internal systems. It argues in particular that: 'lack of adequate corporate governance in the banks seems to have been an important contributory factor in the Asian crisis. The boards of directors and management committees of the banks did not play the role they were expected to play' (Basel Committee 1999b). According to the Committee, good corporate governance includes:

- establishing strategic objectives and a set of corporate values that are communicated throughout the banking organisation;
- setting and enforcing clear lines of responsibility and accountability throughout the organisation;
- ensuring that board members are qualified for their positions, have a clear understanding of their role in corporate governance, and are not subject to undue influence from management or outside concerns;
- ensuring there is appropriate oversight by senior management;
- effectively utilising the work conducted by internal and external auditors;
- ensuring that compensation approaches are consistent with the bank's ethical values, objectives, strategy and control environment;
- conducting corporate governance in a transparent manner.

Some useful insights have been provided by Sinha (1999) who concludes, for instance, that while the regulatory authorities may approve the appointment of non-executive directors of banks, such directors often monitor top management less effectively than is the case in manufacturing firms. Sinha compares corporate governance arrangements in banks and manufacturing firms in the UK and finds that top management turnover in banks is less than in other firms, and that turnover seems not to be related to share price performance. Prowse (1997) also shows that accountability to shareholders, and the effectiveness of board monitoring, is lower in banks than in non-financial firms.

An interesting possibility is the extent to which all this results from moral hazard associated with official regulation and supervision: a further negative trade-off within the regulatory regime. It could be that the assumption that regulatory authorities impose regulation and monitor banks reduces the incentive for non-executive directors and shareholders to do so. The presumption may be that regulators have more information than do non-executive directors and shareholders, and that their own monitoring would only be wastefully duplicating that being conducted by official supervisors. Further research is needed into the role of non-executive directors and institutional investors in the effectiveness of corporate governance mechanisms in banks.

There is a further dimension to this issue. A major market discipline on any firm comes from the market in corporate control where, in principle, alternative managements seek control of companies. It is reasonably well established that there is something of a trade-off between internal corporate governance mechanisms and the power of the market in corporate control (the take-over market). In general, corporate governance arrangements tend to be stronger when the market in corporate control operates weakly. Sinha (1999) argues that this trade-off does not apply to banks, as corporate governance arrangements are weak and so is the discipline of the market in corporate control. It is possible that restrictions imposed on the ownership of banks may reduce the disciplining power of markets.

4.4.7 *Disciplines on the regulator*

Four perspectives reinforce the case for regulatory authorities being subject to strong disciplining and accountability measures: (1) there is an ever-present potential for over-regulation as it may be both over-demanded and over-supplied (Goodhart *et al.* 1998); (2) regulatory agencies have considerable power on both consumers and regulated firms; (3) the regulator is often supplying regulatory services as a monopolist although, in the US, there is scope for banks to switch regulators, and (4) the regulator is not subject to the normal disciplines of the market in the supply of its services.

These issues can be illustrated by the recent experience of the UK which has created a single regulatory authority for all financial institutions and markets. As well as conferring substantial powers, the Financial Services and Markets Bill in the UK gives the Financial Services Authority substantial discretion in the use of its powers. In some respects, the way this discretion will be used will prove to be more significant than the powers the Bill confers. This, in turn, emphasises the importance of the disciplining and accountability mechanisms of the FSA, and of the FSA being open in the way it plans to develop its approach to regulation. The agency has, indeed, been open in this regard (see, for instance, its document *Meeting Our Responsibilities*).

Several accountability mechanisms have been put in place with respect to the FSA. Its objectives have been clearly defined in the Bill, and the FSA reports directly to Parliament. In addition, there is a formal legislative requirement for the FSA to use its resources in the most efficient way, and to make any regulatory burden proportionate to its benefits. The last-mentioned includes a requirement on the FSA to conduct cost–benefit analyses on its regulation. The Bill also outlines a strong set of accountability mechanisms including the scope for judicial review, public reporting mechanisms to the Treasury, requirements for consultation, the creation of Consumer and Practitioner Panels, independent review of its rules and decisions including by the Office of Fair Trading, independent investigation of complaints against the FSA, and an independent appeals and enforcement procedure. A further disciplining mechanisms is the requirement to conduct a cost–benefit study on major regulatory changes.

4.5   Differentiations in the regime

A central theme has been that the two components of the financial stability objective (reducing the probability of bank failures and minimising the costs of those that do occur) are most effectively and efficiently served by a regulatory strategy that optimises the regulatory regime. This is necessarily more complex than myopically focusing upon regulation *per se*. The skill lies in combining the seven key components incorporating various positive and negative trade-offs that may exist between them.

However, there is no presumption for a single optimum combination of the components of the regime. On the contrary, optima will vary between countries at any point in time, over time for all countries, and between different banks within a country at any particular time. The optimum mix of the components of a regulatory regime and of instruments will change over time as financial structures, market conditions and compliance cultures evolve. For instance, the combination of external regulation and market discipline that is most effective and efficient in one set of market circumstances, and one type of financial structure in a country, may become ill-suited if structures change. Also, if the norms and compliance culture of the industry change, it may be appropriate to rely less on detailed and prescriptive regulation, at least for some banks.

Neither does the same approach and mix of components in the regulatory regime need to apply to all regulated firms, or all types of business. On the contrary, given that neither are homogeneous, it would be suboptimal to apply the same approach. A key issue is the extent to which differentiations are to be made between different banks.

Financial systems are changing substantially and to an extent that may undermine traditional approaches to regulation and most especially the balance between regulation and official supervision, and the role of market discipline. In particular, globalisation, the pace of financial innovation and the creation of new financial instruments, the blurring of traditional distinctions between different types of financial firm, the speed with which portfolios can change through banks trading in derivatives, etc., and the increased complexity of banking business, create a fundamentally new – in particular, more competitive – environment in which regulation and supervision are undertaken. They also change the viability of different approaches to regulation which, if it is to be effective, must constantly respond to changes in the market environment in which regulated firms operate.

Space precludes an extensive discussion of these differentiations. Nevertheless, the major determinants may be summarised as follows:

- the expertise that exists within banks and the extent to which reliance can be placed on internal management;
- the incentive structures within banks and those faced by regulators, supervisors and intervention agencies;
- the quality of risk analysis, management and control systems within banks;
- the skills of regulatory and supervisory agencies;
- the nature and efficiency of the basic financial infrastructure of a country: quality and reliability of accounting and auditing; nature, definition and enforceability of property rights; enforceability of collateral contracts; information disclosure and transparency, etc.;
- the existence of financial markets;
- the efficiency of financial markets, most especially with respect to issues such as the extent to which market prices accurately reflect all publicly available information about the true value and risk characteristics of banks;
- the existence of financial instruments to enable banks to mitigate risks;
- the strength of incentives for stake-holders to monitor the risk characteristics of banks;
- the extent of moral hazard created by public intervention (e.g. deposit insurance);
- whether rating agencies provide rating services to investors in banks;
- the complexity and opaqueness of bank structures;
- ownership structures of banks and the extent to which owners are able to effectively monitor banks and influence the behaviour of bank managers to whom they delegate the responsibility of managing the bank;
- the degree of complexity of the business operations of banks;
- the existence or otherwise of an effective market in corporate control in the banking sector;
- the degree of ownership independence of banks from their corporate customers;
- the extent to which decision-making in banks is independent of political influence;
- the capital structure of banks.

With respect to the differences in the optimum structure of the regulatory regime as between countries, it is likely that in developing countries a substantial reliance will be placed on the explicit regulation component. This will reflect, for instance, considerations such as limited banking expertise; relatively unsophisticated techniques of risk analysis and management; a shortage of high-quality supervisory personnel; rudimentary financial infrastructure, financial markets, and financial instruments; absence of rating agencies; limited corporate governance mechanisms, and sometimes close relationships between banks and their corporate customers.

These considerations will vary from country to country though, in general, they imply that for developing countries more reliance probably needs to be placed on formal, prescriptive rules with less reliance on discretionary supervision, incentive structures, market discipline and corporate governance arrangements.

Over time, and as the complexity of banks' operations increases, it is likely that less reliance can be placed on detailed and prescriptive rules. Risk becomes too complex and volatile an issue to be adequately covered by a simple set of prescriptive rules. Also, as markets develop and become more efficient, a greater role can be envisaged for market discipline. Similarly, less reliance may be needed on regulation to the extent that the skills within banks raise the sophistication and accuracy of banks' risk analysis and management systems.

Equally banks within a country are not homogeneous with respect to their skills, risk analysis and management systems, corporate governance arrangements, their overall significance within the financial system, legal, organisational, and corporate structures, or access to markets for capital. These differences may also create differences between banks in the optimum mix of the components of the regulatory regime.

4.6   Shifts within the regulatory regime

Drawing together some of the earlier themes, several shifts within the regulatory regime are recommended in order to maximise its overall effectiveness and efficiency:

- Less emphasis to be given to formal and detailed prescriptive rules dictating the behaviour of regulated firms.
- A greater focus to be given to incentive structures within regulated firms, and how regulation might have a beneficial impact on such structures.
- Market discipline and market monitoring of financial firms should be strengthened within the overall regime.
- Greater differentiation between banks and different types of financial business.
- Less emphasis to be placed on detailed and prescriptive rules and more on internal risk analysis, management and control systems. In some areas, externally-imposed regulation in the form of prescriptive and detailed rules is becoming increasingly inappropriate and ineffective. More emphasis needs to be given to monitoring risk management and control systems, and to recasting the nature and functions of external regulation away from generalised rule-setting towards establishing incentives and sanctions to reinforce such internal control systems. The recently issued consultative document by the Basel Committee on Banking Supervision (Basel Committee 1999a) explicitly

recognises that a major role of the supervisory process is to monitor banks' own internal capital management processes and 'the setting of targets for capital that are commensurate with the bank's particular risk profile and control environment. This process would be subject to supervisory review and intervention, where appropriate.'

- Corporate governance mechanism for financial firms needs to be strengthened so that, for instance, owners play a greater role in the monitoring and control of banks, and compliance issues are identified as the ultimate responsibility of a nominated main board director.

This chapter has emphasised the central importance of incentive structures and the potential for regulation to affect them. The key is how to align incentive structures to reduce the conflict between the objectives of the firm and those of the regulator. It is not a question of replacing one mechanism by another. It amounts to a re-balancing within the regime. It is unfortunate that public discussion of regulation often poses false dichotomies rather than recognising that the key issue is how the various mechanisms are to be combined. To make the case for regulation is not to undermine the central importance of market disciplines. Equally, to emphasise the role of incentives and market monitoring is not to argue that there is no role for regulation or supervision by an official agency.

4.6.1 Recent trends in regulatory practice

Space precludes a detailed review of how regulatory arrangements have been evolving in practice. However, in some areas substantial changes have been made and others are in the pipeline. This section briefly considers some of the trends that are emerging with respect to the international approach to the prudential regulation and supervision of banks. While the BIS would not necessarily adopt the paradigm of the regulatory regime outlined earlier, there are some shifts in approach along the lines outlined in this paper.

When setting capital adequacy standards on banks, the regulator confronts a negative trade-off between the efficiency and costs of financial intermediation on the one hand, and financial stability on the other. Although it is a complex calculation (absent the Modigliani–Miller theorem (which does not, in any case, apply to banks with deposit insurance)) as the cost of equity exceeds the cost of debt (deposits), the total cost of financial intermediation rises as the equity–assets ratio rises. If the regulator imposes an unnecessarily high capital ratio (in the sense that it exceeds what is warranted by the risk profile of the bank) an avoidable cost is imposed on society through a high cost of financial intermediation. On the other hand, a high capital ratio reduces the probability of bank failure and hence the social costs of financial instability. It also means that a higher proportion of the costs of a bank failure are borne by specialist risk-takers rather than depositors.

When judging the efficiency and effectiveness of capital adequacy regulation, four basic criteria are to be applied: (1) does it bring regulatory capital into line with economic capital?; (2) does it create the correct risk-management incentives for owners and managers of banks?; (3) does it produce the correct internal allocation of capital as between alternative risk assets and therefore the correct pricing of risk?; and (4) to what extent does it create moral hazard?

4.6.2   *The BIS approach to capital adequacy*

The problems with the current BIS capital adequacy regime (1988 Accord) are well established. In particular:

- The risk-weights applied to different assets and contingent liabilities are not based on precise measures of absolute and relative risk. This in turn creates incentives for banks to misallocate the internal distribution of capital, to choose an uneconomic structure of assets, and to arbitrage capital requirements. It is also liable to produce a mis-pricing of risks. There is, for instance, an incentive to choose assets whose *regulatory risk weights* are low relative to the *economic (true) risk weights* even though, in absolute terms, the risk weights may be higher than on alternative assets. The distortion arises not because of the differences in risk weights but to the extent that differentials between regulatory and economic risk weights vary across different asset classes.
- The methodology involves the summing of risk assets and does not take into account the extent to which assets and risks are efficiently diversified.
- No allowance is made for risk-mitigating factors such as hedging strategies within the banking book, though allowance is made for risk mitigation in the trading book.
- Almost all loans carry a risk weight of unity whereas the major differences within a bank's overall portfolio exist within the loan book.
- Banks are able to arbitrage their regulatory capital requirements in a way that lowers capital costs without any corresponding reduction in risk.
- The current Basel Accord only applies to credit and market risk.

Some national regulatory and supervisory authorities have discretion in how the Accord is applied (subject to certain minima), and differentiate between banks according to their overall risk profile. So the distortions may not be as serious in practice as the Accord might suggest. Nevertheless, the Accord has flaws. Still, there are many countries where no discretion is allowed and the Basel requirements are adopted precisely.

Partly because of these weaknesses, the Basel Committee on Banking

Supervision has recently proposed a new framework for setting capital adequacy requirements (Basel Committee 1999a). It has issued a substantial consultation document which, when adopted, will represent a significant shift in the approach to bank regulation. This is not discussed in detail here other than to note that it is based on three pillars: minimum capital requirements, the Supervisory Review Process, and market discipline requirements. The proposed new approach can be viewed in terms of the regulatory regime paradigm:

- Substantial emphasis is given to the importance of banks developing their own risk analysis, management and control systems, and it is envisaged that incentives will be strengthened for this.
- The Committee's consultative paper stresses the important role of supervision in the overall regulatory process. This second pillar of the capital adequacy framework will 'seek to ensure that a bank's capital position is consistent with its overall risk profile and strategy and, as such, will encourage *early supervisory intervention*' (italics added).
- In an attempt to bring regulatory capital more into alignment with economic capital, it is proposed to widen the range of risk weights and to introduce weights greater than unity.
- A wider range of risks are to be covered including legal, reputational and operational risk.
- Capital requirements are to take into account the volatility of risks and the extent to which risks are diversified.
- Although a modified form of the current Accord will remain as the 'standardised' approach, the Committee believes that, for some sophisticated banks, use of internal and external credit ratings should be incorporated, and also that portfolio models of risk could contribute towards aligning economic and regulatory capital requirements. However, the Committee does not believe that portfolio models of risk can be used in the foreseeable future. The Committee recognises that use of internal ratings is likely to incorporate information about customers that is not available either to regulators or external rating agencies. In effect, in some respects this would involve asking banks themselves what they believe their capital should be. This is a form of pre-commitment. In practice, while banks will slot loans into buckets according to the internal ratings, the capital requirements for each bucket will be set by Basel. The object is to bring the regulatory process more into line with the way banks undertake risk assessment.
- A major aspect of the proposed new approach is to ask banks what they judge their capital should be. Any use of internal ratings would be subject to supervisor approval.
- Allowance is to be made for risk-mitigating factors.
- Greater emphasis is to be given to the role of market discipline. The

third pillar in the proposed new approach is market discipline. It will encourage high standards of transparency and disclosure standards and 'enhance the role of market participants encouraging banks to hold adequate capital'. It is envisaged that market discipline should play a greater role in the monitoring of banks and the creation of appropriate incentives. The Committee has recognised that supervisors have a strong interest in facilitating effective market discipline as a lever to strengthen the safety and soundness of the banking system. It argues: 'market discipline has the potential to reinforce capital regulation and other supervisory efforts to promote safety and soundness in banks and financial systems. Market discipline imposes strong incentives on banks to conduct their business in a safe, sound and efficient manner.'

- The proposals also include the possibility of external credit assessments in determining risk weights for some types of bank assets. This would enhance the role of external rating agencies in the regulatory process. The Committee also suggests there could usefully be greater use of the assessment by credit rating agencies with respect to asset securitisations made by banks.
- The Consultation document gives some emphasis to the important role that shareholders have in monitoring and controlling banks.

Overall, the new approach being proposed envisages more differentiation between banks, a less formal reliance on prescriptive rules, elements of choice for regulated institutions, an enhanced role for market discipline, a greater focus on risk analysis and management systems, some degree of pre-commitment, and a recognition that incentives for prudential behaviour have an important role in the overall approach to regulation. The new approach would create incentives for banks to improve their risk management methods and to develop their own estimates of economic capital. Equally, there would be powerful incentives for supervisors to develop and enhance their monitoring skills (Stephen and Fischer 2000).

4.7   Assessment

This chapter has introduced the concepts of *regulatory regime* and *regulatory strategy*. Seven components of the regime have been identified: each are important but none alone is sufficient for achieving the objectives of regulation. They are complementary and not alternatives. Regulatory strategy is ultimately about optimising the outcome of the overall regime rather than any one of the components. Regulators need to consider that, if regulation is badly constructed or taken too far, there may be negative impacts on other components to the extent that the overall effect is diluted. However, there may also be positive relationships between the components, and regulation can have a beneficial effect on incentive structures within financial firms.

Effective regulation and supervision of banks and financial institutions has the potential to make a significant contribution to the stability and robustness of a financial system. However, there are limits to what regulation and supervision can achieve in practice. Although regulation is an important part of the regulatory regime, it is only a part and the other components are equally important. In the final analysis, there is no viable alternative to placing the main responsibility for risk management and general compliance on the shoulders of the management of financial institutions. Management must not be able to hide behind the cloak of regulation or pretend that, if regulation and supervisory arrangements are in place, this absolves them from their own responsibility. Nothing should ever be seen as taking away the responsibility of supervision of financial firms by shareholders, managers and the markets.

The objective is to optimise the outcome of a regulatory strategy in terms of mixing the components of the regime, bearing in mind that negative trade-offs may be encountered. The emphasis is on the *combination* of mechanisms rather than alternative approaches to achieving the objectives. The skill of the regulator in devising a regulatory strategy lies in how the various components in the regime are combined, and how the various instruments available to the regulator (rules, principles, guidelines, mandatory disclosure requirements, authorisation, supervision, intervention, sanctions, redress, etc.) are to be used.

Note

1 The author is grateful for invaluable comments on an earlier draft of this chapter from Glenn Hoggarth, Patricia Jackson, Chang Shu and Peter Sinclair and also to Marsha Courchane, Gillian Garcia, Klaas Knot, Davis Marston, Larry Wall and Jean-Pierre Patat. The usual disclaimer applies.

5 Bank capital requirements and the control of bank failure

Richard A. Brealey[1]

5.1 Introduction

Financial markets serve several purposes. They allocate capital to uses with the highest value, they provide mechanisms to ensure that this capital is used efficiently, and in fulfilling these functions they impart valuable signals for companies and governments.[2] Second, they enable payments to be made cheaply and rapidly across large distances. Third, they allow individuals to change the time pattern and riskiness of their consumption. For example, mortgage banks make it possible for someone to buy a house in anticipation of future income, while insurance companies assume particular risks and thereby reduce the probability of sudden reductions in an individual's wealth.

A number of studies have concluded that an efficient and developed financial system promotes economic growth. For example, industries that require large amounts of external funding have grown most rapidly in those countries that have developed capital markets.[3] Similarly, in the USA those states that liberalised their banking sector enjoyed an increase in growth and an improvement in the quality of bank lending. The efficiency of the financial system depends *inter alia* on a legal and regulatory system which protects creditor rights and on a transparent corporate sector. Those countries that have adopted legal, regulatory and accounting measures to enhance their financial markets have also experienced an acceleration in growth.[4]

Within the financial sector, banks play a central role, both in terms of providing liquidity services to savers and of allocating capital. However, their ability to fulfil these functions has been hampered by widespread bank failures. Furthermore, these failures have tended to come not as single spies but in battalions. For example, between 1929 and 1933 there were nearly 10,000 bank failures in the United States. From then until the end of the 1970s, failures averaged only about twelve a year, but with the S&L crisis the number of bank and thrift failures increased dramatically to a total of 2,400 in the ten years ending in 1990.

Between 1970 and 1997 there were eighty-six banking crises affecting sixty-nine countries, in which aggregate bank loan losses exceeded 10 per

Table 5.1 Costs to government of selected banking crises

Country	Period	Estimated cost/GDP (%)	Country	Period	Estimated cost/GDP (%)
Finland	1991–4	8.4	Indonesia	1987–8	80.0p
Japan	1990s	20.0p	Israel	1977–83	30.0
Spain	1977–85	16.8	Korea	1987–8	60.0p
Sweden	1991	6.4	Malaysia	1987–8	45.0p
USA	1980s	2.5	Thailand	1987–8	45.0p
Chile	1981–3	41.2	Uruguay	1981–4	24.2
Argentina	1980–2	55.3	Venezuela	1994–5	18.0

Source: Kaufman (1999)
p = provisional

cent of assets. In each case these losses were roughly sufficient to wipe out the entire capital of the banking system.[5] Table 5.1, which is extracted from Kaufman (1999), summarises the costs of bailing out the banks in a sample of these recent crises.

Although the banking system provides a higher proportion of corporate financing in developing economies, and the cost of bank failure is therefore relatively higher in these countries, banking crises have by no means been confined to developing markets. The cost to the taxpayer of bailing out the S&Ls in the United States was over $150 billion, while the continuing crisis in the Japanese banking system is likely to cost more than ¥80 trillion. Moreover, despite the efforts of bank regulators, the incidence of bank failures has increased. For example, over two-thirds of the eighty-six banking crises referred to above occurred in the second half of the 28-year period.

In this chapter, I discuss the role of capital requirements in reducing bank failure. Section 5.2 considers the causes and costs of banking crises. Section 5.3 discusses the function of capital requirements, while Section 5.4 focuses on the relationship between risk and the required amount of capital. It is impossible to judge the appropriate level of bank capital, without some judgement as to its cost, and therefore Section 5.5 considers the cost imposed by capital requirements. Section 5.6 considers the issue of the appropriate measure of the value of bank assets. Section 5.7 concludes and discusses the implications for bank regulation and the control of bank failure. The issues that I discuss have considerable generality but the setting for the discussion of bank capital requirements is primarily the UK and US banking markets.

5.2   Causes and consequences of banking crises

5.2.1   *The causes of banking crises*

Individual bank failures may result from unauthorised dealing and fraud. However, widespread failure is commonly attributed either to exogenous, self-fulfilling panics that involve a net withdrawal of deposits from the banking system[6] or to losses on the banks' loan books stemming from economic recession. A number of studies have emphasised the relationship between economic activity and banking crises. For example, a study by Benston (1986) of US banking during the period 1875–1919 estimated that the correlation between industrial production in the USA and annual changes in the number of bank failures was −.42. During this period there were only two instances of a sharp increase in bank failures when industrial production did not decline. The direction of causation appears to be from changes in industrial production to declines in asset values and cash flows and so to loan defaults.[7] Crises are typically preceded over a period of about nine months by sharp falls in industrial production, stock prices and foreign exchange reserves.[8]

Widespread distress may arise simply because banks are exposed to correlated shocks. However, it could also result from a domino effect in which the failure of one bank causes further failures. A number of papers have sought to analyse these financial linkages. For example, Allen and Gale (1998) show that the interbank market acts as an insurance market in which banks with a liquidity shortage borrow from those with a surplus. However, if there is an excess global demand for liquidity, such a system of insurance can no longer work. For instance, suppose that every bank holds deposits in one other bank. In this case each bank in turn will attempt to solve the liquidity shortage by liquidating these deposits. In this way the impact of the shortage travels down the chain, so that a relatively small shock to one bank may have a large and widespread impact.

Interbank exposures may also arise through the payments system. This was the main route by which the failure of Herstatt Bank spread to other banks. Real time gross settlement eliminates this source of contagion, but only at the expense of concentrating the losses from failure on the bank's other creditors.[9]

It is an empirical issue how far such financial linkages between banks are likely to cause the failure of one bank to bring about widespread default. Kaufman (1994), in an extensive review of the empirical literature on bank contagion in the United States, concluded that bank runs appear to be largely bank specific and rational, so that contagion 'has occurred only for banks in the same market or product area as the initially affected bank'. Kaufman added that there was 'no evidence to support the widely held belief that, even in the absence of deposit insurance, bank contagion is a holocaust that can bring down solvent banks, the financial system, and even the entire macroeconomy in domino fashion'.

5.2.2 The consequences of banking crises

Banks are not the only providers of capital, and therefore are not alone in suffering periodic losses. In developed economies, a far larger part of any reduction in corporate values is borne by holders of the firms' equity and bonds. For example, the losses borne by US equity holders on 17 October 1987 far outweighed the total losses incurred by the S&Ls in the 1980s. However, as far as I am aware, no-one has seriously suggested that there should be a government bail-out of individuals who suffer losses through their investments in stocks or mutual funds. Yet large amounts of government aid are provided to rescue banks in financial distress and banks are subject to considerable regulatory oversight to limit the likelihood that such government assistance will be called upon. Thus, falls in asset values are regarded as having wider and more serious consequences if they occur in the banking system rather than elsewhere in the economy. It is these additional costs, rather than the amount of the loan losses, that both constitute the costs to society of a banking crisis and justify regulation.

The role of bank regulation is to correct a market failure, which may either arise because the insolvency of a bank involves social costs that are ignored by a value-maximising bank management or because agents are subject to a co-ordination problem.[10] There are three commonly suggested ways that this market failure could come about. The first arises from banks' central role in operating the payment system. The second stems from the way that a banking crisis may restrict credit and accentuate a fall in economic activity. The third potential for market failure comes from the fragility of bank deposits and the costs of monitoring bank solvency.

On the first issue – the operation of the payment system – there appears little to be said. If a serious loss of confidence in the banking system were to lead to a large net loss of deposits and a flight to cash, the consequent disruption to the payment system would severely damage trade. Such dangers, however, are most likely to be associated with war or acute domestic unrest rather than with simply a weak regulatory system.

The second way that a banking crisis may affect economic activity is if it results in credit restrictions.[11] A negative shock reduces bank profits and therefore its equity capital. If this leads it to reduce lending, the economic shock may be accentuated. Of course, the bank could raise additional equity to maintain its lending. However, in financial distress the bank encounters the classic debt-overhang problem,[12] whereby investors are reluctant to contribute more equity even to finance profitable loans if the effect is simply to increase the value of depositors' claims.

If banks are capital-constrained, they may also be induced to hold safer and more liquid assets in periods of recession. This reduces the capital available to smaller firms, that have only limited access to the capital markets. This flight to quality may explain why small and bank-dependent firms appear to be quicker in a recession to cut back short-term borrowing and investment in inventories.[13]

Many of a bank's assets, such as its holdings of marketable securities, survive the bank's failure largely unscathed.[14] The exception is the information that a bank acquires about its customers through its long-standing relationships.[15] While the immediate effects of the loss of this information fall on the contracting parties, it may have a wider cost if it affects the availability or cost of capital for bank customers.

There have been a number of attempts to measure the effect of banking crises on economic activity and, while there are considerable problems in identifying the counterfactual, the apparent impact is large. For example, the IMF has estimated that the aggregate output loss following a major banking crisis has averaged about 11 per cent of GDP.[16]

The third, and somewhat different, motive for regulation arises from implicit or explicit deposit insurance. The standard argument for deposit insurance is that it serves to prevent self-fulfilling bank runs,[17] but governments may also wish to guarantee bank deposits because small depositors are at a disadvantage in monitoring banks, or simply suffer from a free-riding problem.[18] In addition, politicians are likely to be very aware of the social and political costs if depositors were to bear the full brunt of a bank failure.

In the absence of deposit insurance, depositors would demand that the bank takes actions to limit its risk and the bank would, in turn, have an incentive to reduce the probability of a run by providing information to depositors that demonstrates its soundness. In this way the fragility of deposits would act as an important discipline on both depositors and management. But, since deposit insurance lessens that discipline, the government needs to protect the taxpayer against the risk that banks will exploit the existence of insurance by substituting risky assets.

To conclude this section, I should note that the arguments on bank runs and the need for regulation are not all one way. For example, Allen and Gale (1996) observe that, while there are costs to bank runs, there may also be benefits, so that 'an unregulated banking system which is vulnerable to crises can actually achieve the incentive-efficient allocation of risk and investment'. They argue that depositors who find that they do not need to raise cash for consumption will leave their funds in the bank as long as the returns on the bank's loan portfolio are perceived to be high. However, when depositors foresee low returns, they will attempt to withdraw funds and so bring about a panic. This results in efficient risk-sharing between the depositors who have an information motive to withdraw early and those depositors that encounter an unanticipated need for liquidity. If the regulator were to prevent banks from holding portfolios that are vulnerable to runs, then banks would need to hold excess amounts of low-yielding safe assets and to reduce the interest paid to depositors.

5.3 Capital requirements

5.3.1 The role of bank capital

There are a variety of vehicles that could be used to protect a bank against failure. For example, a bank might be required to hedge its loan book against specified risks. But identifying those risks and monitoring the quality of the hedge demands special knowledge on the part of the regulator. By contrast, equity provides a general protection against failure from any source.[19] It also has the advantage that it is patient capital that cannot easily be redeemed by the holders in the event of a banking crisis. Not surprisingly, therefore, bank regulation has focused heavily on capital requirements.

Capital requirements also have an important potential disadvantage, for a binding capital constraint may cause the bank to reduce its lending and so lead to the credit crunch that regulation was designed to avoid.[20] Indeed, it has been suggested that the scramble by US banks to meet the standards of the 1988 Basel Accord led to the US credit crunch of the early 1990s.[21] Some more reassuring evidence is provided by Ediz, Michael and Perraudin (1998), who found that, as UK banks approached the capital constraint, they boosted their capital ratios principally by increasing Tier 1 capital, though they also shifted their assets to those with lower risk weightings.

5.3.2 Are capital constraints binding?

Capital requirements would serve little purpose if banks wished to hold more than the required level of capital. It does appear that, in the absence of any government safety net or deposit insurance, banks have an incentive to demonstrate to depositors that they have a sufficient equity buffer. Thus, in 1840 before government regulation, US banks voluntarily held equity in excess of 50 per cent of assets. As depositors increasingly acquired protection against bank failure, this ratio declined to about 10 per cent,[22] which is significantly less than the amount of equity maintained by finance companies, which do not enjoy implicit or explicit government guarantees.

Capital requirements seem to have contributed to stemming this decline in bank equity. For example, the average risk-weighted capital ratio of G-10 banks rose from 9.3 per cent before the 1988 Basel Accord to 11.2 per cent in 1996. Moreover, the greatest rises were experienced by those countries whose banks were close to, or below, the Basel minimum standards.[23]

In most G-10 countries banks now hold more capital than the regulatory minimum. This may stem from the need for banks to preserve their credit ratings, in which case the capital requirement is immaterial. However, it seems more likely that the surplus capital reflects a perceived need to maintain a buffer to avoid the need for costly adjustments.[24]

5.3.3   *Prompt corrective action*

Imposing capital requirements will not prevent widespread bank failure; that depends on what actions are taken when capital requirements are breached. Delays in taking action encourage gambling for resurrection and the risk of much larger losses.[25] As long as the bank is wound up, sold or reorganised *before* its capital is exhausted, neither uninsured depositors nor the government need suffer loss. Uninsured depositors have less incentive to run and the risk of contagion is reduced.

In the USA, the Federal Reserve had discretionary powers to limit the activities of banks that were capital-impaired, but prompt corrective action became mandatory only under FDICIA. FDICIA divides banks into five categories, varying from those that are 'well-capitalized' to 'critically undercapitalized'. No sanctions are involved for banks in the first two categories, but, when a bank falls into the third category ('undercapitalized' banks), it becomes subject to increasingly severe restrictions on its activities. The weakness of FDICIA lies in the way that banks have been categorised. For example, Jones and King estimate that, under FDICIA, more than half the failed banks during the years 1984–9 would have been classified two years before failure as 'well-capitalized' or 'adequately capitalized'.[26]

In the UK, the FSA also has a policy of early intervention, though it lacks the mandatory basis of FDICIA. Each bank in the UK is given a target ratio, which in many cases is set substantially above the Basel minimum. In addition the bank must at all times meet a lower trigger ratio. As the level of capital falls below the target ratio, the FSA is likely to take regulatory action to ensure that the trigger ratio is not breached.

5.4   Bank risk and capital requirements

5.4.1   *Why risky banks require more capital*

If the values of bank assets evolved smoothly and could be observed continuously and without error, then a bank would need only a minimal amount of equity capital. The bank could be closed down as soon as its liabilities threatened to exceed the value of its assets. But, of course, none of these conditions holds in practice. Some risks, such as a change in a country's fixed exchange rate, are jump risks that do not evolve smoothly. Extra capital is required to protect against such risks. Second, asset values are observed at discrete intervals. The greater the time between calculating the value of the bank's assets and the more variable the value of those assets per unit of time, the more capital is needed to guard against changes in value during that interval.[27] This becomes particularly important if banks are led to engage in asset substitution as their capital diminishes.[28] Finally, capital provides a safeguard against errors in valuing the bank's assets. Here also risk is likely to be relevant, for the higher an asset's risk, the more likely that it will be misvalued. Thus there is a tradeoff between maintaining a high level of equity capital, and increasing the frequency and accuracy of asset valuations.

5.4.2 The Basel Accord

While capital requirements have played an increasingly central role in bank regulation, the development of a well-defined standard is relatively recent. For example, for twenty years from the mid-1950s, US regulatory agencies employed an accounting formula for the desired amount of capital. Innovation in the 1960s and 1970s made this formula increasingly inappropriate and the agencies eventually reverted to a discretionary approach. In 1981, the USA adopted explicit accounting-based standards, and in 1985 regulators required banks to hold primary capital of 5.5 per cent of assets and total capital of 6 per cent.

The international standard for bank capital arose out of discussions between the G-10 bank regulators, which resulted in the 1988 Basel Accord.[29] This not only explicitly incorporated risk into the capital standard but specified a minimum level of bank capital for internationally active banks, that was adopted by each of the G-10 countries.

The Accord defined two tiers of capital. Tier 1 consists of equity, while Tier 2 capital includes subordinated and convertible debt, perpetual preference stock, and general provisions. As a minimum standard, banks are required to maintain Tier 1 capital equal to 4 per cent of risk-weighted assets and total capital of 8 per cent of these assets.

Much of the focus of the Basel Accord was on categorising asset risk and devising a system of risk weights. Because the dominant risk to banks is that of defaults in their loan books, the Accord addressed only the issue of credit risk. It stipulated that all assets should be allocated to one of four risk buckets depending on the type of instrument and the issuer. At one extreme, cash, local currency claims on the country's government, and claims on OECD governments receive zero weighting. At the other extreme, claims on the private sector, claims on non-OECD banks maturing in more than one year, and foreign-currency claims on non-OECD governments all involve a 100 per cent weighting. The Accord also took a stab at categorising the credit risk in off-balance sheet exposures.

The Accord was acknowledged to be only a first step and the Committee announced its intention to go on to look at interest rate risk and market risk. In the event it proved impossible to gain agreement on a capital treatment for interest rate risk, though the Committee published a measurement framework. Market risks – that is, price risk in the trading book and foreign exchange risk for the whole bank – were dealt with in the 1996 market risk amendment.

The Basel Accord made several important innovations. First, it established an international standard, which has since been implemented by some 100 countries. Second, it made formal allowance for risk in computing capital ratios. Third, it took explicit account of off-balance-sheet exposures. Fourth, the 1996 amendment recognised the difficulty that any regulatory system was likely to have in keeping up with best practice, and allowed banks to use an approved internal model for measuring market risk.

One problem with the Basel system of credit risk weightings is the relatively crude categorisation by issuer. For example, all commercial and personal loans (except mortgages) receive a risk weighting of 100 per cent, regardless of the riskiness of the borrower, while the only distinction between sovereign borrowers is that between OECD governments (which receive zero weighting) and all other governments (which receive a 100 per cent weighting). Criticism has also been directed against the fact that claims to non-OECD banks maturing within a year earn a 20 per cent weighting, while longer-dated claims earn a 100 per cent weighting.[30] Finally, the Accord was ill-suited to dealing with credit derivatives, which are subject to a wide variety of national treatments.

These deficiencies would be particularly damaging if banks are tempted to get the largest bang for each buck of capital by concentrating their portfolios in the more risky assets within each of the Basel risk buckets or by securitising the safer portions of their loan books. Concern with the possible extent of such capital arbitrage encouraged the Committee in June 1999 to propose a wide-reaching overhaul of the Accord.

5.4.3   *Proposed revisions to the Basel Accord*

In its 1999 proposals for a new framework, the Committee on Banking Supervision emphasises that capital requirements are only part of the process for ensuring bank soundness and therefore sets out 'three pillars' of the proposed new accord – minimum capital requirements, supervisory review and market discipline. With regard to the first pillar the Committee proposes a number of changes to align capital more closely to differences in credit risk.[31]

A major innovation of the proposed changes is that external ratings would be used for loans to sovereigns, banks and some corporates. Thus, instead of basing the risk weighting for sovereign debt on OECD membership, the Committee proposes to use external ratings to distinguish between sovereign loans, with risk weights varying between zero for the most highly rated sovereigns to 150 per cent for countries rated BB or below.

In the case of corporates, the use of public debt ratings raises a number of issues. For example, an obvious potential difficulty concerns the question of which rating agencies are approved for this purpose and what the system of approval is. In the United States a much higher proportion of firms currently have debt ratings. If an unrated issue were to be treated as very low-quality debt, then non-US banks would face higher capital requirements. The Committee's proposed compromise, therefore, envisages that the highest quality loans (for example, those to corporates with at least an AA rating) would receive a 20 per cent risk weighting, while those rated below B would have a 150 per cent weighting. All other loans would continue to have a 100 per cent weighting. While the final outcome may involve an additional category of loans, there are likely to be some substantial discontinuities in the weightings. Moreover, since less capital is needed for lending to unrated corporates than to those with low ratings, there will be little incentive for firms with low-quality debt to apply for a rating.

As an alternative to using external ratings, the Committee has proposed that banks with reliable internal credit rating systems should be allowed to use them for calculating capital requirements. This more likely proposal mirrors the existing framework for market risk, which gives banks the option of using an approved internal market risk model.

One consequence of the use of either external or internal ratings is that the amount of capital needed to support a particular loan book may vary over time. A fairly dramatic example is that of Korea. Since Korea is a member of the OECD, its government borrowing received a constant zero risk weighting under the original Accord. Under the proposed changes, the risk weightings would vary with changes in Korea's debt rating. As Korean debt was downrated in the second half of 1997, the amount of capital required to support loans to Korea by BIS-area banks would have increased by $6.7 billion.[32] Not only is the capital requirement likely to be more variable but, as loans are downrated, more capital is likely to be required in a recession.

Whilst most of the Committee's focus continues to be on credit risk, it also proposes to introduce a capital charge for abnormal levels of interest rate risk in the banking book and for operational and other risks. This latter charge might be based initially on a measure such as revenues or assets.[33]

5.4.4 The problem with devising risk weightings

There are undoubtedly further improvements that can be made to the Basel risk weightings by improving the estimates of default probabilities on different types of bank loans. For example, one might wish to take account of differences in loan maturity or in security.

There are other important deficiencies in the Basel risk weightings that are more difficult to deal with. Bank failures have commonly been accompanied by a high degree of concentration in the loan book. For example, the Scandinavian, Japanese and Thai banking crises were all associated with heavy exposure to real estate companies. The large losses of US money centre banks in the late 1980s resulted from their exposures to Latin America. But the Basel measures of bank credit risk are concerned only with the risk of individual assets and ignore differences in the degree to which the loan book is diversified, though supervisors may take account of these differences informally.[34]

The Basel Committee undertook a detailed examination in 1998 of portfolio models of credit risk but concluded that it was premature to allow them to be used for calculating capital standards.[35] This reluctance of regulators to tackle the issue of diversification is understandable. Not only would it involve a shift away from the current practice of measuring the risk of individual loans and assigning them to risk buckets, but it would involve some difficult measurement problems. There are two possible approaches to measuring the risk of a portfolio rather than of individual loans, neither of which is straightforward for anything other than the simplest of loan books. The first approach might be to specify a limited number of factors that affect loan returns. For example, one might assume that the variability of loan returns is a function of a market-wide factor that influences all loans and an industry factor that is uncorrelated with the market. To compute the risk of the loan portfolio, one would need to estimate the sensitivity of the bank's loans to these factors and the uncertainty of the returns for each factor. But, quite apart from the difficult data problems, the factor structure is almost certainly more complicated with the degree of diversification depending on the portfolio's geographical, as well as industry, dispersion. The alternative approach, which is to estimate the record of returns on the loan portfolio and to measure directly the variability of portfolio returns is about equally unattractive.

Capital adequacy requirements focus on the differences in risk between banks and therefore in the probability that they will suffer financial distress, but they ignore possible differences in the *cost* of failure. For example, a merger between two banks is likely to lead to a more diversified portfolio of assets and therefore a reduced probability of failure. However, because the combined institutions are now effectively guaranteeing each other's debt, the chance of a major default may be increased. Since the cost of failure is likely to increase with the size of the default, a capital adequacy rule that is simply based on equalising the probability of failure is almost certainly suboptimal. Moreover, the cost of distress in a single bank is likely to depend on whether it coincides with similar problems in other banks. We might be relatively relaxed about the failure of an individual bank when economic activity is buoyant, but much more concerned when it coincides with, and possibly accentuates, declining asset values in other banks.

Hellwig (1995) has pointed out a further problem with regulation that focuses on the probability of the failure of an individual bank. Suppose that a bank borrows and lends at slightly longer maturity to a second bank, which in turn relends at a longer maturity to a third. The maturity transformation undertaken by the system as a whole is greater than is apparent from the analysis of either bank individually. More generally, the variety of linkages between banks is such that the risk to the system cannot be deduced from the risks of individual components.

In sum, the revision of the Basel Accord will probably leave at least three important deficiencies in the treatment of risk. First, it is unlikely to incorporate differences in loan maturity (except in a limited case) or to provide more than an interim solution to the treatment of other sources of risk, such as operational risk. Second, there are no plans to tackle the issue of how well an individual bank's assets are diversified. And third, there is no consideration of differences in the cost of bank failures or their impact on the system as a whole. This is not a criticism of the Committee of Banking Supervision, but only emphasises that there are considerable difficulties in pushing much further with attempts to relate capital requirements to risk.

5.5   The cost of bank capital requirements

While the Basel Committee has devoted considerable effort to the topic of devising appropriate risk weights, far less attention has been paid to the appropriate level of capital. The four per cent and eight per cent minimum ratios of Tier 1 and combined capital lack any clear justification. It is easy to see why this is the case. To know whether a particular level of capital is adequate, the regulator needs to weigh the probability and costs of bank failure against the cost of the extra capital. Our lack of knowledge about the cost of too little bank capital is matched only by our ignorance of the cost of too much.

Banks finance their lending in several ways. For example, they accept deposits from the public; they borrow in the money markets; and they raise equity either through new issues or through retained earnings. Since chequing accounts pay little or no interest, they are sometimes believed to be 'cheap money'. However, chequing accounts do pay benefits in kind – for example, banks may offer free chequing and maintain apparently uneconomic branches for the benefit of depositors. In a competitive banking market, the value of these benefits would need to equal the rate of interest. Regardless of whether this is the case, chequing accounts are a relatively small and declining source of funds and are not the marginal source of capital for most banks.[36] A bank that wishes to expand its loan book has the choice between borrowing in the wholesale markets or increasing its equity base.

Bankers seem to regard it as self-evident that equity capital is a more expensive source of capital than borrowing,[37] but it is not clear *why* this should be so. It is true that the interest rate on borrowing is generally lower than the return that equity holders require, but any increase in borrowing by a corporation increases the risk to equity investors and therefore their required return. Thus debt has an *explicit* cost (the rate of interest) and an *implicit* cost (the increased risk to equity holders). Modigliani and Miller (MM) showed that in perfect capital markets debt is no cheaper than equity, once one recognises both the implicit and explicit costs of debt. The value of the firm and its cost of capital are therefore unaffected by its capital structure. MM's propositions imply that investors would have no difficulty in investing in a company that issues equity to invest in low risk debt, and indeed every day, large amounts of money are invested in the shares of unit trusts and mutual funds that do just that.

If MM's propositions do apply to banks, then equity capital would be no more expensive than debt, and a painless way to reduce the frequency of bank failures would be to increase the capital requirements. However, capital markets are not perfect, and, if they were, there would be no need for banks or other financial intermediaries.[38] Thus, MM's propositions need no longer hold in a world that is complicated by taxes, transactions costs, differences in information, and so on. The existence of such frictions does not in itself suggest that company values can be increased by leverage, and it is clear that many successful non-financial companies thrive using little or no debt. So what is special about banks that would significantly raise their costs if obliged to hold more equity?[39]

5.5.1   *Do textbook arguments for corporate leverage apply more strongly to banks?*

Some of the arguments for leveraging non-financial firms either *do not* apply to banks, or are not relevant to a regulator whose objective is to maximise social welfare. For example, one often-cited advantage to debt is that, unlike dividends, interest payments are deductible for corporate tax. Since the shareholders capture the benefit of this concession, they may prefer the firm to finance by debt rather than equity. But while any tax advantage to leverage is correctly taken into account by bank management, it is merely a transfer payment from the government to the shareholder and should not weigh with a regulator whose *raison d'être* is to take account of externalities.[40]

The MM propositions are concerned with the cost of alternative capital structures, but not with the costs of issuing different securities. Thus one motive for companies to prefer debt to a new issue of equity is that the latter may indicate that management has information that the stock is overpriced.[41] However, this does not apply to equity capital that comes from retained earnings. Nor would equity issues provide such a signal as long as they were made to satisfy a regulatory constraint.[42]

The choice of capital structure can also affect managers' incentives. For example, the cushion provided by equity capital may encourage complacency and waste, while the cash requirements for debt service force managers to forego wasteful capital expenditures and improve operating efficiency.[43] But these incentive effects are not weakened by a capital requirement, which cannot be breached without penalty.

Leverage increases the probability of financial distress and ultimately of bankruptcy. In the case of banks, unless there is a government safety net, the prospect of distress can lead to a run on the bank and the loss of its deposit base. Because bank deposits are fragile and a run on deposits is costly, an unregulated bank has an incentive to maintain a relatively large amount of capital. Any explicit or implicit government guarantee of the bank or its depositors diminishes this incentive and creates a moral hazard problem where the bank maximises the value of the guarantee by asset substitution which increases the probability that the guarantee will be called upon. But, while banks may wish to take advantage of any government guarantee, this consideration should not influence the level of capital that banks should be required to hold. In particular, the required level of capital should not be set below the level that banks would maintain in the absence of any government guarantee. The Basel capital requirement may be quite close to this level.

5.5.2   Are banks special?

It looks unlikely that a counter-argument to an increase in regulatory capital will be found in a simple extension of the literature on the capital structure for non-financial firms. If there are social costs to an increase in capital requirements, it seems that these must arise from the same imperfections that give rise to banks in the first place. For example, Diamond and Rajan (2000) consider the case where a banker has information about the best time to terminate a borrower's business, but the fragility of bank deposits means that the banker cannot expropriate the value of this information without inducing a bank run. Because equity holders are unable to run, they cannot provide this discipline on the manager. Thus, in a world of certainty, banks would maximise the amount of credit that they could grant by financing entirely with deposits.

Where there is uncertainty, a reliance on bank deposits also has a *dis*advantage. In this case, the value of the bank's assets may unexpectedly fall and so prompt a run, even if the banker does not seek to expropriate value for himself. Thus, under uncertainty, banks are faced with a trade-off, where equity capital protects depositors against exogenous risks, but at the same time enables the banker to behave opportunistically. In this case Diamond and Rajan conclude that regulations, which force the bank to hold additional amounts of capital and reduce the fragility of deposits, will reduce the value of the bank's assets and increase its cost of capital.

The Diamond–Rajan analysis depends on two important assumptions. The first is that, through his relationship with the borrower, the banker enjoys an advantage over other possible lenders of when to withdraw a loan facility and liquidate the firm. As this information advantage becomes less marked, the disciplinary effect of a possible deposit run becomes less valuable. Second, this disciplinary effect is negated if deposit insurance removes any incentive for depositors to run. In this case capital requirements, conditional on the existence of deposit insurance, would not affect the cost of capital.

Information asymmetries also motivate Gorton and Winton's (1996) analysis of the cost of capital. They view a bank as providing two unique functions. First, its relationships with borrowers provide it with information about their creditworthiness, which is lost if the bank fails. Second, demand deposits provide a unique source of liquidity to agents who do not know when they will require access to their cash. Because the value of bank equity capital is more informationally sensitive than demand deposits, the two investments are not perfect substitutes. This results in a trade-off in which the cost of failure creates an incentive for banks to issue equity, while the liquidity advantages provided by demand deposits make it costly to increase bank capital at the expense of deposits.

The Gorton–Winton argument may work well for a bank that relies primarily on checking deposits, but, as we noted above, many banks rely heavily on time deposits that do not provide liquidity. Moreover, a bank time deposit offers few unique characteristics and must compete with a number of other money market products.[44]

Thus the puzzle surrounding the bank cost of capital remains unresolved. Textbook arguments for levering non-financial companies may explain why bank managers view equity as costly, but should not weigh with a regulator who is concerned with the broad social welfare. While the informational asymmetries that characterise banking may increase the cost of equity, there is no evidence as to the importance of these effects. For the bank regulator the MM irrelevance propositions are probably no worse a guide to capital structure decisions than for the treasurer of a non-financial company.

5.6   Asset valuation

While the cost of capital may be relatively unaffected by changes in bank capital structure, the relationship between capital ratios and bank failure appears to be relatively weak.[45] As we noted above, despite the increased emphasis in recent years on capital requirements, banking systems seem to have become increasingly prone to crisis. More telling is the fact that crises have hit banks whose capital ratios were well in excess of the Basel levels. For example, the average risk-weighted capital ratio of Swedish banks before the 1990 banking crisis was about 10 per cent, well above the Basel standard.

This continuing fragility in the banking system may partly reflect the fact that many of the risks that banks face are 'jump risks'. For example, some hazards such as fraud may literally become apparent overnight and give no opportunity for remedial action. But the potential for capital requirements to reduce bank failures also depends on the accuracy with which the loan book is valued.

The relevant measure of economic capital is the present (or market) value of assets, less the value that the liabilities would have in the absence of the option to default (in other words, less the amount of the liabilities discounted at the risk-free interest rate). However, in measuring the amount of bank capital, regulators generally look at the book value of the bank's assets and liabilities. Book value is based on the historic cost of assets and, since assets are subject to both interest rate and credit risk, the amount that the bank originally paid for the assets may bear little relationship to their market value.

Book value of assets is measured net of specific provisions. These provisions usually apply only to impaired debt and reflect the expected losses on this debt. They therefore exclude any unrealised losses incurred on debt that is not yet impaired. Banks may also use provisions to manage their capital. For example, before 1989, loan loss reserves in the United States were part of the bank's primary capital and, since additions to these reserves were tax deductible, every dollar of provisions added one dollar times the tax rate to capital. After 1989 the capital ratio calculation effectively excluded reserves from capital, and US banks became less ready to add to the reserves.[46]

Book value is not the correct measure of the assets' economic value. It is also to some degree within the control of the bank, since the bank can enhance book value by realising capital gains and postponing capital losses. One way to postpone capital losses is by forbearance, in other words, rolling over loans to customers that are in danger of default. This is not possible when loans are sold on the open market, for in this case it is clear whether investors think that the new borrowing is enhancing or impeding the company's ability to repay debt.[47]

If the rate of provisioning approximated the change in market values, we would expect that the yearly figures would be independent. In practice this is far from the case. For example, in the case of the big four UK banks during the period 1981–99 the correlation between the rate of bad debt charges in successive years was 0.67, while for the period 1970–88 in the USA the correlation was 0.75.[48]

The obvious solution is to move to fair-value accounting. This has already been adopted in Denmark, and in the United States SFAS 107 requires entities to disclose, where practicable, the fair value of all financial instruments, including the value of bank loan portfolios. Fair-value accounting received a further boost in 1997, when the International Accounting Standards Committee (IASC) set up a working group to develop proposals for an international standard for recording financial items on the balance sheet at fair value.[49] The draft standard is expected to be published in the second half of 2000.

These moves towards fair-value accounting have encountered opposition from banks and, in some cases, regulators. The most common reason given is that many bank assets are opaque and it is impossible to observe market values. This argument is unconvincing. Bankers are making daily decisions on the interest rate to charge on loans, many of which are to existing customers of the bank. It seems difficult to believe that banks can value these loans when they make them, but not subsequently. While there are clearly extra costs for the bank in valuing a loan portfolio and its valuations are less easily verifiable by an auditor or regulator, worthwhile progress on setting capital requirements is unlikely as long as assets are recorded at their book value.

Bank reluctance to move to fair-value accounting also stems from concern that, if market values were to be used in calculating the earnings that are reported to shareholders, earnings could be more volatile. This concern with reported earnings has merit. Although it is not clear whether they would in fact be more volatile, a measure of profits which incorporates changes in the market values of the firm's assets is of little use when valuing the firm.[50] Accounting earnings are designed to provide shareholders with a measure of sustainable earnings and should not include value changes that are random in character and therefore not sustainable.[51]

5.7 Conclusions

Bank regulation and the imposition of capital standards have not prevented banking crises. As Franklin Edwards has commented,

> Ineffectual and out-of-date bank regulation currently poses the greatest threat to financial stability. Contrary to what many would have us believe, the threat to financial stability does not come from the rapid expansion of mutual funds and derivatives markets but from the fragility of banks and banking systems ... Bank fragility is a pervasive and persistent characteristic of economic systems, rather than an exception to otherwise well-functioning financial systems, and financial history suggests that there is a fatal flaw in how banking is traditionally conducted.[52]

What can be done to reduce bank failures? Regulation is certainly not the whole answer. For example, particularly in the case of developing economies, many of the problems derive from inappropriate capital structures in the non-financial sector, which concentrate the risk in the banking system rather than spreading it through the capital markets. The Asian crisis also illustrated the dangers that result when loans by overseas banks are channelled through the domestic bank system and when those domestic banks take on the risks of a maturity mismatch and a currency mismatch. The system of bank governance and control also has an important influence on the quality of bank loans. In particular, there are few countries in which the state has not sought to interfere with bank lending decisions. This suggests that public policy should be directed at the roots of the problem and should not simply ensure that banks can weather the storms.

It seems likely that capital requirements will continue to play a central role in bank regulation. While the current renegotiation of the Basel Accord should improve the system of risk weightings, significant further improvements will need to tackle the difficult issue of correlations. I am doubtful how much scope there is for much progress here without imposing large costs on the banks. More frequent monitoring may be a cheaper and more effective approach than more accurate monitoring.

The difficulty in improving risk estimates will, I believe, force attention back onto three issues. The first is the general level of capital that banks are required to hold. Although there is a common belief that increasing the required level of equity capital would impose large costs on banks, this view sits uneasily with the capital irrelevance propositions of Modigliani and Miller. Of course, the MM propositions are no better than first approximations in a world of imperfect capital markets. However, it is not clear that differences between the costs of equity and debt capital are any larger for a bank than for a non-financial company or that one country's banks would be at a competitive disadvantage if compelled to hold more capital.[53]

While an increase in the level of capital requirements may be the simplest and cheapest way to reduce the incidence of bank failure, its efficacy depends on the accuracy with which bank assets are valued. In particular, it is too easy for banks to disguise problem loans by a practice of forbearance. There is no consistent system of provisions for delinquent loans and the rate of provisioning appears to be a poor proxy for changes in the value of the loan portfolio. The solution is to move towards an explicit system of market value accounting for bank assets. This should be used for regulatory purposes but should not form the basis of reported earnings.

If banks were wound up or sold while their capital still had positive value, all the losses would be borne by the equity holders and there would be no costs to either the depositors or government. Thus capital requirements need to be accompanied by a system of prompt corrective action that restricts the ability of the bank to dissipate capital. Such early regulatory intervention reduces the incentive for banks to increase risks as capital ratios decline, and eliminates the chance of contagion occurring through losses on interbank lending.

Particularly in developed economies, the commercial banks face problems both in their liabilities and assets. On the one hand, individuals are holding a smaller proportion of their wealth in the form of bank deposits. For example, in the United States mutual fund assets are now comparable in importance to bank deposits. At the same time banks have been losing their advantage in lending. This advantage has traditionally stemmed from two features of a bank. First, would-be borrowers can reduce search costs by channelling their business through a bank which has a large pool of potential lenders and depositors and which has access to an interbank market in which it can settle up any net imbalance. Second, to the extent that the bank sees a large portion of the borrower's financial transactions over a prolonged period, it has an information advantage over other possible lenders. However, both advantages are disappearing. At least for large companies, investors have access to credit ratings and to security prices that efficiently impound the information available to a diverse set of investors.[54] At the same time the technology of issuing and distributing securities has made it economic for large companies to raise funds directly from investors. As a result there has been a pervasive tendency for large companies to finance themselves by issues of long-term bonds and equity rather than by bank borrowing. For example, bank share of corporate debt in the United States has declined from 20 per cent in 1979 to about 14 per cent today. Moreover, since the highest-quality borrowers have the easiest access to the capital markets, banks are being forced to make lower quality loans and to turn increasingly to fee-earning activities.

The development of money market funds has potential implications for the long-run development of banks, for as long as the holders of these funds can write cheques against their investment, the shares serve as bank deposits. The funds are invested in a portfolio of safe assets which are held by an independent custodian. Therefore regulation is largely limited to ensuring that the assets are indeed held on behalf of the beneficial owners. There is no need to insure the shares and no question of capital ratios.

The money market fund has created by a back-door the narrow-based bank which was originally proposed by Irving Fisher over 60 years ago. If bank deposits were invested only in safe money-market securities, there would be no need to tinker with the complex structure of deposit insurance and capital requirements. At the same time broader-based banks would continue to raise capital to re-lend to private individuals and industry without any more assurance that those securities are safe than you or I have when we invest in the securities of a non-bank.

There are clearly very strong pressures for banks to stay as strongly regulated entities, with deposit insurance. What may force more radical change is the introduction of new technology, that is, making it increasingly difficult to define a bank deposit. The eventual outcome could be a world in which banks simply provide a choice of more or less risky funds of marketable assets that may be drawn on to make payments.

Notes

1 I am grateful to Fiona Mann, Bill Allen, Glenn Hoggarth, Patricia Jackson and Chang Shu for comments and advice. The views expressed in the chapter are, however, my personal views and do not necessarily represent those of the Bank.

2 For a discussion of the way that banks provide valuable investment signals, see Boyd and Prescott (1986).

3 Jayaratne and Strahan (1996) and Rajan and Zingales (1998). Other studies are reviewed in Levine (1997) and King and Levine (1993).

4 See Levine (1999).

5 Caprio and Klingebiel in Bruno and Pleskovic (1996).

6 For an example of how such panics can arise in the absence of deposit insurance or a committed lender of last resort, see Diamond and Dybvig (1983).

7 See, for example, Gorton (1988). Gorton rejects the alternative view that, even before the US introduction of deposit insurance, banking crises were the result of 'sunspots' or self-fulfilling panics.

8 See Kaminsky and Reinhart (1999).

9 However, real time gross settlement may help to bring problems to light more quickly.

10 For a survey of possible sources of systemic risk in banking, see Dow (2000).

11 See, for example, Bernanke (1983) and Bernanke and Gertler (1989).

12 See Myers (1977).

13 See, for example, Oliner and Rudebusch (1993), Gertler and Gilchrist (1994) and Bernanke, Gertler and Gilchrist (1996).

14 See James (1991).

15 For example, when Continental Illinois Bank appeared likely to fail, the shares of client firms experienced a negative abnormal return of -4.2 per cent. When it became apparent that Continental would be rescued, the stocks of these firms experienced positive abnormal returns of $+2.0$ per cent. See Slovin, Sushka and Polonchek (1993). For evidence that a close relationship with a bank provides small firms with easier access to credit, see Petersen and Rajan (1994).

16 International Monetary Fund (1998). See also Hoggarth, Reis and Saporta (2000).

17 See, for example, Diamond and Dybvig (1983).

18 See, for example, Dewatripont and Tirole (1994).

19 See Merton (1995).

20 See Blum and Hellwig (1995). However, as long as a bank has significant equity, it is less likely to face the debt-overhang problem and more prepared to raise new capital to support lending. The empirical evidence on whether capital-constrained banks adjust their capital or their lending is reviewed in Basel Committee on Banking Supervision (1999a).

21 See Bernanke and Lown (1992), Haubrich and Wachtel (1993), Thakor (1996) and Hancock and Wilcox (1998). For contrary evidence, see Berger and Udell (1994).

22 Berger, Herring and Szego (1995). The authors argue that the creation of the FDIC in 1933 led to a sharp fall in the level of bank capital.

23 See Jackson *et al.* (1999).

24 For example, Berger, Herring and Szego (1995) suggest that the increase in the capital of US banks following the passage in 1991 of the FDIC Improvement Act (FDICIA) reflected an increased value to a buffer stock. Also Ediz, Michael and Perraudin (1998) provide empirical support for the view that banks place value on a buffer and do not let capital ratios decline to the regulatory minimum.

25 For example, Barth, Brumbaugh and Sauerhaft (1986) estimate that delays by FSLIC in closing insolvent S&Ls cost FSLIC about $1.5 million per failed institution.

26 Jones and King (1995).

27 Variability could also arise because a bank changes its assets between valuation dates.

28 On the issue of whether changes in capital requirements encourage or discourage asset substitution, see, for example, Kim and Santomero (1988) and Genotte and Pyle (1991).

29 Basel Committee on Banking Supervision (1988).
30 Some critics have argued that these very low risk weights attached to short-term interbank lending (together with Korea's accession to the OECD) encouraged the large inflow of short-term bank capital into South East Asia.
31 Basel Committee on Banking Supervision (June 1999).
32 Richardson and Stephenson (2000).
33 Operational risk was discussed in Basel Committee on Banking Supervision (1998).
34 For example, in the UK the lower diversification of smaller banks is reflected in higher required capital ratios.
35 Basel Committee on Banking Supervision (April 1999).
36 For example, in the United States checkable deposits amount to 13 per cent of the liabilities of commercial banks.
37 For example, Schaefer (1990) comments, 'Though theory would suggest perhaps a mild preference for debt, there is little evidence that non-financial corporations see capital structure as of fundamental importance. Financial institutions are unusual in the high degree of industry consensus which seems to exist that "capital is expensive".'
38 See, for example, Bhattacharya and Thakor (1993) for a review of the literature on market imperfections and the development of financial intermediation.
39 Miller (1995) argues that the MM propositions do apply to banks, so that the cost of capital for banks is not increased by an increase in the equity proportion.
40 However, if bond mutual funds (unlike banks) can pass through interest income free of tax, banks might be at a competitive disadvantage if they were obliged to issue more equity.
41 See Myers and Majluf (1984).
42 In the case of US banks Cornett and Tehranian (1994) provide evidence that equity issues result in a much smaller drop in price when they are required to meet regulatory standards and are therefore involuntary.
43 These incentive effects of leverage are emphasised by Jensen (1989).
44 Even checking deposits must compete with money market funds and credit cards as a source of liquidity.
45 Lane, Looney and Wansley (1986), Thomson (1991), Avery and Berger (1991), Cole and Gunther (1995).
46 See, for example, Kim and Kross (1998) and Ahmed, Takeda and Thomas (1999).
47 Giorgio Szego (1997) has suggested that there are lessons here to be learned from the securities primary markets, where the underwriter issues securities on behalf of the client. No collusion is possible between the underwriter and potential buyers, and investors independently reassess the value of the securities. In a similar way, he argues, banks could be encouraged to resell loans to unrelated credit institutions or to securitise them. In this way, he argues, one would achieve complete separation between credit-granting and credit monitoring.
48 Provisions are correlated (at least in the UK) with the *level* of defaults, which we would expect to be serially correlated.
49 The proposal envisages recording both assets and liabilities at their fair value. In this case the accountant would need to estimate how asset values were distributed between different claimholders. The arguments for some form of fair-value accounting were set out in International Accounting Standards Committee (1997).
50 The irrelevance of economic earnings for firm valuation is discussed in Treynor (1972).

51 For example, the income statement shows separately 'extraordinary items', which are unlikely to be repeated. Fisher Black discusses why accounting standards are concerned with sustainable earnings in Black (1980).
52 Edwards (1996: 148–9).
53 See, however, my earlier comments on the danger that sudden changes in capital requirements may induce a shortage of credit.
54 The information advantage that banks possessed in lending to the personal sector is also diminishing. The bank that operates a customer's checking account may have no more information about a customer's creditworthiness than his credit card company or credit agencies.

6 Crisis management, lender of last resort and the changing nature of the banking industry

Glenn Hoggarth and Farouk Soussa[1]

6.1 Introduction

This chapter examines the involvement of central banks in crisis management, particularly their role in lender of last resort. The arguments for such intervention are reviewed as well as the costs that such support may entail.

The structure of the financial sector has been changing over the last decade. Consolidation has resulted in the creation of a greater number of big banks. Frontiers between banks and non-banks are in some respects becoming increasingly blurred, and financial institutions and markets are also becoming more global.

6.2 Justification for central bank involvement in financial crises

Why should central banks intervene to support failed financial institutions, particularly banks, but not non-financial ones? Traditionally banks have been thought to possess two distinguishing features: vulnerability to losses of confidence, and large externalities associated with their failure.

A distinguishing feature of traditional banking activity is the transformation of liquid short-term deposits (liabilities) into illiquid long-term loans (assets). Since only a small part of their assets are held in liquid form, banks rely on depositors not withdrawing more than a fraction of their funds at any given time. The withdrawal of a large number of depositors at the same time would result in the forced liquidation of loans at distressed 'fire sale' prices and therefore to insolvency even of an otherwise fundamentally sound bank.

Illiquidity of an individual bank may, in turn, have implications for the financial system as a whole, if the liquidity of other banks is threatened through contagion, direct exposures to the failing bank via the interbank market or the payments system, or the withdrawal of lines of credit from the failing bank. Moreover, the failure of a very large bank or a series of smaller banks, or possibly of a non-bank financial institution, may be a public policy concern in its own right if it impairs the payments system, credit allocation or the wider functioning in the economy. These externalities imply that bank failures, whether generated by pure liquidity problems or by underlying solvency ones, may sometimes justify intervention by the public authorities, although not necessarily by the central bank. But such intervention is justified only if other solutions are not possible and that the benefits to financial stability from such support outweigh the costs involved, particularly the risk of increasing moral hazard.

6.3 Crisis prevention – the financial safety net

Of course, the authorities' involvement in financial stability does not consist solely of managing crises. Rather, crisis management tools are part of a broader safety net, including, in particular, deposit insurance, regulation and supervision.

The widespread existence of retail deposit insurance, at least in developed countries, has reduced – although not eliminated – the likelihood of retail runs. Banks, however, remain vulnerable to withdrawals by uninsured depositors such as other banks and large non-bank institutions. Whether this would occur to fundamentally solvent banks rather than ones that are unsound depends mainly on the efficiency of the interbank market and the transparency of financial institutions. We return to this point below.

Moreover, a drawback of comprehensive retail deposit insurance is that it dampens market discipline. Retail depositors have little incentive to monitor the risks that their banks take on. Banks may be encouraged to take more risks knowing that the benefits of success will go to shareholders and that the cost of excessive risk taking will be borne partly by the (government or private sector) financiers of the deposit insurance scheme. As argued by Benston and Kaufman (1998) amongst others, supervision and regulation are also therefore an important element of the financial safety net to control this moral hazard problem. This is supported empirically by Demirgüç-Kunt and Detragiache (2000) who find, in a sample of sixty-one emerging and developed countries between 1980–97, that in the absence of an effective system of prudential regulation and supervision, banking crises *increase* rather than *decrease* with the generosity of deposit insurance schemes.

The moral hazard problem aside, supervision and regulation are also important tools in discouraging banks from taking risks, which may threaten the stability of the financial system as a whole. This is necessary since banks do not take into account externalities (systemic risk) but only private benefits and costs when assessing their risk–reward strategy. Of course, at the limit, banks could be prevented from taking any risks at all, but this would take away the *raison d'être* of banks as financial intermediaries (George 1997).

Taken together, then, retail deposit insurance, regulation and supervision reduce the risks of systemic crisis but they do not remove it altogether. So the public authorities also need crisis management tools to deal with bank failures. Key among these from a central bank's viewpoint is the willingness to provide, or organise, emergency liquidity support to illiquid but solvent banks, particularly those whose failure would threaten the financial system more widely.

6.4   Lender of penultimate resort – private sector solutions

In the face of a bank failure, the public authorities will usually first attempt to arrange a private sector solution in order to avoid risking taxpayers' money.

In principle, organising private sector liquidity provision may be either the responsibility of the central bank or another official agency (Fischer 1999). However, Giannini (1999) points out that often in the past central banks have fulfilled this role – known as honest brokering. This may be because the central bank is the bankers' bank and at the heart of the monetary and payments system and can provide agency (e.g. escrow) facilities or act as a principal intermediary. As shown in Chart 6.1, a number of central banks in our survey perform this honest brokering role.

However, a liquidity run on a bank could be due either to misinformed doubts about the solvency of the bank concerned or well-founded concerns about its solvency. In the first situation, the central bank could be involved in co-ordinating private liquidity support and/or providing assurances to other banks that the weakened bank is actually solvent. If, on the other hand, there is an underlying solvency problem, then supervisors – whether based in or outside the central bank – often take the lead in organising a take-over or helping to wind-up the failed firm in an orderly manner.

The central bank may have a role in bringing potential lenders together where individual banks, even when known to be solvent, are unable to obtain funds due to co-ordination problems among creditors. Where co-ordination failures are the source of the liquidity problem, there should be no need for the central bank to 'coerce' other banks to lend, as it should be in their interest to do so. If, however, pressure is put on banks to lend, or to lend on terms which do not fully reflect the risks involved, then this would indicate that the problem is not purely one of co-ordination. In such a case, private sector support would, in effect, subsidise the failing bank and reduce market discipline (Goodfriend and Lacker 1999). In any case, co-ordination problems may be difficult to overcome because of the short-term competitive advantage banks with liquidity surpluses experience during a crisis. In these circumstances, 'moral suasion' and regulatory powers may be required to instil a cooperative attitude into what are otherwise keen competitors.

Where the role of public authorities is to convince other banks that a weakened bank is solvent, this may require a greater degree of involvement by the central bank or supervisor. Other banks may be willing to accept the word of a credible central bank and/or supervisor, but it is more likely that the latter will have to demonstrate a bank's viability through, for example, disclosing information about the weakened bank. But this assumes that the authorities have an informational advantage over the private sector concerning the weakened bank, for example, via the supervisor, involvement in the payment system or as part of an application for emergency liquidity assistance. Evidence from Berger *et al.* (1998) suggests that shortly after supervisors have inspected a bank, supervisory assessment on its future performance is more accurate than the market. In contrast, where supervisory information is not up-to-date, market assessments of changes in a bank's performance are more accurate than those of the supervisor. As discussed below, as large banks' assets are increasingly becoming determined by market prices, the advantage from supervisory information may increasingly lie in knowledge of the skills and practices of the bank managers rather than in proprietary balance sheet information.

Past experience suggests, however, that more often than not liquidity problems at individual institutions are the result of well-founded concerns about solvency. When a financial institution is clearly insolvent, the authorities – concerned about the risk to the financial system as a whole – may try to organise private sector *capital* support, such as a take-over.

Historically there appears to have been a tension between the effectiveness of concerted support and the degree of competition in the financial system. Orchestrated liquidity support operations occurred often in the past, such as the Bank of England's co-ordination of the rescue of Baring Bros. in 1890 and the Clearinghouse System in the United States – a private institutional framework in place for dealing with liquidity problems – operating from the 1860s up to the 1910s. Such private sector solutions, however, became less feasible as the degree of competition in the market increased. The Clearinghouse System was brought down, at the beginning of the century, by the marked increased in competition in the key US financial centre, New York. Likewise, orchestrated operations became more difficult to organise in the United Kingdom during the 1980s. This was apparent when the difficulties encountered in the rescue of Johnson Matthey Bankers Ltd, a London bank which had been an active market-maker in the gold bullion sector, in an environment of heightened competition led the authorities to rethink their approach to LOLR support (Capie *et al.* 1994).[2]

The notion that liquidity support should be seen primarily as the responsibility of the institutions operating in the market has, however, remained in countries where competition in the financial system has until recently been somewhat limited, such as Germany, France and Italy. In Germany it was formalised with the creation, in the 1970s, of a semi-private institution (LikoBank) to deal with liquidity problems at smaller banks. The Bundesbank refers to the Likobank as the lender of penultimate resort.

Moreover, even in the competitive Anglo-Saxon financial systems, the handling of the crisis of Long Term Capital Management (LTCM) in 1998, may suggest that in some circumstances a financial institution can be 'too big to fail' even from the perspective of the rest of the private sector. As William McDonough (1998) stated at the time, the failure of LTCM would have had substantial repercussions on financial markets, on which LTCM's counterparties 'voiced their own concerns' so that, in the end, 'a private sector solution ... involving an investment of new equity by Long-Term Capital's creditors and counterparties was reached'.[3]

6.5   Lender of last resort (LOLR)

In some instances, it may not be possible to solve liquidity problems at *individual* banks through organising private sector support. Moreover, liquidity shortages may be experienced by the banking system as *a whole*, in which case a private sector solution – which redistributes the current available liquidity in the market from institutions with surpluses to those with deficits – could not help. When liquidity problems are not caused by underlying solvency problems, central banks will usually consider providing liquidity support. However, there is a distinction between normal day-to-day central bank liquidity support from that provided in an emergency.

As monopoly supplier of base money, central banks satisfy the normal needs of the banking system as a whole for additional liquidity through open market operations and/or standing facilities. Such regular liquidity is supplied on pre-specified good (eligible) collateral, sometimes to a limited number of counterparties. The liquidity needs of the system are therefore met to the extent that the central bank's money market counterparties hold sufficient good collateral, and that they onlend liquidity to banks that do not have regular direct access to the central bank. Thus, the broader (narrower) the institutional access and types of collateral accepted in normal operations, and the more efficient the interbank market, the more (less) likely an illiquid financial institution would be satisfied in normal operations.[4] The distinction between such regular lending and emergency assistance is that, with the former, the rules of access are clear *ex ante,* whereas the latter is typically available only at the discretion of the central bank and only in exceptional circumstances. Also, emergency support may entail a degree of credit risk for the central bank. This is because acceptable collateral may not be available to cover the resulting exposure with complete certainty, even if the recipient becomes subject, as part of the process, to more intensive regulatory scrutiny.

6.5.1 LOLR to the market

Although normal liquidity operations should satisfy the needs of the market, there are circumstances, albeit exceptional and rare, where the market may want liquidity temporarily beyond what is available from these operations. This might occur, for example, when there is a generalised marked increase in uncertainty and flight to liquidity. In such cases, in order to maintain financial stability, the central bank may increase total liquidity to the market as a whole, on a temporary basis, and extend possibly the range of eligible securities that are acceptable in monetary operations. A recent example of the latter occurred over the millennium period when an anticipated increase in the demand for liquidity by the banking system as a whole prompted the Bank of England, and a number of other central banks, to widen the range of acceptable securities in normal operations.

The distinction between emergency lending to the market as a whole and an easing in monetary policy is not clear cut. The instrument used – open market operations – is usually the same in both cases. It will increase the supply of reserve money and may reduce short-term interest rates. Therefore, countries, which do not have independent control of the money supply, will be constrained in providing LOLR to the banking system as a whole. Hence, the three countries in the survey described in Chapter 3 that do not provide LOLR to the banking system – Argentina, Estonia and Bulgaria – do not have either independent monetary policy but instead have currency board systems in operation. The critical distinction between LOLR to the market and an easing in monetary policy is the motivation for the operation. Emergency assistance to the market is an abnormal and purely temporary measure designed to relieve market pressure following some adverse exogenous shock, such as the millennium period in the example above, whereas changes in monetary policy are directed at maintaining longer-term price stability.

6.5.2 LOLR to individual institutions

Central bank liquidity support to individual institutions affects the composition of the central bank's balance sheet but, unlike lending to the market as a whole, need not increase its size. Such lending can be offset by lending less/draining more in normal market operations and so need not conflict with monetary policy – this is why in the Eurosystem, LOLR for individual institutions can be devolved to national central banks without necessarily affecting the Eurosystem's total supply of reserve money.

In a properly functioning interbank market, the inability of an individual bank to borrow funds through the market indicates that it is insolvent or failing. However, even in the most developed and deepest financial markets, the interbank market may not always operate smoothly, and under certain circumstances solvent institutions may be unable to borrow. The literature identifies three reasons why this may be. First, because the interbank market has access only to incomplete information, doubts may arise about the solvency of a bank, which is in fact sound.[5] Second, the interbank market may become more cautious in times of crisis (Flannery 1996). Third, banks may refuse to lend surplus liquidity if they cannot be confident that they will themselves be able to borrow in order to address their own possible future liquidity shortage (Freixas, Parigi and Rochet 1998a).

In the absence of finding a private sector solution, these market failures provide justification for central banks to lend.

6.5.3   *Solvency support*

When a bank is clearly insolvent, it could be liquidated and the creditors paid back with the proceeds (to the extent that these cover liabilities). However, concern about the stability of the financial system as a whole may prompt some form of direct public sector intervention. Systemic risk aside, it is possible that it may be less costly to restructure an insolvent bank than allow it to fail.[6] James (1991), among others, has obtained results showing that the liquidation value of a bank is lower than its market value as a going concern. Guttentag and Herring (1983) also make this point, stating that 'banks usually are worth more alive than dead even when their worth alive is negative'. Public intervention in clearly insolvent banks can be divided into three broad categories: publicly assisted acquisitions of failing banks by healthy private banks, public direct acquisition of failing banks, and outright bail out (Goodhart *et al.* 1998).

In practice, although the central bank would probably advise on the systemic consequences of failure, as shown in the result of the survey of 36 countries in Chapter 3, it would not usually provide solvency support itself. Rather the government would need to make a decision on whether or not to provide risk capital to prevent failure in order to maintain financial stability or on other criteria (e.g. for social reasons). That said, it may not be possible to draw a clear distinction between a true liquidity and a solvency problem, especially in the time often required to make a decision and allocate responsibilities. Goodhart and Huang (1999) argue, for example, that when the central bank is approached by a bank for liquidity support, it does not have time to verify whether or not the bank is solvent. If the central bank provides support to a bank that is revealed later to be insolvent, it will incur a direct financial loss as well as suffering a reputation cost. The central bank will therefore, in practice, need to weigh the probable cost of providing capital to a possibly insolvent bank against the cost of the instability that its failure could generate. In practice, many central banks would not be in a position to absorb the losses arising from lending to what is revealed to be an insolvent firm independently, and therefore they may require a government guarantee of the exposure (Goodhart and Schoenmaker 1993; Goodhart 1999).

Empirical evidence on the resolution of bank defaults suggests that failing banks are more often rescued rather than liquidated. Goodhart and Schoenmaker (1995), for example, gather evidence on the effective resolution policies in 24 countries. Out of a sample of 104 failing banks, they find that 73 resulted in rescue and 31 in liquidation. Santomero and Hoffman (1998) also find that public authorities in the United States have been reluctant to liquidate banks in the past. They find that access to the discount window in the United States between 1985 and 1991 was often granted to banks with poor CAMEL ratings[7] that later failed. (Access was granted, they argue, in order to keep institutions afloat – even those which were known to be insolvent – so as not to impose further costs on the deposit insurance fund which had suffered large losses.)

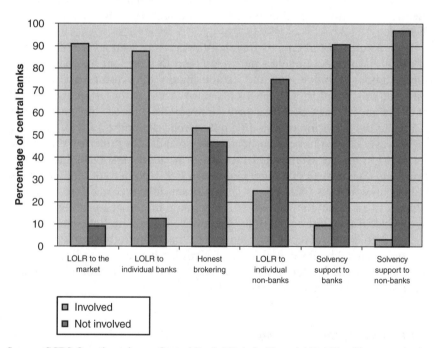

Source: CCBS Questionnaire on Central Banks' Role in Financial Stability. The countries in the sample are Argentina, Australia, Brazil, Bulgaria, Canada, Chile, Cyprus, Czech Republic, Denmark, Estonia, Hong Kong, Hungary, India, Indonesia, Ireland, Latvia, Malawi, Malaysia, Malta, Mexico, Netherlands, New Zealand, Norway, Peru, Poland, Russia, Singapore, Slovenia, South Africa, South Korea, Sri Lanka, Sweden, Thailand, Uganda, UK and Zimbabwe. For more details see Chapter 3.

Chart 6.1 Central banks' role in crisis management

6.6   Terms and conditions for LOLR

If exercised too leniently, banks may expect liquidity support from the central bank 'as a matter of course' (Bagehot 1873). Indeed, if liquidity support is extended on terms more favourable than are available in the market, it ceases to be lending of *last* resort altogether. It is for this reason that Bagehot's 'rules' proposed, among other things, that lending be made at a rate that is high relative to the pre-crisis rate. This, he believed, would ration access to liquidity and decrease the moral hazard problem. Also, a penalty rate was thought to be a fair price to pay for the protection offered to the failing bank through the provision of liquidity or to cover the central bank's risk exposure (Humphrey 1989).

Solvency support, on the other hand, may have two adverse effects on bank behaviour (Freixas and Rochet 1997). First, it gives the bank managers and shareholders incentives to take additional risks so as to maximise the subsidy implicit in rescues. Second, the possibility that the official sector will prevent an insolvent bank from failing may reduce the incentives for uninsured creditors to monitor the behaviour and performance of the institutions to which they have lent (Kaufman 1991; Rochet and Tirole 1996).

Both Thornton (1802) and Bagehot (1873) were well aware of this risk of moral hazard. As Bagehot put it, 'any aid to a present bad bank is the surest mode of preventing the establishment of a future good bank'. Bagehot's proposal to lend only on security reflects the attempt to eliminate the moral hazard capital provision entails. Indeed, his 'rules' refer strictly to the provision of liquidity, not solvency, support.

However, as we have seen, it may be socially desirable for the public sector to intervene even when faced with a clearly insolvent institution. Prati and Schinasi (1999) and Giannini (1999) point out that, in many industrial countries, authorities have often felt the need to advance support even when confronted with a genuine insolvency problem. Moreover, since it may not be possible to draw the distinction between a liquidity problem and a solvency problem in the time required to make a LOLR decision, central banks may find themselves inadvertently lending to insolvent institutions. Under modern financial conditions, therefore, it is not clear how readily Bagehot's rules still apply.

6.6.1   *Penalty rates and conditionality*

The idea of lending at a penalty rate is often challenged and, in practice, emergency lending to individual solvent institutions has sometimes been made without applying a premium over the current notional market rate (Goodhart and Schoenmaker 1995; Prati and Schinasi 1999). This divergence from Bagehot's rules has several justifications: lending at a high rate may

i   aggravate the bank's crisis (Crockett 1996; Garcia and Plautz 1988);
ii send a signal to the market that precipitates an untimely run, unless it is provided covertly; and
iii give the managers incentives to pursue a higher risk/reward strategy to get themselves out of trouble ('gamble for resurrection').

These risks may be more likely in modern financial systems where clearly solvent financial institutions should normally be able to obtain liquidity from the interbank market.

Whether or not they apply penal rates, however, central banks, in conjunction with supervisors (where separate), typically do impose conditionality in providing LOLR. For example, borrowers may be asked to provide financial data while they are borrowing and develop plans that would allow them to restore their access to market sources of funds. Also they may be subject to supervisory actions which limit their ability to engage in various activities.

6.6.2   *Transparency or constructive ambiguity?*

Bagehot recommended that central banks pre-announce their policies in advance of crisis to reduce uncertainty. In fact, central banks purposely do not usually pre-announce in order to reduce moral hazard. As Corrigan (1990) argued, by introducing an element of uncertainty into the provision of support, pressure can, in principle, be maintained on banks to act prudently, since the latter will not know individually whether they will be rescued or not. Such 'constructive ambiguity' is, by definition, difficult to pin down and formalise. An informal definition of the notion can be found in a recent G-10 Report which states that:

> any pre-commitment to a particular course of action in support of a financial institution should be avoided by the authorities, who should retain discretion as to whether, when and under what conditions support would be provided. In addition, when making such a decision, it is important to analyse rigorously whether there is a systemic threat and, if so, what options there may be for dealing with systemic contagion effects in ways that limit the adverse impact on market discipline.
>
> (BIS 1997)

As this passage makes clear, *ex ante* constructive ambiguity is a complex notion, encompassing, besides uncertainty as to whether intervention will take place at all, also uncertainty regarding both the *exact timing* of the intervention and the *terms* and *penalties* attached to any particular intervention.

Ambiguity regarding whether intervention is actually taking place, which implies that liquidity assistance may be provided covertly, might be desirable either to avoid 'imitation effects' within the banking system or where, due to the bank's size and operational ramifications, the handling of an individual bank's problem risks itself triggering systemic repercussions (Enoch, Stella and Khamis 1997).

When a panic has already set in, however, it is sometimes recognised that management of the crisis, including support operations, may usefully be made public. This is because transparency during a crisis may reduce uncertainty and thereby have a calming effect on financial markets. This was the rationale behind the announcement of extraordinary provision of liquidity over the millennium period, described above. Also, in the UK, the Bank of England announced its willingness to provide extra liquidity to borrowers with good collateral in the wake of the Barings failure (see Annex 2).

Ambiguity regarding the conditions attached to liquidity support, in turn, may be needed to keep managers and shareholders uncertain as to the cost they will have to bear should a firm's illiquidity result from imprudent behaviour (Crockett 1996).

The downside of constructive ambiguity is that it places a large degree of discretion in the hands of the agency responsible for crisis management. As in other fields of economic policy-making, discretion raises a time-consistency problem: while it is in the interest of the authorities to deny their willingness to provide a safety net, *ex post* they may later find it optimal to intervene. Lack of transparency enables them to avoid having to justify treating differently what the general public may perceive as identical situations. Enoch, Stella and Khamis (1997) argue that central bank discretion in handling individual cases could be balanced against firm rules for disclosure after the event.[8] Indeed, as the IMF's Code of Good Practices on Transparency in Monetary and Financial Policies itself testifies, an effort is currently being made in this direction (IMF 1999).[9]

In practice, the effectiveness of constructive ambiguity as a check on moral hazard can be expected to be greater to the extent that there exist procedures for 'punishing' the managers and shareholders of imprudently managed intermediaries. Furthermore, the effects of moral hazard have often been contained by rules directly constraining or indirectly encouraging banks and other financial intermediaries to act prudently, including in managing their capital and liquidity.

6.6.3   *Collateral*

As discussed earlier, the distinction between liquidity and solvency problems is seldom clear-cut. Given this uncertainty, central banks will, where possible, want to secure their lending with acceptable collateral, helping also to limit moral hazard. A central bank may accept a broad range of collateral provided it meets some basic threshold criteria for credit quality, protecting itself by taking a margin commensurate with the level of credit risk and the quality of collateral. In order to protect the central bank from incurring losses, acceptable collateral should be debt instruments issued or guaranteed by financially sound entities. It should also not be issued by the counterparty to the central bank or where the creditworthiness of the issuer is dependent on that of the counterparty, and should not fall due for repayment before the maturity date of the monetary operation they collateralise (see Laurens 1997). However, in some countries, for example those with less developed financial markets, there may be a limited amount of good marketable collateral available. Even in more developed financial markets, asset prices can fluctuate substantially and the market value of the collateral could decrease beyond the central bank's safeguards. In this event, central banks may extend the range of eligible collateral, although this may not always be possible when collateral of a sufficiently high quality is scarce.

There may therefore be circumstances in which a central bank lends to an institution which turns out later to be insolvent, and the collateral value has fallen below the amount the central bank has lent. A clear exit strategy in such an event is desirable. Moreover, the costs should be allocated in such a way as to fall in the first instance on shareholders of the firm concerned. If the costs are beyond the shareholders' liability, additional resources may need to be sought from a private sector recapitalisation.

6.7   Crisis management, consolidation and the changing nature of the banking industry

There has been a marked increase in consolidation in most developed banking systems in the past decade, resulting in larger and more complex firms than existed before. This has raised a number of issues for the current practice and institutional structures for crisis prevention and management. To the extent that the failure of large firms cause, or were thought to cause, greater systemic disruptions than small ones, this would raise the issue of whether some or more institutions were 'too big to fail'. Consolidation is also occurring between domestic banks and non-banks and between cross-border financial groups. Although this may reduce the risk of individual firm failure to the extent that there are net benefits from sectoral or cross-country diversification, any failure may propagate increasingly across financial industries and countries.

6.7.1   Institutional size

The consolidation process may increase the number of banks that are *thought* by the private sector to be 'too big to fail'. This may be particularly a concern in countries where concentration in banking is already very high and where consolidation is not accompanied by the development of capital markets that would offer borrowers an alternative source of funding. If so, there would be a potential for large banks to take more risks in the expectation of support. This is because, in the absence of a policy of punishing bank shareholders and managers in the event of a rescue, shareholders may encourage managers to take greater risk, as they would benefit from the greater reward if the strategy is successful, but not expect to bear the full costs if it fails. In principle, uninsured creditors could temper excessive risk-taking. In practice, such market discipline will be missing if these creditors expect to be bailed out if a large bank fails. However, excessive risk taking could be constrained through regulating the activity of risky banks by more intensive inspection, and ensuring that such banks have sufficient capital and adequate risk management systems to absorb unexpected losses. Also it should be made clear, as mentioned earlier, that any financial support would be conditional on disciplinary measures on those responsible for the failure, particularly managers and shareholders, reducing their incentive to take excessive risk provided by such support. Nonetheless, if creditors not covered by explicit deposit insurance expect to be bailed out in the case of failure of a big bank, then such banks will receive a funding subsidy, and thus a competitive advantage, *vis-à-vis* small banks (see Soussa 2000).

Consolidation may have reduced the probability of firm failure to the extent that risks are reduced through diversification. Everything else being equal, however, the failure of a large firm would pose a larger systemic threat than the failure of a smaller one. Given that the process of consolidation may have increased the systemic costs of individual firm failure, additional policies may be required to ensure that firms and markets are better able to withstand shocks, such as improved risk management supervision and more firm disclosure to increase market discipline, and reduce the likely contagion once firms fail through continuing to improve the international financial infrastructure, such as through developing liquid and secure interbank markets and payment systems.

6.7.2   *Bank conglomerates and non-banks*

Traditionally, public sector safety nets have been centred on banks rather than other financial institutions because of the risk that fundamentally sound banks can become insolvent following an ill-informed liquidity run and that widespread banking failures could have systemic consequences. However, disintermediation has made this distinction less clear cut. Banks can increasingly be weakened by the failure of non-banks either through direct exposures or indirectly through the disruption caused to financial markets. Moreover, consolidation between traditional banks and non-banks has blurred this distinction, to some extent, particularly when non-banking activities within conglomerates cannot be ring-fenced and thus can cause losses to the banking business. An important question here is whether the non-banking activities can be incorporated within conglomerates without affecting the banking activities. In principle, an institutional structure consisting of subsidiaries with separate capital bases might potentially limit contagion. In practice, there may be large transactions between subsidiaries and the risk of reputational contagion.

Since banks have also expanded their investment banking activity, the speed with which insolvencies occur may have increased (for example, Barings). On the other hand, since bank conglomerates hold a larger share of liquid assets, the likelihood of true liquidity problems, other than when there is a generalised increase in market uncertainty, may have declined. The complexity of banks' balance sheets has also increased. This may make it more difficult for public sector authorities to judge whether problems are primarily ones of illiquidity or insolvency.

Central banks still tend to regard the distinction between banks and non-banks as sufficiently clear to concentrate any potential central bank liquidity support on banks. This is reflected in the responses to the survey where three-quarters of central banks confine liquidity support to banks.[10] However, as in the case of banks, where non-banks are thought to pose a systemic threat, the central bank and/or supervisor may attempt to orchestrate private sector support. The US Fed's response to the LTCM crisis is a case in point.

6.7.3 Globalisation

The growing integration of international financial markets and expansion in cross-border merger activity raises a number of challenges for current institutional structures, or at least how they are implemented in practice. The failure of a large bank or disruption to an important financial market would increase the likelihood of pan-regional or even global instability either through a common shock hitting financial firms or markets in several countries at the same time or through a shock affecting a firm or market in an individual country, more likely spreading to firms or markets in other countries. This emphasises the need for cooperation and information sharing amongst national supervisors – including both bank and non-bank – and central banks to prevent such crises occurring. It also requires arrangements in place between national central banks, as well as national supervisors and ministries of finance, when solvency is seriously in doubt, questionable, to manage such crises.

In the case of cross-border banks, there is already a number of bilateral Memoranda of Understanding (MOUs) in place between national banking supervisors whereby information is exchanged and meetings are held regularly. However, a recent EC Report ('Brouwer' Report 2000) suggested a number of recommendations to improve the practical functioning of the institutional framework for financial stability in Europe. These suggestions are equally applicable at the global level:

• more bilateral information sharing and cooperation within and across countries between bank supervisors and those of non-banks, and across country between supervisors and central banks, such as in analysing financial trends;

- a more formal structure to deal with the possibility of regional or global financial crises. This could include, for example, clarifying and extending the concept of the co-ordinating supervisor(s) for the large financial groups and clarifying the division of responsibilities between home and host supervisors in the case of winding-up a bank operating across borders;
- convergence in supervisory practices, which can significantly enhance the efficiency of national supervisory authorities involved in monitoring cross-border financial institutions.

There is also a question of how best to prevent and manage financial problems at branches of foreign-owned banks. Supervision is mainly the responsibility of the home supervisor and they, together with the home central bank (if separate), would be expected to take the lead in the case of problems at branches located abroad. In order to perform this task the home supervisor may need greater access to information on affiliates in the host country. On the other hand, the potential systemic threat of bank failure, if any, may be most acute in the host country. This could become a particular problem in small countries if branches of foreign banks account for a large share of the domestic banking system. Here the home supervisor and central bank may be willing to accept liquidation without necessarily fully taking into account the systemic consequences in the host country. The co-ordination problem between home and host central bank may be particularly acute when the host central bank is located in a small emerging country.

The increasing need for timely information to assess both solvency and potential systemic risk, and the increase in complexity of financial firm structures both across sectors and countries, suggests the need to modify approaches to supervision and to increase market discipline. This is recognised in the proposed changes to the Basel capital standards for international banks (see Chapter 5). Supervision is likely to be increasingly focused on firms' risk management systems rather than formulaic capital standards. Also, an increase in the transparency of firms' performance and risk profile may enhance market discipline, particularly by other financial firms and credit rating agencies. This will be more effective if creditors do not believe that a broad implicit safety net is in place.

6.8   Conclusion

Central banks' involvement in crisis management has traditionally focused on banks and is justified by the vulnerability of banks to liquidity crises, and the potential impact that bank failures can have on the financial system and the economy as a whole. However, it is recognised that the distinction between liquidity and insolvency is not clear-cut in practice, and that in any case, externalities also apply to the failure of clearly insolvent banks. For these reasons, central banks have been involved in supporting failing banks, either indirectly by facilitating private sector solutions, or directly by acting as lender of last resort, either to individual institutions or the market as a whole. This involvement has been part of a broader safety net which also includes deposit insurance and supervision.

However, various costs arise from official support to failing banks, especially solvency support. There are direct financial costs in the explicit provision of risk capital to insolvent institutions, and in losses incurred through providing liquidity to banks that later prove insolvent. More importantly, by insuring banks against the costs of liquidity or solvency problems, the provision of support may result in banks (and their creditors) behaving less prudently (the moral hazard problem). The scope of such support, and the terms and conditions on which it is extended, should therefore be as limited and stringent as the maintenance of financial stability will allow.

In recent years there has been a marked increase of consolidation in financial firms in many countries. In the process, banks have grown, expanding into non-traditional banking activity and into other countries. The increasing complexity of international banks is resulting in a switch in focus of supervision towards firms' risk management systems and the desire for more firm disclosure to enhance market discipline. It has also emphasised the need to reduce the systemic effects of individual firm failure by improving the firewalls between banks, such as through the adoption of real time gross settlement payments systems and a secured interbank market. It has also stressed the importance of co-ordination and cooperation between central banks and other institutions involved in crisis prevention and management, in particular bank and non-bank supervisors and ministries of finance, both domestically and increasingly across country.

Annex 1: Case study – UK small bank crisis 1991–2

Background   In the early 1990s a group of about 40 small UK banks came under liquidity pressure. On the liabilities side of their balance sheet, they were heavily reliant on wholesale deposits from foreign banks, building societies, local authorities and big industrial companies, as well as other banks.

Foreign banks, particularly those from the United States and Japan, became increasingly nervous over the depth and duration of the UK recession and reduced their sterling claims on UK banks from over $110 billion to $76 billion between end-1990 and end-1992. This initiated the liquidity pressure on the small banks. Local authorities – whose deposits made up over 10 per cent of total deposits at 12 smaller banks – were under pressure to be more discerning where they place their funds and soon followed the foreign banks in withdrawing. This trend was strongly reinforced when BCCI was closed down. The bigger UK banks were also under cyclical pressure to contract their balance sheets and improve the quality of their assets. Meanwhile the assets of these small UK banks were becoming increasingly vulnerable to the recession, particularly as it affected the property values supporting their loans.

Action   The first warning of problems was provided by the supervisors, then part of the Bank of England, who had information on the pressures growing at these institutions. The supervisors produced weekly reports on a 'watch list' of banks which were most vulnerable, and whether they were systemically important.

The Bank used its relationship with the financial markets, particularly the clearing banks, to acquire quantitative and qualitative information to help assess the seriousness of the small bank problem and its likely systemic impact – for example, the likelihood that a bank run would spread to other small but sound banks and building societies. There were on-going discussions from mid-1991 onwards with key personnel from all the large banks.

The small banks identified as problem cases were told to strengthen their liquidity or reduce their total assets given the reduction in lines to them. Their total assets declined by over 25 per cent between end-1990 and end-1992. Three small banks – Chancery, Edington and Authority – were allowed to fail in early 1991. Since the Bank did not consider such failure as a systemic threat to the system, no emergency support was provided at this stage.

The wholesale market continued to shrink during 1991, accelerated by the closure of BCCI. As the bigger picture became more threatening, one particular institution (National Mortgage Bank) ran into a liquidity crisis – its auditors could not certify that it had enough assurance of liquidity to allow it to continue to operate. It was then that the Bank decided to provide support to that and to a small number of other banks, partly because the risks of contagion to other, larger banks were judged to have increased materially. Although we cannot run a controlled counterfactual experiment, the Bank was clear at the time that, had it not acted, the liquidity crisis would have spread.

The Bank made provisions in respect of loans given to these small banks. These reached a maximum of £115 million in 1993. In the case of National Mortgage Bank (NMB), the institution that necessitated the major part of the provision, the Bank guaranteed initially (in 1991) a consortium of 10 banks against loss if they continued to offer a credit line of £200 million. This was increased to £250 million in March 1992 and to £400 million in September 1992.

The Bank acquired NMB from its parent company at end-September 1994. This changed the form although not the substance of the Bank's support. This acquisition, which was for the nominal sum of £1, was to facilitate better control over the process of realising the assets. In recent years the NMB group has made good progress in realising its assets and reducing its operations and costs. As a consequence, the Bank has been able to release some of its provisions. By end-February 1999, provisions amounted to £74 million, down more than £40 million from their peak five years earlier.

Issues raised   A common adverse shock to a number of *small* banks can have broader implications for financial stability, particularly in recessions when balance sheets are already likely to be fragile.

Where crises build-up gradually, information flows to the lender of last resort from the supervisor and the private sector are important in evaluating illiquidity/insolvency and systemic risk.

Annex 2: Case study – Barings, February 1995

Background   Barings was a family-owned merchant bank, one of the oldest and most reputable in London.

On Friday, 24 February, it was made known to the Bank of England by Barings' senior management that its securities subsidiary in Singapore had made large losses on Japanese Government Bonds (JGBs) and Japanese equity positions and held large uncovered positions (options) in the Japanese stock market (Nikkei index). The trades had been made by a single trader on the floor of SIMEX who had fraudulently concealed them in reports to Barings' offices in Singapore, Tokyo and London. Barings' senior management requested the Bank of England's support.

The actual amount of losses was not known immediately for two reasons: (i) the fraudulent trader had tampered with the accounting books and so there was a general concern that the P & L statements were not reliable. A group of auditors had to recreate the transactions by investigating the trading journal entries on a trade-by-trade basis, a process that was resource intensive; (ii) even if the exact number and type of transactions had been known, their value was uncertain as they could not be realised until trading started again in Japan on the Monday morning (Sunday evening UK time). At that time, the Nikkei was expected to fall by between 5–10 per cent since it was known that Barings' (very large) position was to be liquidated.

Action   A decision on whether or not support would be extended had to be reached by the time trading started in Japan on the Monday morning local time (Sunday evening UK time) since insolvent institutions are barred from trading. The authorities therefore had the weekend to determine their response. As the auditors' reports came in during the course of the weekend, it was becoming increasingly clear that the size of the losses probably rendered Barings insolvent.

The question therefore arose whether or not the systemic implications of Barings' failure justified the commitment of public funds. The overall judgement was that, since bilateral exposures were relatively limited and the source of Barings' failure was a specific case of fraud, the threat of contagion in the UK financial system or more widely was not large enough to justify the commitment of public funds.

Against this background, the Bank invited private parties with a potential interest in seeing Barings' continue as a going concern to consider providing liquidity support and/or purchasing Barings (e.g. other UK merchant banks worried about reputation contagion, UK clearing banks concerned about the reputation of the City of London, international investors who held similar positions to Barings in the Japanese market). It was not, however, possible to place a ceiling on the already large losses because of the uncertainty of additional losses generated when trading began on the Monday. Therefore, private sector support was not in the end offered.

The Bank was also in liaison with the Japanese authorities as the failure of Barings was likely to have an impact on the Nikkei (and thus on Japanese financial stability). The Japanese authorities made the Bank aware of the rules in the Japanese stock market. In particular, they confirmed that the sale of Barings' position would have to be made on the market, re-affirming the fact that any potential buyers would have to accept the risk of a worsening of the position when the Japanese market re-opened on the Monday morning.

Without a private buyer or the possibility of allowing Barings to trade the next day, Barings announced on the evening of Sunday, 26 February (GMT), that it was seeking an administration order. In case of a market disturbance, the Bank made public its willingness to provide adequate liquidity to the 'UK banking system'.

Once Barings was in administration, it faced a variety of problems since it could not use its own nostro accounts because of the strong possibility that payments would be seized. The Bank facilitated transactions by interfacing with the market on Barings' behalf. In effect the Bank used its own correspondent bank network and counterparts while protecting its own position by taking collateral. It also acted as a sub-custodian for the funds under management.

Issues raised   The relative calm in the wake of Barings' collapse indicates that faced with an idiosyncratic shock – in this case fraud – even reputable banks can fail without serious systemic implications.

The usefulness of supervisory information may be limited when failure occurs suddenly, because of an event such as a fraud or a marked decline in asset prices.

In certain circumstances, a central bank's transparency over its willingness to provide liquidity to solvent institutions may prevent panic (in this case an announcement of the Bank's willingness to provide sufficient liquidity to the banking system as a whole).

There are potential difficulties associated with determining the extent of losses arising from derivative trading. The Barings case was relatively straightforward (the trader's positions were simple put options whose value depended on

> movement in the Nikkei), but when financial engineering is more complex, asset valuation becomes more difficult.
>
> The central bank has an important role in crisis resolution other than emergency liquidity assistance. For example, it may help to maintain orderly markets through facilitating the winding down of a failed bank's positions.
>
> Barings was an example where there was a possible systemic implication in more than one country (UK, Singapore and possibly Japan) but where the home central bank took the lead in handling the crisis.

Notes

1 Farouk Soussa is currently on secondment from The Bank of England to the Financial Services Authority. We would like to thank Bill Allen and Paul Tucker for helpful comments and Xavier Freixas and Curzio Giannini for collaboration on earlier work in this area. The views expressed in this chapter are the authors and not necessarily those of the Bank of England.

2 It should be noted, however, that the more recent failure of Barings in 1995 was because the magnitude of Barings' losses were uncertain since open positions in derivatives markets made the risk to potential creditors unquantifiable (see the overview in the annex and also evidence given before the Treasury Select Committee by Eddie George, Governor of the Bank of England (Treasury and Civil Service Committee 1995)).

3 Statement before the Committee on Banking and Financial Services in the United States Congress, October 1998.

4 However, a continuous recourse by an individual bank to a regular standing facility may be an early warning to the central bank and supervisors of a structural liquidity or solvency problem.

5 Under such circumstances, even a bank with collateral that would normally be accepted would not be able to borrow if there was residual legal uncertainty over the title of the collateral. Within Europe, efforts to remove this friction include the introduction of repurchase agreements and the European Union Settlement Finality Directive, which aims at reducing legal uncertainty and harmonising transaction laws across the European Union.

6 Note that this also provides further justification for extending liquidity support to illiquid, solvent but non-systemic banks.

7 CAMEL ratings are scores assigned by US supervisors that reflect their judgement of a bank's Capital, Asset quality, Management, Earnings and Liquidity.

8 This is exemplified by the Bank of England's handling of the small banks crisis in the early 1990s where, at the time, it was not made public that the Bank was providing assistance to a small number of small banks. After the direct systemic threats were averted, however, the Bank then disclosed its operations to the public and accounted for its actions. See, for example, *Bank of England Annual Report*, various issues and Appendix 1 for a summary of the small banks crisis).

9 'aggregate information on emergency financial support by financial institutions should be publicly disclosed through an appropriate statement when such disclosure will not be disruptive to financial stability' (IMF 1999, para 7.3.1).

10 Even where non-banks have access in principle, they are less likely in practice than banks to face either underlying liquidity problems or to pose a systemic threat.

7   International capital movements and the international dimension to financial crises

Peter Sinclair and Chang Shu[1]

7.1   Introduction

Financial crises often have a crucial international dimension. Should countries seek to limit or prevent international capital movements, or should they permit them without restriction? What benefits and risks do they bring?

This chapter aims to address these questions. It starts by examining the major effects of international capital movements, negative and positive (Section 7.2). The relative merits of different methods of restricting or controlling them are also discussed. We then turn to the analysis of financial crises in the open economy, and to the volatility of international capital movements (Section 7.3). While Sections 7.2 and 7.3 deal primarily with *theory*, Section 7.4 explores capital controls in *practice*. It surveys evidence about their effects, and presents a description of the capital control regime adopted in Chile. The main conclusions are gathered in Section 7.5.

7.2   Capital movements across the exchanges: curse or blessing?

In fact, international capital movements are both curse and blessing. From the standpoint of national welfare, the advantages must outweigh the drawbacks, at least under suitably simple assumptions. There are, however, undeniable disadvantages, which are peculiarly apparent to the central bank.

We begin with the disadvantages of capital inflows and outflows (7.2.1), and then turn to their benefits (7.2.2). Some provisos are presented (7.2.3), followed by a discussion of capital flows as intertemporal trade (7.2.4). Attention is then directed (7.2.5) to the relative merits of different methods of limiting international capital flows.

7.2.1   *Negative aspects of capital inflows and outflows*

International capital movements have certain negative aspects. These are especially evident to central bankers.

When capital flows in from abroad, countries attempting to hold an exchange rate peg have to accept a build-up in reserves, whether they like it or not. Then they face the problem of possibly very large rises in domestic monetary aggregates, which are usually far from easy to neutralize by sterilization. If financial markets are well developed, sterilisation tends to raise bond yields, all else equal, triggering further inflows, and it may entail budgetary costs. Worse, if sterilization is, as so often, incomplete, they have to face the upward pressure on the price level that monetary expansion should, all else equal, sooner or later, induce. The prices of domestic assets, including real estate, are bid up. So, too, are the prices of non-traded goods, particularly services; and labour markets tighten, with ensuing increases in the pace of money wage increases. Inflation targets are liable to over-run.

Directly or indirectly, the inflow of foreign capital adds to the country's productive capacity. But it also exerts upward pressure on wage rates, and some other key prices. When exchange rates are fixed, it is probable that capital inflows add more to aggregate demand than supply. Hence the potential, sooner or later, for higher domestic inflation. At the very least, capital inflows make it difficult to avoid an induced monetary expansion.

If the exchange rate is floating freely, capital inflows typically generate appreciation. This time pressure on the domestic-currency price level is negative, not positive. But undershooting an inflation target may be deemed just as disagreeable as exceeding it. This is not least because of the damage that may result to profits, production and employment in traded industries (compared with the fixed exchange rate case), and the knock-on effects this can bring, at least in extreme cases, to the balance sheets of commercial banks.

Finally, there is the worry that capital inflows may quickly change direction, and lead to outflows. The larger the stock of foreign capital in an economy, the greater the potential volume of subsequent capital outflows over the exchanges.

International capital outflows pose other difficulties. Pressure on the exchange rate is negative. Preventing depreciation, in practice, may mean losing foreign exchange reserves. Domestic interest rates may have to be increased to stem the outflow, but sterilization – even if feasible – is likely to entail bond purchases, which may push interest rates in the opposite direction. Incomplete sterilization leads to monetary contraction, and an inevitable deterioration in the quality and performance prospects of a large slice of commercial banks' domestic loans. The Hong Kong example in 1998 shows that exchange rates can be defended successfully against speculative attack. But defence is neither cheap nor easy. And the list of currencies whose parities had to be reduced, abandoned, or surrounded by broader bands in the face of speculative attack in the past decade, is not a short one. It includes Argentina, Brazil, Britain, Finland, France, Indonesia, Ireland, Italy, Norway, South Korea, Malaysia, Mexico, Russia, Spain, Sweden and Thailand.

Yielding to the pressure on the exchange rate implies depreciation. The home prices of imported goods and exportable goods are bid up. Although this threat to inflation is essentially only one-off, and depends on what caused the capital flow, exactly how it is distributed over time is hard to tell in advance. The magnitude and speed of exchange rate pass through to the domestic price level vary country by country and, within countries, over time as well. Pass through is more rapid when labour markets are tight, and apt to be bigger in smaller countries, with large ratios of trade to national income. Inflation targets are overshot, possibly by large margins. Exchange rate depreciation is particularly uncomfortable when the domestic private (or public) sector has large debts denominated in foreign currency, as is highly likely for developing countries. Then there is the risk, so well exemplified by Thailand in 1997, of an explosion of worries about the quality of bank loans and the solvency of the domestic banks themselves. This can only lead to positive feedback on the capital account of the balance of payments. Domestic and foreign actors scramble to transfer still more funds abroad, unless the exchange rate collapses so far that all market participants agree that it can hardly drop any further.

In sum, international capital outflows can be highly disruptive to both monetary and financial stability. The central bank has to opt between the macroeconomic downturn frequently induced by a successful defence of the exchange rate, on the one hand, and the perils of a burst of inflation, possibly exacerbated by solvency problems, when it acquiesces in an exchange rate slide on the other. Neither prospect entices.

Small wonder, then, that the case for taxing, restricting or discouraging international capital movements is often viewed sympathetically by the central banking community. The sheer scale of international capital movements in contemporary conditions is bewildering; and, following widespread liberalization, they appear to be growing much faster than central banks' foreign exchange reserves. Given the undoubted and increasingly serious threats they imply for financial and monetary stability, nostalgia for the quieter times of earlier decades is all too understandable.

7.2.2   The gains from international capital movements

It is well to remember, however, that international capital movements can be a blessing, too. For one thing, the current account of the balance of payments may be volatile, and accommodating private capital flows, often engineered by interest rate decisions enacted by the central bank, provide an invaluable method – often really the *only* method – of financing them.

For another, there are important real-economy effects, which should in principle be favourable on balance, that stem from international movements of capital.

What prompts capital to move from country A (a developed economy, for example) to country B (a developing one) it is that it is expected to offer a higher yield in the destination country than the source. If expectations are fulfilled – and on average, sooner or later, they really should be – it is efficient that this transfer should occur. A movement of capital from A to B will depress yields in B and raise them in A. The world's stock of capital cannot be correctly allocated if yields in different countries or sectors differ. Reallocation, so as to equalize yields, should increase the world's total output – and indeed succeed (ideally at least) in maximizing it, subject to the relevant constraints of technology, knowledge and other resources.

Country A, where the stock of capital goes down, will experience an undeniable fall in domestic output, relative to trend. In country B, where capital goes up, domestic output will increase, too. If capital does actually yield more in B than A, the gain in B's domestic output will exceed the drop in A's. But national income should go up in both countries. The capital which moves from A to B is presumably owned by residents of country A. This means that a stream of dividend, profit or interest income will be paid out by B to them. This stream forms part of A's national income (but not domestic product). It is also part of B's domestic product (but not its national income). B's national income rises too, but by much less than its domestic output.

In fact, national income in *each* of the two countries should rise by about one-quarter of the product of two numbers – the volume of the international capital transferred, and the original difference in yields between the two countries that occasioned it. This formula holds exactly if the relationship between the stock of capital and the yield upon it is linear, competition is perfect, taxes are negligible, expectations about yields are exactly fulfilled and the capital movement is taken to the limit where the gap in yields is eliminated. Brenton *et al.* (1997) may be consulted for more details on these points.

If national income ought to rise in both countries, it is likely that both countries can be said to gain higher welfare, too. The simplest (if controversial) definition of economic welfare in a country is simply the level of its national income. There may be snags, which complicate the picture somewhat. For example, equilibrium real wages drop in A, which loses capital. This may alarm a government that weights wages more heavily than profits in its conception of welfare. It also poses a risk of (at least temporary) unemployment there when wage rates are sticky.

In country B, there is redistribution from domestic profit to labour, of which its government might approve or disapprove. There are also tax effects, which may be complex, and are liable to increase B's gain at the expense of Λ's if B levies taxes on the profits A's residents make there. B also stands to gain from any technology transfer associated with the international capital movement (and A may even gain from this too, in certain circumstances, as Grossman and Helpman (1992) demonstrate). If the investment turns out to be less profitable than anticipated, B is insulated if it was financed by equity held by A's residents, but exposed if it is bond-financed. But, snags aside, the key point is that the international capital movement ought to be beneficial for both economies, taken in the round. The largest capital flows across the exchanges that the world has ever observed, when measured in proportion to estimated world income or trade, occurred in the decades before 1914 from Britain. The classic 'cliometric' study on this by McCloskey (1970) calculated that these must have been of considerable benefit to both Britain and the destination countries, on all but the most extreme and improbable assumptions.

7.2.3 Some provisos

The central tendency of international capital movements ought to be favourable, therefore, in both source and destination countries. The overall tendency to gain should materialize, at least, if the transferred funds are wisely invested, and expectations of return are broadly correct. These provisos are important. If it is the public sector that does the investment, financed by overseas loans, history is replete with examples of over-optimism, and mega-projects that proved to be socially and commercially unsuccessful. Many domestic private sector investments turn out unprofitable too. In either case, the value of the extra output is modest, very probably below the interest costs. The country's credit rating is liable to deteriorate, too. The effects of that might be pervasive and prolonged. Some good prospects *ex ante* turn out to be failures *ex post*. The reverse is also true. However, no-one, not even the central bank, has an infallible crystal ball.

Particular difficulties arise when information is incomplete and asymmetric. As we shall see in Section 7.3, these asymmetries may cause some uninformed firms to copy each others' investment decisions, under the impression that the latter know something the former do not. Essentially the imitator generates externality effects, for example on the profits of other firms, which may well be negative. In the banking sphere, new entrants, whether foreign or domestic, are liable to bring benefits to depositors and lenders in the form of keener prices. But the erosion of incumbents' profits may ultimately increase the risks of illiquidity and insolvency. Striking an ideal balance between competition and safety, as we saw in Chapter 1, would set the number of banks somewhat lower than a policy of free entry would imply. Finding this point of balance is challenging enough in a closed economy. In an open one, it is still more daunting.

If capital imports come in a rush, there may be serious difficulty in digesting them, and ensuring that they produce the good harvest hoped for. Banks' ability to monitor and maintain the quality of domestic loans is strained. This problem of adjustment costs, which may have an externality element, may be adduced as an argument for a regime of capital inflow taxes, perhaps with a preannounced tapering to discourage bunching. Difficulties in absorbing large capital inflows are particularly likely for small countries with relatively undeveloped financial systems, and also after a period where capital imports have been low, or hitherto controlled.

In this connection, it is worth recalling that most of the trillion US dollars of sovereign loans to the Third World in the 1970s and early 1980s was disbursed on large projects of doubtful merit. Further, on average, some 70 cents of each dollar lent ended up as private capital re-exports (Heffernan 1986). Tax-avoidance and diversification motives will have contributed to this. The end result of this unfortunate episode was a credit famine and a lost decade of slow growth for the borrowing countries, and a banking crisis engulfing several of the main lenders.

Nonetheless, the financing problems posed for central banks are normally transitory in character. By contrast, the real benefits to national income, in both source and destination countries, should be permanent, or at least far more long-lasting. Unwelcome surges or falls in inflation rates and exchange rates, or the costs of containing or preventing them, may be serious, but they should decay much faster than the stock of capital depreciates.

A strong distinction is usually drawn between direct and portfolio international capital movements. Foreign direct investment consists of (or at least includes) the creation of new assets in one country, funded in part or whole by residents of another. Foreign portfolio investment, by contrast, denotes the acquisition of title to (some share of) existing assets, generally located in or otherwise related to the destination country; title transfers to source country residents. In practice this distinction, like others such as those between long-term and short-term capital movements, or transactions in equity and bonds, is blurred at the edges and hard to draw with precision.

It is tempting to think of direct or long-term capital movements as the vehicle of net benefits of the kind outlined above, and portfolio or short-term movements (unless deliberately engineered by the authorities to accommodate other flows across the exchanges) as nothing but a grievous nuisance. But this temptation should be resisted. Portfolio inflows from A to B will raise the price of financial assets in B, lowering the cost of capital there, and inducing physical investment in B, by B's residents or others, as a result. So B's domestic product will increase eventually, with much (but not all) of this rise balanced by profit, dividend or interest income paid to A's residents, just as in the direct investment case. The timing of these developments is different, but the end result is essentially the same. Financing problems for the central bank are very much the same for both direct and portfolio inflows, too. Both of them generate inflows on the capital account of the balance of payments. Both threaten to push up the monetary aggregates and/or the exchange rate, and thereby alter the course of inflation.

This means that there is really no intrinsic workable distinction between 'beneficial' and 'unhelpful' international capital movements. All capital movements, whether direct or portfolio, long-term or short-term, are ultimately rather similar in their effects, and in the challenges they pose for central banks as they attempt to retain financial and monetary stability in the face of them.

Another way of thinking about international capital movements, whether direct or portfolio, is that they give poorer, faster-growing countries a quicker route to prosperity than the prospect of building up capital from domestic savings alone. The latter path leads eventually to higher national income, but may take many generations to accomplish. The former allows the country to raise its domestic product towards international levels much more swiftly. Effectively, it pre-empts the capital stock it would otherwise have accumulated itself over decades or centuries. The price of the quick route is the transfer of profit or interest income to overseas creditors or equity-holders. In normal circumstances it can be shown that this price is well worth paying.[2]

7.2.4 *International capital movements as intertemporal trade*

Yet a further aspect of international capital movements is that they permit residents to smooth out their consumption in the face of random shocks to their technology, endowments or resources (or to consumer preferences, at home or abroad, which create disturbances in the country's terms of trade). If opportunities to borrow or lend on international markets were withheld, home country consumption would display a jagged pattern over time, because the values of exports and imports would always have to go up and down together. Providing these opportunities is tantamount to a kind of consumption insurance. So long as the insurance is given on fair terms, it will be worth buying. If the terms were unfair, people would buy less insurance, and perhaps none, but they would not be worse off on average than if the insurance had been denied them completely.

In essence, what access to international capital markets permits is trade over time, and trade across contingencies. International trade in goods and services exerts profound effects, some damaging but generally beneficial on average, except in very special circumstances. This certainly applies for small countries, which cannot influence the terms on which they trade. For them, official obstacles to trade, like tariffs and quotas, can never be ideal: any net advantage they secure can always be had more cheaply by keeping free trade and removing the source of the problem – a distortion of some kind – directly at source.

It is only when the direct solution is unavailable that trade barriers are worth thinking about. Even then they can usually be shown to be less beneficial than other indirect solutions, such as taxes or subsidies or regulation. These remarks really also apply to large countries, too. For them, a sufficiently low tariff on imports or tax on exports is advantageous. What they gain from improved terms of trade can then exceed what they lose from reduced trade volume. But this is never efficient at the world level, and all countries, even large ones, can be shown to be still better off by trading freely and, if needs be, accepting some set of international transfers between them. To make matters worse, the costs of lobbying for trade barriers have to be brought into the picture. These can be sizeable, often gobbling up any net gain and more.

Exactly the same arguments apply to restrictions on international capital movements. Cases can be constructed where they do harm (although such cases are invariably 'non-standard' in some way). But in such cases they do harm because of some market imperfection or distortion, which stops them giving the undeniable net benefits that would have to accrue in simple, standard cases. Ideally one should try to get rid of the distortion directly. If that is impossible or too costly, there should be a second-best, roundabout route to trying to rectify the problem, which does not involve restricting capital movements. This indirect route, or really, a set of indirect routes, because there may be a vast number of them, is 'second best'. Restricting international capital movements is typically inferior to the second best. So it is 'third best', if that.

What international capital movements represent then, to a large extent, is 'inter-temporal trade'. Countries swap claims on consumption at one date for claims on consumption at another. Normally, both parties should gain from this trade. Why else would they conduct it? Such swaps may arise for a variety of reasons. Disquiet does attach, however, to one of these possible reasons: suppose residents of one country are less patient than residents of another. The former will borrow from the latter initially, enjoying the additional consumption early on that such trade permits.

Later, the time will come when the debtor has to start repayment. In some extreme cases, such as those explored, for example, by Lucas (1992), the creditor could come to own all the debtor's capital. The debtor is reduced to the status of a beggar. This is far from healthy. The borrower may come to regret bitterly the debts he acquired, and wish he had not. In a community whose government believes economic actors are liable to borrow more than is strictly good for them, there is a case for limiting that borrowing. Even here, there is a superior policy to hand, however: taxing consumption and subsidizing saving for domestic residents, within a framework of free international capital movements.

Self-sufficiency in goods and services is, in general, a thoroughly unwise objective for countries. Where it has been pursued most vigorously, as in Albania for much of the post-war period, its adverse consequences are plain. Banning international capital movements is tantamount to an attempt to impose self-sufficiency over time. It forces home residents to match their aggregate spending with their aggregate income in each and every period. Restrictions on international capital movements are a step in this unwelcome and ill-advised direction. It is only when capital movements are demonstrably damaging – laundering the proceeds of crime, for example, or in the exigencies of a protracted war – that active steps to prevent them are well-advised.

To this we must add the fact that international capital movements resemble international trade in another respect: they are rather hard to prevent. As we shall see in Section 7.4, controls have diminishing impact over time. Regulations may be bypassed. New rules might be waterproof for a while, but they invariably create a search for loopholes to obviate them. The incentive to search is strong when home and overseas asset yields diverge widely, and these are usually the circumstances when restrictions are in force. When a loophole is uncovered, it will be used heavily, and news of its existence will percolate through the banking and corporate fraternity until it is plugged.

Multinational firms can invoice for transactions between their divisions or affiliates in different countries more or less as they choose. Enforcing truthful revelation of shipment values is well nigh impossible. Multinational banks may learn to exploit fine print in regulations to their advantage, or even be tempted simply to disobey them. The days when large banks and large companies produced their outputs in just one country are long since over. And even nationally-based companies and banks are not immune from contacts with their like abroad, nor blind to the possible gains to be had from arbitrage with them just beyond the limit of the law.

So 'asset' smuggling cannot realistically be stopped entirely. Closer and wider surveillance, and stiffer penalties for transgressions, can reduce the amount of asset smuggling, but only an incorrigible optimist could hope to eliminate it. Surveillance is costly; penalties are not always enforceable, and legal process to secure them is slow, complex, expensive and uncertain. As Hammond (1990) argues, there are times and places when the existence of a market has to be accepted as a constraint on policy – and not necessarily a good in itself. That constraint may be modified by policy actions, but not removed in its entirety.

Just as with trade in goods and services, for trade over time or in contingencies, free trade must generally be better than no trade, and, in simple cases at least, it must also be better than restricted trade. Restricted trade can be preferable to free trade in the presence of certain market imperfections. However, free trade must be superior to restricted trade under two conditions: if these market imperfections can be corrected at or close to source, and if side-payments can be made, if needs be, to compensate any losers.

Furthermore, any form of capital controls, or restrictions on 'trade over time or contingencies', suffers from certain important drawbacks. As we shall see in the next section, history shows that they do not prevent foreign exchange crises (although they may help to contain them). They are liable to circumvention. They tend to narrow the range of sources of funds available to finance domestic investment, and therefore raise its cost; and they are apt to narrow the range of investment opportunities for domestic savers, and sacrifice opportunities for reducing risk.

Our conclusion must be that there is a general presumption that international capital movements are more blessing than curse. There are groups of individuals who lose from their effects, but the balance of benefits against costs should normally be positive. Even when it is negative, as it can be, the underlying reason is some form of market failure, which is better addressed at or close to source, than by attempting to restrict or prevent them. It falls to central banks to cope with the serious but essentially temporary difficulties of maintaining order in financial markets as they occur.

7.2.5   *Comparing different types of capital control: the theory*

Capital movements may be discouraged by taxes, or subjected to quantitative controls (quotas). What can be said about their relative merits?

Taxes and quotas are equivalent in certain circumstances. These arise when quantities or prices can be set at any level, when licences to export or import are auctioned, and in the absence of uncertainty or market imperfection. All these conditions need to hold for equivalence. In practice, they do not. Auctions of state assets are quite common, sometimes with quotas on foreigners' purchasers. A few auctions of import licences for goods have been observed. However, quantitative limits on capital exports or imports are apt to be discontinuous and binary, and invariably non-revenue yielding. They are either 'on', and prohibitive, or 'off'. They bring no receipts to the authorities.

These features make taxes on capital flows look much more appealing than quantitative restrictions. The rate of tax may be raised or lowered as deemed necessary. The fiscal authority earns revenue from them. Quantity controls have an all-or-nothing character (although they may discriminate, for example between domestic and foreign residents) and they yield nothing in the way of tax receipts. However, there is one argument that may point in favour of quantitative controls. Given the limited size of foreign exchange reserves, and unpredictable character of international capital movements, any possible commitment to an exchange rate parity will be easier to honour when capital exports are banned rather than taxed. It would be very hard to calculate the tax rate at which capital exports dry up.

In the somewhat special circumstances when a country is justified in restricting international capital movements, there could be some exceptional occasions, such as warfare or a grave recession, when a temporary outright ban may be preferred to taxation, because of the greater predictability of its effects on the reserves. Generally, however, taxation will be more appropriate.

Taxes can be set on either inflows or outflows of capital, or on both. Which is preferable? The time-consistency argument for the volatility of international capital flows, which we shall consider in Section 7.3, points strongly in favour of *inflow* controls. These have the advantage of giving the foreign investor greater certainty of return, and therefore (given risk aversion) a larger volume of inflows. More important, the host government has an incentive to deliver unexpectedly large outflow taxes; their anticipation by foreign investors may cause capital flows to dry up completely. A policy of taxing capital inflows only may therefore be superior to one of taxing outflows. There is one caveat to this. The qualification relates to the asymmetries of reserves management. Capital outflows pose a more urgent and worrying threat than capital inflows, when the authorities are determined to defend an exchange rate parity. An unexpected and penal tax on outflows, which the authorities announce that they aim to reduce over time, will be of much more use in these conditions than a tax on capital inflows.

What taxes on inflows or outflows may do is to create a zone of inertia, where capital movements, in or out, fail to respond to changes in the variables that would ordinarily affect them. This will certainly arise when investment decisions are at least partly irreversible. The inertia is well described, for the closed economy, by Dixit (1997), who also considers the costs of adjusting labour as well as capital. Both inflow and outflow taxes will tend to make capital more expensive for domestic firms, although there can be circumstances when the stock of capital (at home) will be higher than it would have been without them.

Lastly, capital movements may be contained by a system of dual exchange rates. Many African, Asian, European and Latin American countries have employed this at various times. A standard example is the introduction of a separate foreign exchange market for financial and asset transactions (the 'financial exchange rate') as opposed to transactions linked to international trade, which are conducted on the commercial exchange rate. Belgium initiated a dual exchange rate system of this kind in 1954. In the early 1970s, Belgium was followed here by France and Italy. These dual systems lasted into the later 1980s. The UK's investment dollar market for home residents operated until 1979.

Another instance is provided by South Africa (1985–95). The South African case has recently been explored in depth by Farrell (2000), of the South African Reserve Bank. Among numerous other conclusions, Farrell finds only quite limited empirical support for the view that the dual exchange rate system, when in force, insulated the domestic economy and domestic monetary variables from external developments. This is important, because the main theoretical appeal of dual exchange rate systems, urged, among others, by Dornbusch (1986) and Fleming (1974), is that they *can* insulate domestic monetary policy from overseas shocks and capital flows. Their drawback is that they impede international capital movements whose long-run effect, as we have seen, should, on balance, be benign, and that they might result in a misalignment of the commercial exchange rate on which current account transactions are conducted.

7.3   Financial crises and capital movements

7.3.1   *Financial crises in the open economy*

One key difference between the open economy and the closed one is that the former introduces a hitherto absent price: the exchange rate. If two (or n) countries each have separate currencies, there will be one $(n-1)$ independent exchange rates. The exchange rate is the price of an asset that can collapse or jump instantaneously. This is as true of fixed-but-adjustable regimes as floating ones, although jumps that entail band revision are obviously rare events in the first case.

A currency crisis is not the same event as a bank crisis. But the two can occur together, and causation can run both ways. The discovery that a major bank may be in trouble can provoke a loss of foreign exchange reserves as market participants re-evaluate risks on the country's public and private sector obligations. This is especially likely if the bank in distress is thought to affect the rest of the domestic banking system. Equally, an exchange rate tumble can spread poison to the perceptions of the solvency of a domestic institution with large unhedged liabilities in foreign currency. Marion (1999) provides an excellent analysis of the parallels and differences between banking and foreign exchange crises.

A central bank's decision not to support a bank feared to be insolvent, if this leads to its failure, clearly precludes the option of granting that support tomorrow when news about its balance sheet may improve. But deciding to grant support today preserves the option of keeping the bank alive later. This asymmetry makes the parallel between official reactions to banking and currency crisis inexact, since foreign exchange intervention, and parity or interest rate revisions, are not technically irreversible. There is some temptation for the financial authorities, especially for central banks that also supervise and regulate, to defer the decision to close a troubled bank, in the hope of better news. By contrast, a currency crisis requires an instantaneous response. A currency crisis is also more transparent. For aficionados of Charles Dickens, awaiting the chance of better news, or 'waiting for something to turn up', is known as 'Micawberism'. Micawberism in dealing with ailing banks is a chronic temptation in the eyes of central bankers alarmed by the dangers of using emergency lending in inappropriate circumstances.

The implications of a decision to open an economy to international capital movements depend on the degree of sophistication of the country's financial system. When this is high, the main effect will be to align its set of nominal interest rates on their foreign counterparts, after due allowance for risks and anticipated exchange rate and inflation trends. Further, domestic residents gain freedom to diversify portfolios. International capital movements allow them to smooth expenditure in the face of income fluctuations, an option previously unavailable in aggregate. The liberty to trade intertemporally with the rest of the world enlarges their opportunities, and should enhance any *ex ante* measure of economic welfare.

If the country's financial system is relatively undeveloped, there are further potential gains. Many domestic residents, previously forced as individuals, and not just in aggregate, to synchronise payments with receipts, can now split them if they prefer. The country's domestic financial institutions gain access to a more elastic supply of assets to buy and a more elastic demand for their liabilities. This may well translate into cheaper loans and better-remunerated deposits, for their customers at home. One may see keener-priced, and possibly lower-risk, longer-term financial instruments of all kinds. If foreign-owned financial firms are admitted, there should be intensification of competition, reinforcing these effects.

If we focus more specifically upon the risks to financial stability, an open door to international capital movements alleviates some dangers and creates others. Suppose the stochastic disturbances affecting domestic asset prices are less than perfectly correlated with those abroad. When a sophisticated financial system is opened up to cross-border lending and borrowing opportunities, the country becomes exposed to disturbances of foreign origin for the first time. On the other hand, disturbances originating at home should have less effect upon the availability and cost of credit. As with the switch from a free-floating to a fixed exchange rate, residents swap better insulation against domestic shocks for greater vulnerability to foreign ones. Sudden changes in foreign investor sentiment will cause pervasive and possibly unwelcome effects at home, for example.

On the negative side, the gains from stronger competition for loans and deposits that should follow the admission of foreign financial institutions need, as we saw above, to be set against the heightened risk of bank failure. Narrower interest rate spreads bring lower profits to financial institutions. If this effect lasts, weakened profit flows aggregate over time to a narrowing of the gap between the stocks of assets and liabilities. Insolvency risks go up. Further, the country's financial system becomes vulnerable to some risk, slight perhaps, that a healthy domestic subsidiary of a foreign bank is pulled down by troubles abroad. No amount of assiduous supervision of local subsidiaries can prevent this.

At a more abstract level, Newbery and Stiglitz (1984) warn us that free international trade could conceivably make everyone worse off everywhere, in a world where futures and insurance markets are incomplete. In a self-sufficient country, random shocks affecting the supply of a particular good give their producers a form of income insurance, as prices and outputs swing in opposite directions. Free trade might stabilise prices, but risk-averse producers everywhere would switch to less shock-prone products; and this could serve to harm everyone. The general point here is that a policy of liberalization may induce subtle negative effects on welfare when markets are incomplete.

The first formal treatments of currency crises are due to Salant and Henderson (1978) and Krugman (1979). Flood and Garber (1984) provide some extensions, and Flood and Marion (1998) a valuable survey of later literature. A crisp and very illuminating account of currency crises is given recently by McCallum (2000). The central idea is that a fixed exchange rate peg between a pair of currencies is unsustainable if, all else equal, the nominal money supply, or domestic credit, keeps rising faster in one of the two countries than in the other. How long the peg can last depends on the level of foreign exchange reserves in the country where credit or money grows faster. The size of the gap in money growth rates matters too.

The crisis will not happen when the reserves of the country with faster-growing money actually run out. It should occur earlier than this. Given perfect foresight, static real incomes, and the absence of stochastic disturbances, three things will occur simultaneously at the point of crisis. The exchange rate will suddenly start to slide at the rate of relative money growth. The short nominal rate of interest will jump from the previous, rest of world level by the rate of anticipated exchange rate depreciation. There will be a steep decline in foreign exchange reserves, as domestic residents adjust to the higher rate of interest by reducing their real money demand. The magnitude of the tumble in reserves is larger (and hence the date of crisis comes earlier), the greater the (semi) elasticity of money demand to the rate of interest.

Several refinements can be made to this basic story. For example, the monetary authorities may keep domestic credit growing at its overseas level in the absence of a speculative attack, but decide to yield to it, if it happens, and subsequently allow domestic credit to rise at a faster rate. These ideas, explored by Obstfeld (1996) make expectations of a currency crisis self-fulfilling. Defending an exchange rate peg could be very costly, entailing temporarily high short-term interest rates, short-term sacrifices in output and employment, and, if the battle is ultimately lost, anyway, losses from unprofitable intervention in foreign exchange markets as well. To be set against this is the loss in the monetary authorities' reputation, and the costly consequences of higher inflation expectations, if the exchange rate is forced off its peg and subsequently follows a sliding path.

In an important recent contribution to the currency crisis literature, Morris and Shin (1998) find fault with the 'bootstraps' concept that a crisis occurs if and only if it is expected to occur. While this may be perfectly true, it does not explain anything: why should speculators suddenly come to expect a crisis? Instead of perfect and common information about economic fundamentals governing a country's equilibrium exchange rate, Morris and Shin argue that foreign exchange market participants receive imperfect and dissimilar signals about the fundamentals. Speculators are heterogeneous, but each is more willing to sell the currency the more probable he thinks that others will. Further, the monetary authorities have perceptions of the benefits and costs from fighting a speculative attack.

The fundamental signal could be so good that the authorities would fight any attack, or so bad that they could seek to devalue or depreciate without the slightest puff of adverse wind. Between these limits, an exchange rate peg is vulnerable to attack. A Morris–Shin *equilibrium* currency crisis arises when a critical mass of speculators attack it. For this, the distribution of the signals about fundamentals must be such that two conditions hold. First, enough speculators opine that the beliefs of other speculators are sufficiently adverse to trigger selling. Second, the perceptions of the net cost of fighting this attack on the part of the authorities, inferring what they can about the speculators' expectations, are too large as well.

7.3.2   *The volatility of international capital movements*

On a month-by-month basis, and even more so day-by-day, capital movements explain nearly all the volatility in external payments and exchange rates. Yet, as Flood and Rose write, '[exchange rate volatility] is a critical feature of the landscape; it has no analogue in domestic finance; and it is poorly understood' (1999: 670).

There are many possible factors contributing to the volatility of international capital movements. We shall consider two leading ones, in the following two subsections, and mention other relevant issues in Section 7.3.2.3.

7.3.2.1   *The time-consistency argument*

The first reason for the volatility of international capital movements, the 'time-consistency argument', runs as follows. Time-consistency problems arise, in general, whenever the best long run *ex ante* plan of actions differs from what you may wish to do, in a particular period, *ex post*.

Foreign direct investment, for example, is hard to undo, and particularly hard to undo quickly. The host government will generally see benefits in attracting it. It promises higher employment, an improved trade balance, more output, and as was seen earlier, even an increase in national product, after the deduction of repatriated profit flows. But once the investment is undertaken, the overseas owner of the new asset is vulnerable to an unexpected change in tax arrangements or regulations that reduces the income flow from it. Outflow capital taxes are an obvious example, and Turkey's restriction on overseas income repatriation late in 1999 provides an instance. The host government has an incentive to enact such changes, especially if its thinking is dominated by short-term considerations of benefit to its fiscal and external balances.

Overseas investors may trust the host government's promise not to tax them unexpectedly once, but this trust will be renewed only if the promise is kept. When the promise is broken, they will anticipate similar 'surprise' taxation, at least for some interval of time. This constitutes a form of punishment for the host government. The minimum credible promise of retrospective taxation is found where the host government's incentive to renege is just balanced by the discounted cost of punishment. At such a point, two outcomes are possible – some capital inflow, or none.

The first equilibrium is very brittle. A rise in the overseas rate of interest, for example, would raise the minimum credible level of taxation. The cost of the exclusion phase following reneging drops too much. One could see a sudden, discontinuous switch to the no-foreign-capital equilibrium. That would mean that foreign capital already in the country would quit as soon as it could. The same thing could happen if the government was thought to have become less patient, possibly because of an impending election or with fears of a coup.

An exogenous rise in the domestic stock of capital would have a similar potential effect. So too, would an adverse shock to domestic income: this would create a need for borrowing to sustain imports and consumption. A rise in the foreign interest rate could generate compound effects, by depressing world prices of the country's exportables, for example. That would reinforce short-term borrowing needs. In all such circumstances, the country may be tempted to borrow against its reputation, by impounding a larger than promised share of profits destined for overseas investors. The First Law of Credit Markets states that you can borrow when you can prove you do not need to. When the need for credit is most pressing, it is hardest to secure. Worse still, that is precisely when existing creditors and investors become keenest to pull out.

This 'time-consistency' argument closely resembles the idea that an announced inflation target should be credible. Here a credible target just balances possible benefits from surprise inflation (temporarily higher output, lower real debt servicing costs) against the costs of higher expected inflation later on. The argument, first due to Barro and Gordon (1983a, b), and later embellished by Backus and Driffill (1985a, b), Rogoff (1985) and Vickers (1986) among others, has proved very influential. It underlies much of the case for central bank independence. Essentially it turns on the idea that the best long-run *ex ante* rule (zero inflation in that case, zero taxation on foreign capital income in ours) may not appear the best short-term, *ex post* guide to action by those in government.

In the context of international capital movements, the argument is of particular relevance to developing countries. Changes in foreign investor sentiment are especially critical here. Establishing a record of consistent, modest taxation on overseas owners' local profits is difficult. Investors are always on the lookout for signs that policy may change unexpectedly. Very large inflows or outflows could be triggered by small perceived changes in the key parameters. The model described above is constructed on the basis of a given unit of time it takes investors to extricate themselves from an investment; of course this will vary across investments. The basic ideas sketched out here can readily be extended to allow for sunk costs, depreciation, imperfect competition, risk aversion and many other phenomena.

In the case of short-term, portfolio international capital movements, the inflation and direct investment time-consistency arguments actually intertwine. Each country, the Barro and Gordon argument would suggest, has a minimum credible inflation target. This depends positively on its government's rate of time-preference, or impatience, and on the value it places on any benefits from unexpected inflation. It varies negatively with a term related to the cost of inflation. If country A's lowest credible inflation target exceeds country B's, A's currency should be expected to depreciate, on average, by the difference between them.

Many of the factors that could suddenly increase the value of the minimum credible tax rate on foreign investors' income, would translate into a higher rate of expected exchange rate depreciation. Domestic and foreign residents could react by transferring funds into foreign currency, and to the maximum extent that they could, if domestic interest rates were not raised at once to prevent it. If the country is on a fixed-but-adjustable exchange rate regime, an immediate currency crisis may result, as investors come to predict an imminent devaluation. All this could be exacerbated by fears that foreign exchange controls could be imposed, or reimposed. And even overseas investors who have lent in *foreign currency* may have cause to fear that devaluation could trigger bankruptcy on the part of those of their debtors with unhedged positions. They may have no direct foreign exchange risk themselves, but they do face counterparty risk, which is clearly linked in this case to exchange rate risk.

The essential message remains. Capital movements are predicated upon a delicate balance of various economic and political forces, all of them liable to vary sharply over time. Small changes in these variables could transform an economy from one which attracted large amounts of overseas capital to one that did not.

7.3.2.2 *Disparate information*

We saw that the Morris–Shin model of currency crises turned critically on heterogeneous information. A second reason for the volatility of international capital movements turns on the disparities of the streams of information that come available to actual and potential asset holders.

Consider equity. The market value of a business turns primarily on market beliefs about five main factors. These are the current trend level of its profits, x, current and expected tax rates on profits, how fast those profits are expected to grow, the evolution of the risk-free rate of interest, and, lastly, the relevant risk premium to be added to the rate of interest. If the last four can be summarized by the single variables t, g, r and p, representing long-run average equivalents, the market value of the business should be inversely proportional to $(r+p-g)$. It should be directly proportional to $x(1-t)$. So together, r, p, g, t and x determine market value. For completeness, one should add the possible role of other variables, such as beliefs about takeover bids, revaluations of stock or other assets, and the like. Often the gap between $r+p$ on the one hand, and g on the other, may be slender. That means that even tiny changes in beliefs about one of these can produce large changes in the value of the business.

One key element here is the variability of profit income, x, and of beliefs about it. Lower profits imply reduced income for equity-holders directly, by reducing retained income per share, if not dividends. For creditors, they could raise the spectre of possible non-performance. Credit ratings would then deteriorate. In either case, the market value of the relevant asset should drop. Where financial markets are relatively undeveloped, or the assets in question are unquoted, what would otherwise appear as price changes might manifest itself as a sudden change in the availability of external finance. In the aggregate, that could mean a sudden drying up of capital inflows to the corporate sector.

Information takes longer to reach some market participants than others. This is especially true of information, or guesses about future information, that straddles geographical boundaries. One reason why assets change hands is because buyers and sellers have different beliefs about future yield prospects. Portfolio capital flows arise when residents of one country trade assets with residents of another. When overseas investors' information sets do not coincide with locals', there is a potential for large capital flows of this character.

Profits are a fickle residuum. Efficiency wage considerations create rigidities in real wage rates. The costs of hiring and firing make labour something of a fixed factor of production. The owners of businesses are better placed to absorb or lay off risk than their employees, whose aversion to risk is another phenomenon that tends to insulate real wages, and/or employment levels, from the vicissitudes of product prices and technology. An economy's profits, the residual claims on its output, are a shock absorber. No one can know at the time whether an unanticipated change in profits that a shock may bring is temporary or permanent, or indeed even, possibly, the start of a continuing trend. Market participants will make different guesses.

Overseas investors, on average as a group, may form different opinions from domestic investors. For example, overseas investors are better placed to make informed guesses about new entry or technological breakthroughs by rival firms abroad, export prospects, and movements in world prices of relevant inputs or substitutes. Home investors may know more about future domestic regulation and tax policies, intended actions of rival local firms, labour market developments and conditions affecting the firm's home sales.

Home and overseas investors' information disparities go further. Overseas investors will probably have a firmer grasp of relevant world macroeconomic trends affecting the interest and profit growth rates. They should have richer information, too, about other foreign economies thought to be comparable or closely linked. Some ingredients affecting the risk premium, also, may be better visible abroad. When it comes to domestic political and labour stability, the intentions and survival prospects of governments, and local factors affecting the economy's future growth prospects or takeover bids, home investors may well be much more knowledgeable than foreign ones.

Stocks change hands when opinions differ about their true values. The informational advantage overseas investors enjoy about relevant broader world developments may have substantial significance for many other domestic stocks, in related sectors or others. Some of the variables about which local investors are likely to have superior knowledge are more microeconomic and firm-specific in character. The stage is now set for the possibility of news that triggers broadly based buying or selling orders by overseas investors, and trades with worse (or differently) informed local investors. That will provide a basis for a sudden, and possibly large, international capital movement. Alternatively, it may be locals with the better aggregate information, about local politics for example, in which case international capital movements are still expected, this time in the opposite direction (inward if the news is bad, outward if good). Contagion may develop when foreign investors extrapolate belief revisions about one economy to another with which it appears to share some common features.[3]

7.3.2.3   Other reasons for international capital volatility

There are several other elements that contribute to the volatility of international capital movements.

For one matter, under fixed-but-adjustable exchange rates, speculators can make one-way 'sure thing' bets on parity changes on what seem very favourable terms, at times when these look imminent. This extends, with somewhat less force, to managed floats as well. Exchange control might make this awkward, particularly for domestic residents; but there will usually be informal foreign exchange markets in which foreign residents can transact, and these may display a similar phenomenon when the central bank intervenes on them, too. Only freely floating exchange rates avoid the problem. Or rather, under free floating, the problem metamorphoses into one of lurches, up or down, and often decidedly unwelcome, in the home price of foreign currency, with consequent knock-on effects on the home price level.

A second further source of volatility in capital movements relates to the government's fiscal position. Suppose that taxes are cut, or government spending raised, from an initial position of budget balance. If the exchange rate is freely floating, the immediate effect will be appreciation; if it is fixed, the real exchange rate should gradually edge upwards, too, as a result of labour market tightening and induced terms of trade effects. If the tax or spending changes are not reversed for a while, upward pressure on the real exchange rate is repeated. Later on, rising government debt, and mounting debt charges paid partly to foreigners, should lead to a *fall* in the real exchange rate. Greater competitiveness will, sooner or later, be needed to create the export surplus to pay the higher overseas debt charges.

At some point, therefore, there should be a sharp change in direction in the exchange rate (if freely floating) or in capital movements (if not). But when? Domestic and overseas observers may form different views on this, with the potential for huge swings in investor sentiment and serious financial crises. In the view of at least one observer, it was misjudgements about the substitutability of one government's debts for another's that underlay the failure of Long Term Capital Management (Dunbar 2000). Buchs (1999), and Aghion, Bolton and Fries (1999) emphasize the crucial role of fiscal difficulties in Russia's currency crisis in 1998. With the Russian example in mind, Fry and Sinclair (1996) show how uncertainty, and changes in uncertainty, about future fiscal policy can trigger large changes in domestic inflation, the internal counterpart to exchange rate swings in the open economy.

Then there is the problem of imitation. Withdrawing funds from a country in large amounts tends to be a public act. It is nearly as visible as queuing outside a bank to remove assets in a bank run. 'What do they know that we don't?' other market participants will start to ask. The traditional menagerie in asset markets consists of bulls and bears. To these may be added, as in Sinclair (1990), elephants, dormice, pigs, goats and sheep.

Elephants believe in mean reversion. They are chartists, perhaps, with very long memories. They expect a return to long-run averages, for real exchange rates or interest rates, for example. Dormice are noise traders that like to sleep on their portfolios. Dormice hate paying commissions. They may be sufficiently confident in market efficiency, too, to transact only when they have to. Pigs enjoy (or think they enjoy) access to some private information that makes them insider traders. Goats are economists who lack insider knowledge but back their theories about the likely paths of asset prices. These theories are rich and numerous, if not always mutually consistent – and get well honed when it comes to trying to explain the past. And sheep just watch what other actors appear to be doing and follow them, free riding on what they take to be their superior wisdom or knowledge. Asymmetric information is the basis for this behaviour: the sheep ask, 'What can it be that they know that I don't?' and decide that imitation is cheaper, and probably more remunerative, than trying to find out the answer.

The 'flocking' behaviour of sheep tends to accentuate trading volumes and price movements. It may explain 'international contagion', such as the genesis of the financial crisis in Argentina in the wake of Mexico's troubles in 1994, or the ripples that spread through much of Asia after the Thailand crisis of 1997. In the context of firms, it can generate excess entry to particular industries, and worryingly so in the banking sector. It can contribute powerfully to bubbles, and particularly so if the sheep react with a lag. It can account for the tendency to short-term serial correlation in asset price changes. Pigs and goats may initiate trade and asset price changes, which sheep infer, after a lag, as a signal to buy what has gone up or sell what has dropped. The theory of flocks of sheep, or 'herds' as they are often known, has been greatly enriched in domestic settings by Banerjee (1992). The positive feedback generated by sheep in financial markets can contribute to Shiller's phenomenon (2000) of 'irrational exuberance'. Morris and Shin (1999) stress the point that the externalities created when one banker or trader mimics another constitute an important argument against pure *laissez-faire*. For Morris and Shin, regulation is an appropriate response to that.

If imitation is generic to international capital movements, taxing them, at a sufficiently modest rate, may be beneficial after all. In an international context, it seems likely that dormice will be predominantly local; that there will be many domestic pigs with some element of special local knowledge; and that many overseas participants are apt to be sheep. There might also be a few foreign elephants, who graduate from single-country time series to multi-country panel econometrics.

Whatever causes volatility in capital movements, taxing or restricting them is an understandable (if questionable) policy reaction. Essentially, there are likely to be net costs of doing this in the long run, but certain possible short-run advantages that may outweigh them, temporarily, at times of crisis. Inflow controls may be helpful for small economies, when besieged by massive capital inflows they cannot digest, at least so long as they are light, temporary and market-based (imposed as a tax). Temporary outflow controls might also have a place as a last resort for countries suffering the aftermath of a currency crisis of exceptionable gravity. But the general presumption should be that their use is ill-advised, and that the balance of advantage is against them in all normal circumstances. This said, what can we learn from the evidence about the imposition of capital controls in practice, and their effects? This is the subject to which we now turn.

7.4 Capital controls in practice

Discussions in the previous Sections have shown that free international capital movements can bring substantial benefits, and yet they also pose difficulties in macroeconomic management, and threats to financial stability. Some countries have resorted to capital controls to deal with these difficulties. This section will discuss issues related to countries' recent experiences with capital controls. Section 7.4.1 sets out some of the objectives that countries seek to achieve by imposing capital controls, while Section 7.4.2 asks whether capital controls have been effective in achieving these objectives. Finally this section concludes with a case study.

7.4.1 Why do countries use capital controls?

The proposal of using capital controls as one way to deal with the difficulties that capital flows bring was put forward by Tobin in 1978. In surveying the theoretical literature on capital controls, Dooley (1996) observes that capital controls may be understood and justified as a second best solution in terms of their welfare effects. More recently, turmoil in the emerging markets has prompted renewed interests in capital controls. Eichengreen *et al.* (1995) are among many of those who advocate 'throwing sand into the wheel' of international financial markets.

Countries have imposed capital controls to achieve a wide range of objectives. Table 7.1 lists some of the objectives that have been suggested as arguments for capital controls, and measures of capital controls that could be used to achieve the policy objectives. The objectives broadly fall into the following categories.

7.4.1.1 Preserving resource allocation

Earlier practices of capital controls are largely on capital outflows aimed at preserving domestic resources in the following ways. They facilitate the taxation of wealth and interest income, and prevent the loss of tax receipts (Bakker 1996).

In some countries, capital controls are imposed in an attempt to hold domestic interest rates below their equilibrium level, and to prop up the exchange rate. Lower domestic interest rates create an excess demand for credit, and allow the authorities to control its allocation. They also help to contain the cost of servicing national debt, increase the demand for domestic currency, and thereby raise seigniorage. Capital controls may prevent domestic capital from fleeing to other economies with higher rates of interest.

Table 7.1 Objectives and measures of capital controls

Objectives	Capital control measures	Purpose	Measures (IMF classification) and examples
Preserve resources for domestic use	Outflows: long-term flows	Prevent domestic savings leaving the country, which represents a drain of domestic resources.	Controls on outward credit operations, direct investment, real estate transactions, overseas deposits and loans both by banks and individuals.
Protect and develop the domestic financial sector	Inflows and outflows: long-term flows	This is the infant industry argument. Sheltering the domestic financial sector from foreign competition might help the sector to develop.	Controls on direct investment, real estate transactions, deposits and loans in both, by banks and individuals in either direction.
Restrict foreign ownership of domestic assets	Inflows: long-term flows	Political considerations.	Controls on inward foreign direct investment and real estate transactions. For example: Mexico: Article 27 of the Constitution.
Financial repression	Outflows: long-term and short-term flows	Some countries maintain interest rates at an artificially low level. Accompanying measures are needed to prevent capital from going abroad to seek higher returns.	Prevailing in developing countries. Can be imposed on any type of capital transactions.
Macroeconomic autonomy	Inflows and outflows: short-term flows	Capital controls allow countries to maintain the interest rate at a level different from the one prevailing in the global capital markets.	Controls on capital and money markets.
Correct balance of payments imbalance	Inflows and outflows: short-term flows	Allow correction of balance of payments imbalance without monetary expansion or contraction.	Controls on capital and money markets. US: interest equalisation tax, 1963–74. Germany: Berdepot scheme, 1972–4.
Prevent capital flows volatility	Inflows: short-term flows	Enhance macroeconomic stability	Controls on capital and money markets. Chile: URR.
Prevent financial destabilisation	Inflows and outflows: short-term flows	Enhance financial stability.	Controls on capital and money markets. Chile: URR.
Maintain exchange rates	Inflows and outflows: short-term flows		Controls on capital and money markets. Dual exchange rates in many developing countries.

7.4.1.2   *Macroeconomic management*

Capital controls are often imposed to assist macroeconomic objectives such as correcting external imbalances, maintaining the exchange rate and enhancing macroeconomic autonomy. Let us take these objectives in turn. First, balance of payments imbalance may stem from economic conditions such as different economic cyclical positions, terms of trade shocks, changes in domestic macroeconomic policy, changes in global economic conditions, and consumer preferences. Second, many developing countries maintained a fixed exchange rate regime prior to the 1997–8 crises, and saw capital controls as a useful device for lowering the cost of defending parities. Third, in the current climate of globalisation and free capital movements, the authorities lose a great deal of control on the domestic economy.

In the face of an external imbalance, the authorities have four options:

1   allow the exchange rate to adjust; *(In Floating FEX System)*
2   use unsterilised intervention; *(Increase monetary aggregates)*
3   use sterilised intervention; and *(Backing currency rate of exchange*
4   impose capital controls. *by using (FEX reserves)*

Countries with a fixed exchange rate are reluctant to take up the first option immediately. Unsterilised intervention can help the country to regain equilibrium due to the automatic adjustment in the money supply. However, the counterpart to this is the fact that, as the authority loses control of the money supply, monetary aggregates might reach undesirable levels, with the potential for inflationary (or disinflationary) pressure. Sterilised intervention may curb capital flows in the short run, but is costly and can encourage further capital flows. Due to the weaknesses of the first three options, McKinnon and Oates (1966) show that it is not possible to maintain a fixed exchange rate, full capital mobility and independent policy simultaneously. One option must give. This is known as the 'incompatible trinity' (McKinnon and Oates 1966; Obstfeld and Taylor 1998). In weighing their options, some countries opted to use capital controls.

Incompatibility trinity

7.4.1.3   *Contain capital flow volatility and financial instability*

We have already seen how capital flows may imperil financial stability. Capital flows often induce banks to act imprudently, rendering the banking sector vulnerable to external shocks. They are notoriously volatile. Quite often they come when least wanted, and leave when least convenient. Some countries have imposed capital controls to fend off capital inflows in order to reduce market volatility and enhance financial stability. It also merits emphasis that West European, post-war history lends no support to the view that capital controls prevent foreign currency crises.

7.4.1.4 Financial sector development

It is also argued that capital controls and other measures limiting foreign entry into the domestic financial sector may assist its development by limiting foreign competition.

Some empirical studies have investigated which economic factors are most important in affecting policy-makers' decisions to impose capital controls. Grilli and Milesi-Ferretti (1995) find that capital controls are more likely to be imposed in countries with a less independent central bank, less developed tax system, higher share of government expenditure, and less open fixed exchange regime. These findings show that those countries with relatively dirigiste policy-making, or where imprudent macroeconomic management tends to lead to internal and external imbalance, often resort to capital controls. In a cross-country study, Johnston and Tamirisa (1998b) explore a wider set of economic features that might underlie the decision to impose capital controls. They find that among the different determining factors, capital controls are largely determined by institutional and structural characteristics. Extensive domestic regulation is associated with fewer capital controls, while financial repression is associated with more. Higher levels of taxation are often supported by controls on outflows. Rossi (1999) also finds that stronger prudential regulation and more effective supervision tend to be associated with fewer capital controls, while higher deposit insurance tends to be associated with higher capital controls.

7.4.2 *Capital control instruments*

There has been a wide range of capital controls in practice. The IMF's *Annual Report on Exchange Arrangements and Exchange Restrictions* gives detailed information on countries' policy towards capital movements. Table 7.2 presents the IMF's framework to classifying capital controls.

Important distinctions may be drawn between controls on capital *inflows* and those on *outflows*, and controls on *short-term* as against *long-term* capital flows. Capital controls on outflows were more prevalent in developing (and several developed) countries before the 1980s, as the primary concern of these countries was then financing balance of payments deficits and preserving capital for domestic resources. Since surges of private capital flows have posed difficulties for macroeconomic management and financial stability in recent years, capital controls in emerging markets have shifted focus towards inflows. In fact, some emerging market countries have relaxed controls on capital outflows as part of the response to large capital inflows. Different objectives for capital controls call for different types of capital controls. For example to prevent foreign ownership, inflow controls are needed on direct investment and equity, while to

Table 7.2 Types of capital transactions that can be subject to controls:
IMF classification

Inflows	*Outflows*
1. Capital and money markets	
Shares or other securities of a participating nature	
Purchase locally by non-residents	Sale or issue locally by non-residents
Sale or issue abroad by residents	Purchase abroad by residents
Bonds or other debt securities	
Purchase locally by non-residents	Sale or issue locally by non-residents
Sale or issue abroad by residents	Purchase abroad by residents
Money market instruments	
Purchase locally by non-residents	Sale or issue locally by non-residents
Sale or issue abroad by residents	Purchase abroad by residents
Collective investment securities	
Purchase locally by non-residents	Sale or issue locally by non-residents
Sale or issue abroad by residents	Purchase abroad by residents
2. Derivatives and other instruments	
Purchase locally by non-residents	Sale or issue locally by non-residents
Sale or issue abroad by residents	Purchase abroad by residents
3. Credit operations	
Commercial credits	
To residents from non-residents	By residents to non-residents
Financial credits	
To residents from non-residents	By residents to non-residents
Guarantees, sureties and financial backup facilities	
To residents from non-residents	By residents to non-residents
4. Direct investment	
Inward direct investment	Outward direct investment
	Controls on liquidation of direct investment
5. Real estate transactions	
Purchase locally by non-residents	Purchase abroad by residents
	Sale locally by non-residents
6. Provisions specific to commercial banks	
Non-resident deposits	Deposit overseas
Borrowing abroad	Foreign loans
7. Personal capital movements: deposits, loans, gifts, endowments, inheritances and legacies	
To residents from non-residents	By residents to non-residents
Settlements of debts abroad by immigrants	
Transfer into country by immigrants	Transfer abroad by emigrants
8. Provisions specific to institutional investors	
	Limits (max.) securities issued by non-residents and on portfolio invested abroad
	Limits (max.) on portfolio invested locally

reduce market volatility, it is controls on short-term flows that will appeal most. The final column of Table 7.2 suggests what measures of capital controls in the IMF classification might be relevant to achieve a particular policy objective.

Capital controls can take the form of direct (adminstrative) controls or indirect (market-based) controls. Direct controls can involve outright prohibitions, explicit quantitative limits or an approval procedure for capital transactions. They seek to influence the volume of financial transactions directly. Market-based controls discourage capital flows by making capital transactions more expensive, and can affect both the volume and price of financial transactions. Examples include explicit or implicit taxation of cross-border financial flows, and dual or multiple exchange rate regimes.

7.4.3 How effective are capital controls?

This section surveys countries' experiences with capital controls to see how effective they have been in achieving their objectives. We begin with a brief discussion on how to gauge the degree or the intensity of capital controls. This is followed by an evaluation of studies offering evidence on the effectiveness of capital controls. We conclude with an analysis of the system of capital controls employed in Chile.

7.4.3.1 Indices used to gauge the degree of capital controls

Measures of the degree of capital controls enable observers to examine the extent to which capital controls have proved effective. Different measures have been proposed to gauge the degree of capital controls. Klein and Giovanni (1999) use a dummy variable which takes the value of one during periods when some form of capital controls are imposed, and zero otherwise. Another simple measure is the length of the period during which some form of capital controls are in place. Some more refined measures of capital controls employ the detailed descriptions of different types of capital controls published by the IMF, as in, for example, Johnston and Tamirisa (1998a,b). Another possibility is to use detailed data for economies to construct capital control indices on a country-by-country basis. For example, in studying the effects of capital controls in Brazil, Cardoso and Goldfajn (1998) construct indicators of capital controls according to changes in legislation relating to taxes and restrictions on capital inflows and outflows.

7.4.3.2 The effectiveness of capital controls

The effectiveness of capital controls is assessed on the basis of whether they have achieved their objectives (such as maintaining exchange rate stability, increasing monetary policy autonomy, or enhancing or preserving macroeconomic and financial stability). To evaluate whether capital controls achieve policy objectives, studies have explored the following aspects:

- The volume and composition of capital flows. Do capital controls reduce the volume, volatility of capital flows, and encourage a portfolio shift towards longer-term capital flows?
- The differential between the domestic and world short-term interest rates. If capital controls are effective, can the monetary authority maintain domestic interest rates at a level that differs from some global benchmark market rates?
- Effects on the path of real exchange rates. Do successful capital controls reduce pressure for real appreciation or depreciation?

Space constraints preclude more than a brief summary of some selected recent attempts to answer these questions.

THE VOLUME AND COMPOSITION OF CAPITAL FLOWS

Some evidence suggests that capital controls have affected the volume and composition of capital flows. Cardoso and Goldfajn (1998) conclude that Brazil's net capital inflows were reduced by controls on inflows, and increased by controls on outflows. The effect peaks after five months, but fades fast after six months. Further looking into disaggregated capital flows, they find that capital controls reduce debt and equity flows, but not, apparently, flows of foreign direct investment. In their study, Montiel and Reinhart (1999) also distinguish different types of capital flows, and find that capital controls reduced short-term and portfolio flows, and increased foreign direct investment in a group of Latin American countries.

A recent IMF report by Ariyoshi *et al.* (1999) analyses capital controls, noting that they had varying policy objectives in a number of countries. Their study included Chile and Thailand. Capital controls seem to have changed the composition of capital flows and lengthened the maturity of loans to these countries. However, capital controls were ineffective in other countries embraced by the study. Obstfeld (1998) remarks that it is easier to prevent destabilising outflows by limiting inflows than trying to stop capital outflows directly.

THE INTEREST RATE DIFFERENTIAL AND THE REAL EXCHANGE RATE

Differentials between domestic and overseas interest rates are another variable that capital controls have been found to affect. Studying capital controls in a group of Latin American countries, Edwards (1998) finds that they can support a wedge between the domestic and world interest rates. After capital controls have been imposed, the differential adjusts more sluggishly. Capital controls have therefore allowed the monetary authority to exercise a greater influence on domestic interest rates, Edwards concludes, but further research will be needed to quantify its magnitude. In one of few studies on their real exchange rate effects, Edwards finds that capital inflow controls have some success in affecting real exchange rate appreciation, but the effects appear modest and short lived.

OTHER ASPECTS OF CAPITAL CONTROLS

Ariyoshi *et al.* (1999) believe that, even in those countries where capital controls have had some effect, successes are achieved because capital controls are applied in a general context of sound macroeconomic management and economic reforms. They point to the limitations of capital controls. No single measure of capital controls is found to be effective across all the countries. Capital controls tend to be circumvented very quickly, in increasingly sophisticated financial markets. More effective capital controls have to be more comprehensive, and therefore more distortionary in the sense that a wider range of asset prices are driven away from the equilibrium values they would have otherwise commanded. Reinhart and Smith (1997) also echo this conclusion. In their calibrated theoretical model, they find that, due to low intertemporal substitution of consumption in developing countries, capital controls need to be high to be effective. Welfare gains on capital controls are small, and can be lost rapidly.

The point that capital controls tend to succeed when part of a wider macroeconomic adjustment and reform programme, is a recurring theme in the recent literature in the area. In reviewing the pros and cons of capital account liberalisation, Cooper (1999) also believes that the important message is that the effectiveness of capital controls depends on the accompanying policy and economic environment. Neely (1999) emphasises that capital controls do most harm when used to try to defend inconsistent policy.

Another finding is that capital controls, while they can serve some prudential purposes, cannot substitute for prudential measures (Ariyoshi *et al.* 1999). Neely (1999) stresses that it is not desirable to replace capital controls with simultaneous financial reform and prudential regulation.

There are also studies linking capital controls with financial crises. Rossi (1999) investigates the links between capital account liberalisation, prudential regulation and supervision by examining their impact on the probability of crises as well as the interaction among them. He finds that financial fragility increases with the lenience of prudential regulation, the coverage of depositors' safety net, and the extent to which capital controls are levied on outflows. Controls on capital outflows are not significant in affecting the probability of currency crises, while capital controls on inflows are found to reduce the probability of currency crises.

7.4.3.3   *Practical difficulties, and undesirable features of capital controls*

Some practical difficulties in implementing capital controls have also been identified. First, with the fast growing sophistication in financial markets, market participants often very quickly discover ways of circumventing capital control measures by shifting to, or creating, products not subject to them. Second, in an effort to curtail undesirable capital flows, restrictions on capital flows may interfere with desirable capital and current account transactions. In a broader context it may hamper the development of the financial sector, a sector that is crucial in transmitting monetary policy, and facilitating economic growth by mobilising savings to finance domestic investment. Another problem is the fact that, while capital controls often aim to reduce short-term capital flows, short-term and long-term flows are very hard to tell apart. This problem also leads to difficulties in interpreting studies on the effectiveness of capital controls.

7.4.3.4   *Problems with empirical work*

The studies cited above should be treated with some caution since there are a number of problems in assessing the impact of capital controls. First and foremost is the fact that there is no generally accepted measure of the intensity of capital controls.

A second difficulty is the data on different types of capital flows. As noted earlier, one test of the effectiveness of capital controls is their effect on the volume and composition of capital flows. However, short-term and long-term flows are hard to distinguish. Claessens *et al.* (1995) test the time series properties to see which types of flows, FDI, portfolio and long-term capital flows, are more likely to be sustainable. They find that there is no time series property inherent in any type of capital flows, and argue that the conventional balance of payments labels for capital flows such as the short-term and long-term capital flows may not be very informative.

Another difficulty in studying the impact of capital controls is that there might be a two-way causal link between capital controls and capital flows. As is clear from earlier discussions, capital controls are often imposed in response to large and volatile flows. Cardoso and Goldfajn (1998) provide empirical evidence that capital flows influence policy decisions on capital controls. One should bear this in mind when interpreting the results from studies on the effects of capital controls. In addition, any quantitative studies on the relationship between capital controls and capital flows need to address the issue of endogeneity in estimation.

Yet another problematic issue is how to disentangle the effects of capital controls and other factors. Changes in capital flows, real exchange rates and interest rate differentials after the imposition of capital controls may well be attributed to other factors such as changes in prudential regulation, macroeconomic development, and financial reforms, rather than solely, if at all, to capital controls *per se*.

A final issue is a general one. The fact that the technology for answering empirical questions in all areas of applied economics is advancing so rapidly does not just lead one to discount the results of much past econometric work. It also makes one diffident about claiming too much for current work, either. In a world beset by differential information, non-linearities, the possibility of multiple equilibria, and non-stationarity for so many relationships, phenomena all highly pertinent to the issue of international capital flows, current econometric methods may suggest inferences that future researchers will not treat with much respect. To that extent, the insights that theory can provide acquire more importance.

7.4.3.5 A case study of capital controls

Among the Latin American countries, Chile was an early reformer. In response to a financial crisis in the 1980s, Chile embarked on a comprehensive programme of macroeconomic stabilisation and structural reform. Macroeconomic stabilisation aimed at reducing inflation, fiscal and current account deficits, while the economic restructuring programme encompassed fiscal, trade, financial, labour market reforms and privatisation.

Since 1990 Chile has experienced surges of capital flows. One factor that prompted the inflows is the fact that the newly appointed independent Central Bank Board of Chile initiated an inflation reduction programme and tightened monetary policy in 1989–90, in response to overheating and a relaxed fiscal stance. This happened at a time when world interest rates were falling, making Chile an attractive investment opportunity. More fundamentally, Chile's success in macroeconomic stabilisation and restructuring programmes enhanced the country's credit rating. Furthermore, as memories of the early 1980s sovereign debt crises faded, there was an increasing willingness around the globe to invest in emerging markets at this time.

The large influx of capital allowed for gradual elimination of some exchange and capital controls in Chile. However, at the same time it posed difficulties for macroeconomic management, and imperilled macroeconomic and financial stability. In 1991 the Chilean authorities found themselves in a dilemma. Should they choose to lower interest rates when the economy was clearly already expanding fast? Or should they allow the Peso to appreciate, endangering the country's external competitiveness? In these difficult circumstances, Sachs, Tornell and Velasco (1996) show that the Chilean authorities responded with:

i   substantial and repeated sterilised foreign exchange market intervention, particularly in 1990–2;
ii a transfer of public sector deposits from commercial banks to the central bank;

iii   a crawling peg targeting the real exchange rate; and
iv   the imposition of capital controls.

The Chilean authorities used a combination of direct and indirect controls on capital flows. Direct controls included a minimum stay requirement for direct and portfolio investment, and a minimum rating requirement for domestic corporations borrowing abroad and extensive reporting requirement on banks for all capital account transactions. The notable market-based control was the unremunerated reserve requirement (URR). Under this scheme a dollar denominated one-year mandatory deposit was imposed on nearly all foreign capital inflows associated with foreign debt or portfolio investment. The URR was initially imposed in June 1991, on foreign loans at a rate of 20 per cent. As this coverage was not universal, loopholes remained open. Over time its coverage was extended to non-debt flows that had become a vehicle for short-term portfolio flows, although this still could not close all the loopholes. The rate was also raised from 20 per cent to 30 per cent. As capital flows declined, resulting from contagion from the Asian crises, the URR was lowered from 30 per cent in June 1998, and eliminated in September 1998.

Chile emerged from the Tequila crisis in 1994–5 relatively unscathed. It actually had a mild nominal and real appreciation of about 10 per cent, and its international reserves increased in this period. The stock market fell somewhat, but soon bottomed out. The prices of Chile's sovereign debt were hardly affected.

Chile's performance during the Tequila crisis is often cited as a successful story of capital controls. However, it is highly debatable to attribute Chile's relatively strong performance solely to their imposition. When the URR was introduced, Chile had made impressive improvements in stabilisation, macroeconomic management, and in its prudential framework.

The strengthening of the prudential framework is particularly noteworthy. Chile has gradually established high disclosure standards, stringent rules for loan classification and provisioning, strict limits on connected lending and on banks' exposure to foreign exchange risks and clear procedures for correction for liquidity or solvency problems. The following statistics reflect the soundness of the Chilean banking sector (Ariyoshi *et al.* 1999):

- a low level of non-performing loans: 1.68 per cent of total loans (on 31 March 1999);
- a reasonable level of provision for bad loans: 127 per cent of non-performing loans;
- compliance of all banks with the BIS capital adequacy ratio; and
- an average capital adequacy ratio of 11.5 per cent.

There is no consensus with regard to the effectiveness of the URR. Due to the methodological difficulties discussed above, quantitative studies which assess the effectiveness of the URR have not reached firm conclusions. Some studies find that the URR did increase the degree of autonomy of monetary conduct, and allowed a persistent real interest rate differential between Chile and the global market (Simone and Sorsa 1999). However, Simone and Sorsa (1999) argue that continued sterilisation may also have contributed to this real interest rate wedge. The URR did not seem to have much impact on the real exchange rate (Edwards 1998; Simone and Sorsa 1999). The URR seems to have had some success in altering the composition of capital flows, although this finding needs to be interpreted cautiously as there are large discrepancies in statistics on short-term capital flows.

Edwards (1998) also looks into other aspects of capital controls. He finds that capital controls have helped to reduce stock market instability and insulate Chile from some external shocks. However, they are not able to isolate the country from large ones. Furthermore they have increased the cost of capital for small firms. He concludes that the effectiveness of capital controls in Chile may well have been exaggerated.

7.5 Concluding remarks

This chapter has examined the international dimension to financial stability. Drawing the analogy with international trade in weighing the benefits and difficulties capital flows bring, we argue that there must be a general presumption that international capital movements are, on balance, favourable in their welfare effects. Consequently any policy to restrict or tax them needs to be viewed with some scepticism. Any advantage it might confer will often be available at lower cost using other instruments. Nonetheless, we recognise that there can be some circumstances in which the case for capital controls, at least on a temporary basis, is strong, and we have scrutinised the relative merits of different types of control, generally preferring taxes on inflows to other types.

The evidence casts some doubt on whether capital controls are effective in achieving their assumed policy objectives. The main messages that emerge from our survey of findings on countries' experiences with capital controls are:

- There is no single capital control measure that is universally effective.
- Capital controls may have some effects in the short term in, for example, affecting the volume and composition of capital flows, creating an interest rate differential between the domestic and world economy. However, the effects tend to disappear very quickly.
- For capital controls to achieve maximum insulation, they need to be high and comprehensive. In this case their likely long-run welfare effects may be more harmful. They also impose administrative costs

on the private and public sectors, and may be an invitation to corruption.

- Capital controls tend to be more effective if they are accompanied by suitable macroeconomic policy, and as part of financial and economic reform programmes.
- Although they may have merit from a prudential standpoint, capital controls are no substitute for sound prudential regulation.

Notes

1 Without implicating them in any errors, we should like to thank Bill Allen, Charles Goodhart and Glenn Hoggarth for very helpful comments.
2 This argument has particular appeal in the case of transition economies, but rather less so for much of South East Asia.
3 Morris (2000) provides an excellent recent analysis of the theory of contagion in markets.

8 Some concluding comments

Alastair Clark

Many contributions to this volume are concerned with the question of how to promote financial stability. Regulation is of course one important instrument, but I would underline David Llewellyn's view that regulation is only one instrument among many. Chapters 1, 2, 3, 5 and 6 give an indication of some others, especially from the point of view of central banks. Even for those central banks that have never regulated, or have ceased to regulate, surveillance (at both the microeconomic and the system levels), crisis management and strengthening the financial infrastructure remain of central concern. There is also the interesting question, discussed by Peter Sinclair in Chapter 1, and Richard Brealey in Chapter 5, of how far and in what ways financial stability policy and monetary policy interrelate. Past experience illustrates clearly the contribution which stable macroeconomic and specifically monetary conditions can make to financial stability; and conversely the threat to financial stability posed by erratic or inconsistent monetary policy.

As a way of gathering together some of the conclusions from this book, I have picked out five issues that lie at the centre of current discussions on financial stability.

The first is *transparency*. Transparency is crucial to the efficient functioning of private markets, on which both national and international capital flows increasingly depend, and for that reason has recently been receiving much attention. The present debate about international standards and codes is one manifestation. As time goes on, the pressure from lenders and investors for transparency is more likely to grow than subside. And correspondingly, the pressure on borrowers, both companies and countries, to meet best practice in this area is also likely to increase, for fear of seeing their access to financial markets becoming constrained.

The second issue – in some ways the obverse of the first – is the *use of information*. Charles Goodhart subtitles part of Chapter 3 'Information, information, information'. Relevant information is of course invaluable to central banks, regulators and other public authorities with financial stability responsibilities. Both for them, and for private market participants, information is of particular importance in the context of risk assessment. But is the available information always used, or used to full effect? Such evidence as we have about this is not particularly encouraging. One issue in this area is the structure of rewards and incentives more generally within firms. For example, do firms place too much emphasis on *initiating* business as opposed to the *ex post* return, and could this mean that those taking lending and investment decisions pay less attention to information which might help in assessing longer term risks than they ought to? Information is not of course costless to obtain and the dissemination of information is not costless either. But if lenders and investors ignore the information available to them, or make only limited use of it, the benefit from its provision is rather obviously diminished!

The third item is the tension between *global businesses and national jurisdictions*. This is an intriguing if far from novel issue. It has long been familiar in the context of taxation, but it arises equally with regulation. Excessively burdensome regulations can divert footloose financial business to jurisdictions which are more tolerant of doubtful practices, or less able to detect them. If a country's authorities choose the scope and character of its regulatory regime in isolation and without coordination, there is a risk that 'regulatory arbitrage' will drive towards undesirably lax regulatory regimes. This concern has of course been a principal motivation for international regulatory cooperation. But such cooperation, both multilaterally and bilaterally, is also vital for the day-to-day oversight of firms which operate across national borders, given the absence of – and the absence of a legal basis for – an international regulatory agency. The disjunction between international firms and national jurisdictions nevertheless leaves a set of problems to be addressed. These include: the congruence, or otherwise, of national laws on insolvency; the oversight of firms based in some so-called 'off-shore' countries; and arrangements for the provision of emergency liquidity assistance, to banks especially, which is discussed at several points in this book, and particularly in Chapter 6 by Glenn Hoggarth and Farouk Soussa. On this last topic, Juliette Healey's survey evidence in Chapter 2 highlights one aspect – the issue of *who* provides emergency liquidity assistance – in the light of the wide variety of practice across different national central banks.

Surveillance is the fourth issue. There has understandably been concern that recent debt problems could have arisen with very little prior warning. How might we improve upon such performance? Analysis has not produced a set of magic indicators of impending financial crises. There are significant Type I and Type II errors associated with all of the macroeconomic – as well as the microeconomic, firm-specific – variables which have been suggested as candidates. There might however be value in focussing more closely on balance sheets than 'traditional' IMF-style surveillance allows, so as to identify possible currency and maturity mismatches (which, as Peter Sinclair and Chang Shu emphasise in the previous chapter, played such a large role in the 1997/98 crisis in Asia).

The fifth and final point is *crisis management*. Here the roles of the public and private sectors in country debt workouts, and the relationship between them, are particularly important. I would emphasise two points. First, that as a straight matter of fact, the public resources available to respond to a crisis are strictly limited and in most cases are likely to be much less than the scale of *ex ante* private sector financial exposures; and second, while the obligation of debtors to meet their obligations is paramount, it is unrealistic to work on the basis that they will, come what may, be able to do so. We have yet to devise a fully satisfactory approach to the handling of such crises, at least in cases where systemic disruption is threatened. Nonetheless, some of the elements of a reliable mechanism may be in place. These include: contingent credit lines for both private and public sectors; the promotion of what have come to be called 'country clubs'; and, in certain circumstances, the adoption of a standstill on payments with more or less formal endorsement by official institutions and lenders overseas, while orderly arrangements for resolution of a crisis are made.

These five issues illustrate just a few of the considerations, going beyond regulatory intervention, which are relevant in maintaining and regenerating financial stability. The list is certainly not exhaustive: strengthening market infrastructure, for example, through improved payments systems, is an obvious omission.

Financial stability has recently received growing attention in international financial discussions. The International Monetary Fund's Financial Sector Assessment Programmes are acquiring increasing importance. The creation of the Financial Stability Institute in Basel in 1999 is a valuable practical manifestation of this growing attention. Financial firms are becoming more and more diversified, sophisticated and multinational. Supervising and regulating them is getting harder, and international coordination is increasingly necessary.

Financial stability policy is much less tidy than monetary policy. For monetary policy, there is typically an explicit objective (for the rate of inflation, or monetary growth, or the exchange rate). Financial stability policy has to do with containing or preventing inherently low probability events with potentially very high costs, such as failures of big banks with the consequential knock-on effects. It is easy to see when a monetary target is missed, and often to see why, but assessing the degree of success in safeguarding financial stability is much harder. It would be naïve to think that the paucity or absence of financial crises is necessary or sufficient for inferring success in this department.

What of the future? Financial markets will surely continue to develop rapidly. New instruments will widen the menu of products available to investors, and pose new challenges to regulators and others sharing in the task of safeguarding financial stability. Geographical boundaries will come to mean even less. Central banks and regulators will have to respond by strengthening international cooperation, trying to keep up with the pace of financial innovation, and making ever-cannier use of all the information which could warn them of impending trouble. It may also mean paying more attention to reward structures and incentives *within* financial firms, so that the behaviour of individual portfolio managers, loan officers etc., is better aligned with the objectives of the firm, and the objectives of the firms are consistent with the public policy interest in financial stability.

One day we might be able to put a tick against the various goals implied in these comments, though personally, I rather doubt it. The international financial system and the interactions which are crucial to the maintenance, or not, of financial stability, are just too complex. But we can certainly do better. Whatever happens, the task of attempting to preserve financial stability will remain taxing but vitally important – and a challenge, I hope, in relation to which the present book provides some helpful insights.

Appendix 1 Minutes of the Bank of England's 7th Central Bank Governors' Symposium
2 June 2000

The subject for the morning session was 'Financial Stability and Central Banks'. The discussion was based on the Report written by Richard Brealey, Alastair Clark, Charles Goodhart, Juliette Healey, Glenn Hoggarth, David Llewellyn, Chang Shu, Peter Sinclair and Farouk Soussa. The proceedings were introduced and chaired by Eddie George, Governor of the Bank of England. After presentations of the papers Governor George invited the three discussants, Governor Mboweni of South Africa, Governor Massad of Chile, and Deputy Governor Grenville of Australia, to comment.

Discussants

Governor Mboweni (South Africa) raised four issues of particular relevance for developing countries. First, the fundamental issue of confidence. The regulatory structure might be in place but if confidence in a particular bank was eroded that alone could potentially destroy the bank concerned and damage the banking system. In South Africa analysts divided banks into two categories: A1 for the very large banks and A2 for the rest. The market perception was that problems were more likely to arise among banks in the A2 category, and that could become self-fulfilling. Second, a distinction should be drawn between financial stability and *banking* stability. It would be mistaken for Central Banks to become obsessed with banking stability to the point of endangering financial stability: it was quite acceptable to allow banks to fail from time to time. Third, there was a question about how far central banks should worry about non-bank financial institutions such as LTCM. Finally, where should banking supervision be located, inside or outside the central bank?

Governor Massad (Chile) noted that, faced with global financial volatility, a small, open country like Chile faced two basic options: to suppress volatility or to try to live with it. The rationale for regulation was that markets were incomplete so that instability would be damaging. But attempting to suppress volatility could have the effect of restricting it to one sector, which could lead to sharp changes in relative prices. For example, in 1979 Chile had a fixed exchange rate regime and a current account deficit of 14 per cent of GDP. That forced real interest rates up, which caused asset prices to collapse. The banking system had to be bailed out at a cost of 35 per cent of annual GDP. This experience suggested that central banks' contribution to financial stability could be to help spread the impact of shocks across markets. Moving from a volatility-suppressing to a volatility-accommodating regime was not easy and many countries had not made the change until they had no other choice. In Chile, by contrast, a gradualist approach had been followed: the Central Bank had worked with the supervisory agency on the exchange rate and interest rate mismatch limits to be applied to commercial banks; the exchange rate target band had been extended: unremunerated reserve requirements on capital inflows gradually reduced to zero; the minimum duration restriction on foreign capital flows reduced; and banks had been authorised to deal in forward foreign exchange. In September 1999 the peso had been permitted to float. Encouragingly, since then, its volatility had been lower than that of many other major currencies. The volatility-accommodating approach was not without risk. There could be a greater exposure to bank failure, for example, so the strengthening of regulation and supervision should be emphasised, although it should be borne in mind that the optimal rate of bank failures was not necessarily zero.

Deputy Governor Grenville (Australia) said that he would focus on the issue of capital flows. Few would disagree with the general proposition that international capital flows were 'a good thing', although it was possible to think of instances, for example prior to the Asian crisis, where capital had been used to finance projects not of the highest priority. So why was it so difficult to get the advantages of capital flows without the disadvantages – most notably, excessive volatility? One problem was 'model uncertainty' – that financial markets did not have a clear view of what the fundamental value of the exchange rate and other economic variables should be. A second problem was that domestic financial markets in emerging countries tended to be small and fragile – fragile because they had only recently moved to a more deregulated environment, which involved institution-building and could not be done overnight. In responding to those problems it was important to be bold: globalisation created the need for new rules and one should not be apologetic about that. Some of the hardest issues were distributional, such as private/public sector 'burden sharing'. But in those areas too, rules were required.

Question and answer session

Governor George said he would like to focus the discussion on two issues. First, the extent of the role of the central bank in promoting financial stability; and second, distinguishing between countries' vulnerability to internal and to external shocks and what could be done to moderate that.

Governor Thiessen (Canada) thought that what central banks contributed to the promotion of financial stability was an economic perspective. But trying to define precisely what that meant in terms of the work done within the central bank had been incredibly difficult in Canada. Payments and settlements were certainly one area where problems could become systemic. Beyond that, domestic financial markets and the international situation were monitored closely: while it was usually impossible to foresee shocks, there was an opportunity to mitigate their consequences internally.

Governor Tošovský (Czech Republic) saw price stability and financial stability as two sides of the same coin. Instability in the financial system made monetary policy less effective, and monetary policy mistakes could destabilise the financial system. The institutional location of banking supervision was not important, provided the Central Bank had access to supervisory information. The role of the central bank in transition economies was often very broad, extending to the promotion of legislation, cultivation of markets and advising the government in the privatisation of the domestic banking sector.

Governor Venner (Eastern Caribbean) thought that the decision as to whether to locate banking supervision within or outside the central bank depended partly upon the size of the country. In smaller countries the central bank often had diverse responsibilities – for example, to act as an 'honest broker' between domestic and overseas banks, and to promote high standards of corporate governance and of auditing. Therefore the intellectual stature and credibility of the central bank was very important. This raised potential conflict of interest issues for the central bank, but in practice it was very difficult for the central bank to detach itself from such subjects.

Governor George noted that the experience of the Bank of England had been similar in that it had become involved in issues such as corporate governance because it had the experience and the capacity to do so, not because of any prior assigned responsibility.

Governor Bonello (Malta) was uncomfortable with the argument that the location of banking supervision did not matter provided data were shared.

In his experience the conduct of supervision was an invaluable source of intelligence and leading indicators that might not be available in the bare statistics.

Governor Afxentiou (Cyprus) said that he could not see how a central bank could act to promote financial stability unless it was the supervisor.

Governor Gunnarsson (Iceland) said that in his country a separate agency had been in place since the start of the year 1999 with responsibility for all financial regulation. There had initially been concern within the central bank at the possibility of losing information about the banking system, but experience of operating the new arrangements had so far been favourable. Senior officials of the central bank no longer found supervisory issues crowding out their consideration of monetary policy. The role of the central bank in maintaining financial stability had been included in the relevant legislation. A division of the central bank was now devoted to that, looking at the issues more broadly than hitherto.

Governor Al-Sayari (Saudi Arabia) noted that in developing countries technical expertise was limited, and that it could be spread too thin if there were to be both a central bank and an independent supervisory agency.

Managing Director Koh (Singapore) agreed that the success of the central bank depended on its ability to attract human talent, and that the integration of supervision within the central bank broadened career opportunities. *This was particularly important for smaller countries like Singapore.* Another advantage was that, as financial markets developed, the central bank could respond more flexibly. Regarding globalisation, Mr Koh said, while he fully supported the work of the Basel Committee, more thought could usefully be given to two aspects: first, the flow of information between home and host supervisors, where it seemed to be assumed that, in general, the flow would be from host to home; and second it should be borne in mind that financial instability could affect both home and host markets.

Governor Fraga (Brazil) commented that the central bank certainly had to look at payment systems. In conducting supervision, the challenge was to look beyond individual institutions to draw out risk aggregation issues. Regardless of the location of the supervisor, the central bank would need to do this kind of work.

Governor Mohohlo (Botswana) said that in order to conduct supervision effectively it was advisable for central banks to attract skills in, among other related fields, accounting and finance: she wondered whether Professor Goodhart's survey of economists and lawyers working in central banks extended to these categories of professionals and what the results were.

Professor Goodhart said that the study included the specified skill areas; it so happens that the survey results were inconclusive in this respect. The full results will be made available to interested parties in due course.

Governor Aziz (Malaysia) said that, in conducting an evaluation of the soundness of the banking system, it was important to look beyond the current state of the banking institutions and to be forward looking. In particular, this diagnostic had to consider the implications of alternative potential domestic economic scenarios, of the possibility of external shocks and the implication of new technology. To effectively do this, Bank Negara found it very helpful to draw upon the expertise across the bank including from the operations, regulation, supervision and economics departments. During the Asian crisis, this approach allowed the authorities to put in place a comprehensive restructuring programme at an early stage in the crisis and in so doing was able to minimise the cost of the crisis on the system. Also, in an emerging market economy such as Malaysia, the central bank played an important role in the development of the financial infrastructure. Having the financial policy, operations and supervision functions integrated within the central bank was helpful in achieving this objective.

Governor Williams (Barbados) thought that the appropriate institutional arrangements had much to do with the sophistication of the economy. Where the economy was rudimentary it was important to combine functions; where markets were more developed a separate regulatory institution might be more appropriate. But if a central bank had overall responsibility for maintaining financial stability, it must be in a position to take preventative measures, so there was a risk for any central bank that was not the supervisor.

Deputy Governor Güemez (Mexico) said that supervision was conducted outside the central bank in Mexico, but the central bank retained the power to regulate the foreign currency activity of banks. The central bank took the view that, in order to maintain financial stability, it must be able to ensure that the banking system was not taking imbalanced, or illiquid, foreign exchange positions.

Governor Alweendo (Namibia) observed that, while some central bank Governors had argued that it was quite possible for them to meet their financial stability responsibilities without conducting supervision, the removal of supervision from them had followed political initiatives, and was not at their own volition. His own feeling was that financial stability was inseparable from supervision – parting them muddied responsibility.

Governor Brash (New Zealand) made three points. First, he thought that the distinction between suppressing volatility and accommodating it was an important one. The experience of New Zealand had also been that its currency had been less variable since its change of regime. Second, there was a trade-off between regulation and market efficiency. In New Zealand banking legislation aimed to create incentives for banks to behave prudently. But banking supervision had been retained for two reasons: the threat of contagion through payment systems, and the implied public guarantee of the banks. Third, regarding foreign ownership of banks, Governor Brash thought that if central banks in small economies wanted a banking sector that was sound, innovative and competitive, overseas banks would have to play a large part.

Governor Sanusi (Nigeria) thought that the quality of banks' management was a crucial factor. That created a dilemma for the central bank: if it 'approved' individuals there were moral hazard issues – but if it did not then it might not get the 'right' people. A second point was that Nigeria had experienced difficulties with non-bank financial institutions which had sprung up outside the supervision of the central bank. Subsequent failures in that sector had adversely affected the banking system. In respect of a volatility-suppressing versus a volatility-accommodating regime, Governor Sanusi asked whether in some circumstances disclosure could be self-defeating.

Governor Mboweni (South Africa) commented that non-bank financial institutions were very difficult to deal with. The central bank had to police them through the banks it *did* regulate.

Governor Massad (Chile) said that his country required very full disclosure from financial institutions, including non-banks, through standard forms based on those in use in industrial countries like the United States.

Chief Executive Yam (Hong Kong) commented that the responsibility of central banks to make markets work better was an important one, and that an integrated approach was helpful in achieving that goal. But provided there was a high degree of cooperation between institutions, the precise institutional arrangements probably did not matter.

Governor George spoke briefly about the experience of the Bank of England. He agreed very much with the comments that financial stability went much further than simply supervision, and that monetary and financial stability were in practice closely connected. As regards institutional arrangements, the erosion of distinctions between different types of financial institution in the UK's large and developed financial system had created parallel pressure for a single regulator. At the same time, the movement towards consumer protection as the primary goal of regulation suggested that the central bank was not the best place to locate a single regulator. Having established a single regulator, it was essential to maintain close relationships with it, including interchange of staff. Before the hiving off of supervision there had been fears that the establishment of a separate regulator would damage career prospects in both the regulator and the central bank. But, in fact, increasingly supervision had required specialist skills such as accountancy, and economists had become reluctant to move to the supervision area from outside. So while careers had lost scope, they had gained consistency.

Appendix 2 Central Bank Governors' Symposium participants

Heads of delegation

Sir Edward George
Governor
Bank of England

Mr Julian Francis
Governor
Central Bank of The Bahamas

Mr Keith Arnold
Governor
Central Bank of Belize

HE Sheikh Abdulla Bin
  Khalifa Al-Khalifa,
Governor
Bahrain Monetary Authority

Dr Arminio Fraga Neto
President
Banco Central do Brasil

Mr Carlos Massad
Governor
Banco Central de Chile

Mr Josef Tošovský
Governor
Ceska Narodni Banka

Mr Momodou Bajo
Governor
Central Bank of The Gambia

Dr Stephen Grenville
Deputy Governor
Reserve Bank of Australia

Dr Marion Williams
Governor
Central Bank of Barbados

Mrs Cheryl-Ann Lister
Chairman
Bermuda Monetary Authority

Mrs Linah Mohohlo
Governor
Bank of Botswana

Mr Gordon Thiessen
Governor
Bank of Canada

Mr Afxentis Afxentiou
Governor
Central Bank of Cyprus

Mr Dwight Venner
Governor
Eastern Caribbean Central Bank

Dr Kwabena Duffuor
Governor
Bank of Ghana

Mr Joseph Yam
Chief Executive
Hong Kong Monetary Authority

Dr Gyorgy Suranyi
President
Magyar Nemzeti Bank

Mr Birgir Isl Gunnarsson
Governor
Sedlabanki Islands

Dr Bimal Jalan
Governor
Reserve Bank of India

Mr Derek Latibeaudiere
Governor
Bank of Jamaica

Mr Micah Cheserem
Governor
Central Bank of Kenya

Sheikh Salem Abdul Aziz Al-Sabah
Governor
Central Bank of Kuwait

Mr Stephen Swaray
Governor
Central Bank of Lesotho

Mr Michael Bonello
Governor
Central Bank of Malta

Mr Rameswurlall Basant Roi
Governor
Bank of Mauritius

Dr Ellias Ngalande
Governor
Reserve Bank of Malawi

Dato' Dr Zeti Aziz
Governor
Bank Negara Malaysia

Mr Guillermo Guemez Garcia
Deputy Governor
Banco de Mexico

Mr Ernesto Gove
Deputy Governor
Banco de Mocambique

Mr Thomas Alweendo
Governor
Bank of Namibia

Dr Joseph Sanusi
Governor
Central Bank of Nigeria

Dr Donald Brash
Governor
Reserve Bank of New Zealand

HE Hamood Sangour Al-Zadjali
Executive President
Central Bank of Oman

Mr Abdulla Khalid Al-Thani
Governor
Qatar Central Bank

Mr Victor Gerashchenko
Chairman
Central Bank of Russia

Mr Hamad AlSayari
Governor
Saudi Arabian Monetary Authority

Mr James Koroma
Governor
Bank of Sierra Leone

Mr Yong Guan Koh
Managing Director
Monetary Authority of Singapore

Mr Rick Houenipwela
Governor
Central Bank of Solomon Islands

Mr Manik Nagahawatte
Deputy Governor
Central Bank of Sri Lanka

Mr Tito Mboweni
Governor
South African Reserve Bank

Mr Martin Dlamini
Governor
Central Bank of Swaziland

Mr Daudi Ballali
Governor
Bank of Tanzania

Ms Amoy Chang Fong
Deputy Governor
Central Bank of Trinidad & Tobago

HE Sultan Bin Nasser Al-Suwaidi
Governor
Central Bank of the United Arab
   Emirates

Dr Louis Kasekende
Deputy Governor
Bank of Uganda

Mr Andrew Kausiama
Governor
Reserve Bank of Vanuatu

Dr Jacob Mwanza
Governor
Bank of Zambia

Dr Leonard Tsumba
Governor
Reserve Bank of Zimbabwe

Bank of England

Mr David Clementi
Deputy Governor

Mr Paul Tucker
Deputy Director

Mr Nigel Jenkinson
Deputy Director

Mr Bill Allen
Deputy Director

Mr Ian Plenderleith
Executive Director

Mr Alastair Clark
Executive Director

Sir Peter Petrie
Professor Dick Brealey
Professor Peter Sinclair
Ms Juliette Healey
Professor David Llewellyn
Miss Chang Shu
Mr Glenn Hoggarth
Mr Farouk Soussa
Professor Alec Chrystal
Mr John Townend
Mr Gabriel Sterne
Mr Joe Ganley
Mr Lavan Mahadeva
Ms Meghan Quinn

Others

Mr Sergio Amaral
Ambassador for Brazil
Banco Central do Brasil

Mr Guillermo Le Fort
Director of International Affairs
Banco Central de Chile

Mr Herbert Carr
Principal Administration Officer
Central Bank of The Gambia

Mr Momodou Ceesay
Director of Research
Central Bank of The Gambia

Dr Kwabena Kwakye
Deputy Head, Research Department
Bank of Ghana

Mr John Herbert Kitcher
Chief Representative
Bank of Ghana

Mr Eddie Yue
Admin Assistant to the Chief
  Executive
Hong Kong Monetary Authority

Miss Josie Wong
Chief Representative, London
  Office
Hong Kong Monetary Authority

Mr Sandip Ghose
Executive Assistant
Reserve Bank of India

Mrs Myrtle Halsall
Divisional Chief
Bank of Jamaica

Mr Mark Lesiit
Personal Assistant to the Governor
Central Bank of Kenya

Mr Chang-Ho Choi
Chief Representative for London
Bank of Korea

Mr Nabil Al-Saqabi
Manager, Governor's Office
Central Bank of Kuwait

Ms Gail Makenete
Director, International Finance
Central Bank of Lesotho

Dr Ahmed Razi
Manager, Economics Department
Bank Negara Malaysia

Mr Jitendra Bissessur
Senior Research Officer
Bank of Mauritius

Dr Clara de Sousa
General Manager
Banco de Mocambique

Mr Adelino Pimpao
Director of Research & Economics
Banco de Mocambique

Mr Mihe Gaomab
Special Assistant to the Governor
Bank of Namibia

Dr M. Ojo
Director of Research
Central Bank of Nigeria

Mr M.O. Durosmim-Etti
Assistant Director, Foreign
  Operations
Central Bank of Nigeria

Dr O. Uchendu
Special Assistant to the Governor
Central Bank of Nigeria

Mr Fahad Faisal Al-Thani
Director
Qatar Central Bank

Dr Bu-Buakei Jabbi
Board Director
Bank of Sierra Leone

Mrs Dolcie Thorpe
Secretary to the Board
Bank of Sierra Leone

Dr Xolile Guma
Advisor to the Governor
South African Reserve Bank

Dr Anila Bandaranaike
Additional Director, Bank
  Supervision
Central Bank of Sri Lanka

Mr John Kimaro
Deputy Director, Communications
Bank of Tanzania

Mr Francis Chipimo
Senior Economist
Bank of Zambia

Dr Hoe Ee Khor
Senior Executive Director
  (Economics)
Monetary Authority of Singapore

Professor Brian Kahn
Deputy Head of Monetary Policy
South African Reserve Bank

Mr Bernard Vilakati
Director, Internal Finance
Central Bank of Swaziland

Mr Edward Katimbo-Mugwangya
Executive Director Supervision
Bank of Uganda

Mr Willard Manungo
Assistant Director (Economic
  Research)
Reserve Bank of Zimbabwe

References

Abel, A.B. and Eberley, J. (1999) 'The Effects of Irreversibility and Uncertainty on Capital Accumulation', *Journal of Monetary Economics*, 44, 339–77.

Abrams, R. and Taylor, M. (2000) 'Issues in the Unification of Financial Sector Supervision', IMF Working Paper 213.

Aghion, P., Bolton, P. and Fries, S. (1999) 'Financial Restructuring in Transition Economies', *Journal of Institutional and Theoretical Economics*, 155, 51–79.

Aghion, P. and Howitt, P. (1992) 'A Model of Growth Through Creative Destruction', *Econometrica*, 60, 323–51.

Aghion, P. and Howitt, P. (1998) *Endogenous Growth Theory*, MIT Press, Cambridge, MA and London.

Ahmed, A.S., Takeda, C. and Thomas, S. (1999) 'Bank Loan Loss Provisions: A Re-examination of Capital Management, Earnings Management, and Signalling Effects', *Journal of Accounting and Economics*, 28, 1–26.

Alba, P., Bhattacharya, G., Claessens, S., Ghash, S. and Hernandez, L. (1998) 'The Role of Macroeconomic and Financial Sector Linkages in East Asia's Financial Crisis', *mimeo*, World Bank.

Alfon, I. and Andrews, P. (1999) 'Cost–Benefit Analysis in Financial Regulation: How to do it and How it Adds Value', Financial Services Authority, *Occasional Paper No. 3*, September.

Allen, F. and Gale, D. (1996) 'Optimal Financial Crises', Working Paper, Wharton School, University of Pennsylvania, December.

Allen, F. and Gale, D. (1998) 'Financial Contagion', Working Paper 98–31, Wharton School, University of Pennsylvania, October.

Ariyoshi, A. *et al.* (1999) 'Country Experiences with the Use and Liberalization of Capital Controls', IMF Report.

Avery, R.B. and Berger, A.N. (1991) 'Risk-Based and Deposit Insurance Reform', *Journal of Banking and Finance*, 15, 847–74.

Backus, D. and Driffill, J. (1985a) 'Inflation and Reputation', *American Economic Review*, 75, 530–8.

Backus, D. and Driffill, J. (1985b) 'Rational Expectations and Policy Credibility Following a Change in Policy Regime', *Review of Economic Studies*, 52, 211–21.

Bagehot, W. (1873) *Lombard Street: A Description of the Money Market*, H.S. King, London.

Bakker, A.F.P. (1996) *The Liberalization of Capital Movements in Europe*, Kluwer, Den Haag, London and Boston.

Banerjee, A.V. (1992) 'A Simple Model of Herd Behavior', *Quarterly Journal of Economics*, 110, 797–817.

Bank for International Settlements (1997a) *Real-time Gross Settlement Systems: A Report Prepared by the Committee on Payment and Settlement Systems of the Central Banks of the G-10 Countries*, Basel.

Bank for International Settlements (1997b) *Core Principles for Banking Supervision*, Basel Committee on Banking Supervision, September.

Bank for International Settlements (1999a) *Sound Practices for Managing Liquidity in Banking Organisations*, Basel Committee on Banking Supervision, Basel.

Bank for International Settlements (1999b) *The Monetary and Regulatory Implications of Changes in the Banking Industry*, BIS Conference Papers 7.

Bank for International Settlements (2000) *Annual Report*, June, Basel.

Bank of England (1999) 'The Financial Stability Conjecture and Outlook', *Financial Stability Review*, Bank of England, Issue No. 6, June.

Barro, R.J. and Gordon, D. (1983a) 'Rules, Discretion and Reputation in a Model of Monetary Policy', *Journal of Monetary Economics*, 12, 101–21.

Barro, R.J. and Gordon, D. (1983b) 'A Positive Theory of Monetary Policy in a Natural Rate Model', *Journal of Political Economy*, 91, 589–610.

Barth, J.R., Brumbaugh, D.R. and Sauerhaft, D. (1986) *Failure Costs of Government-Regulated Financial Firms: The Case of Thrift Institutions*, Federal Home Loan Bank Board, June.

Barth, J., Caudill, S., Hall, T. and Yago, G. (2000) 'Cross-Country Evidence on Banking Crises, Financial Structure and Bank Regulation', paper presented at Western Economic Association International Conference, Vancouver, June.

Basel Committee on Banking Supervision (1988) *International Convergence of Capital Measurement and Capital Standards*, BIS, Basel, July.

Basel Committee on Banking Supervision (1998) *Operational Risk Management*, BIS, Basel, September.

Basel Committee on Banking Supervision (1999a) *Capital Requirements and Bank Behaviour: The Impact of the Basel Accord*, Bank for International Settlements, BIS, Basel, April.

Basel Committee on Banking Supervision (1999b) *Credit Risk Modelling: Current Practices and Applications*, BIS, Basel, April.

Basel Committee on Banking Supervision (1999c) *A New Capital Adequacy Framework*, BIS, Basel, June.

Basel Committee (1999d) *Enhancing Corporate Governance for Banking Organisations*, Basel Committee on Banking Supervision, BIS, Basel.

Benink, H. and Llewellyn, D.T. (1994) 'Fragile Banking in Norway, Sweden and Finland', *Journal of International Financial Markets, Institutions and Money*, 14, 314, 5–20.

Benston, G.J. *et al.* (1986) *Perspectives on Safe & Sound Banking*, MIT Press, Cambridge, MA.

Benston, G.J. and Kaufman, G. (1995) 'Is the Banking and Payments System Fragile?', *Journal of Financial Services Research*, September, 10.

Benston, G.J. and Kaufman, G. (1998) 'Deposit Insurance Reform in the FDIC Improvement Act: The Experience to Date', *Federal Reserve Bank of Chicago*, second quarter, 22, 2, 2–20.

Berger, A.N. and Davies, S. (1994) *The Information Content of Bank Examina-*

tions, Proceedings, Conference on Bank Structure and Competition, Federal Reserve Bank of Chicago.

Berger, A.N., Davies, S. and Flannery, M. (1998) *Comparing Market and Regulatory Assessments of Bank Performance: Who Knows What When?*, Federal Reserve Board Working Paper, March.

Berger, A., De Young, R., Genay, H. and Udell, G.F. (2000) 'Globalisation of Financial Institutions: Evidence from Cross-Border Banking Performance', *Brookings–Wharton Papers on Financial Services*, 3.

Berger, A.N., Herring, R. and Szego, G. (1995) 'The Role of Capital in Financial Institutions', *Journal of Banking and Finance*, 19, 393–430.

Berger, A.N. and Udell, G. (1994) 'Did Risk-Based Capital Allocate Bank Credit and Cause a "Credit Crunch" in the United States?', *Journal of Money, Credit and Banking*, 26, 585–628.

Bernanke, B. (1983) 'Non-monetary Effects of the Financial Crisis in the Propagation of the Great Depression', *American Economic Review*, 73, 257–63.

Bernanke, B. and Gertler, M. (1989) 'Agency Costs, Net Worth, and Business Fluctuations', *American Economic Review*, 79, 14–31.

Bernanke, B.M., Gertler, M. and Gilchrist, S. (1996) 'The Financial Accelerator and the Flight to Quality', *Review of Economics and Statistics*, 78, 1–15.

Bernanke, B.M. and Lown, C. (1992) 'The Credit Crunch', *Brookings Papers on Economic Activity*, 205–39.

Bhattacharya, S., Boot, A. and Thakor, A.V. (1998) 'The Economics of Bank Regulation', *Journal of Money, Credit and Banking*, November, 745–70.

Bhattacharya, S. and Thakor, A.V. (1993) 'Contemporary Banking Theory', *Journal of Financial Intermediation*, 2–50.

Billett, M., Garfinkel, J. and O'Neal, E. (1998) 'The Cost of Market Versus Regulatory Discipline in Banking', *Journal of Financial Economics*, 48, 333–58.

Black, F. (1980) 'The Magic in Earnings: Economic Earnings versus Accounting Earnings', *Financial Analysts Journal*, 36, 3–8.

Black, J. (1994) 'Which Arrow? Rule Type and Regulatory Policy', *Public Law*, June.

Blinder, A. (2000) Conference presentation *in Monetary Policy-Making Under Uncertainty*, European Central Bank, Frankfurt.

Bliss, R. and Flannery, M. (2000) 'Market Discipline in the Governance of US Bank Holding Companies: Monitoring vs Influency', Working Paper Series Federal Reserve Bank of Chicago, WP-00-03, Chicago, March.

Blum, J. and Hellwig, M. (1995) 'The Macroeconomic Implications of Capital Adequacy Requirements for Banks', *European Economic Review*, 39, 739–49.

Board of Governors of the Federal Reserve System (1994) 'Views on the Consolidation of Bank Supervision and Regulation', Memorandum presented to the United States Committee on Banking, Housing and Urban Affairs, March.

Bolton, P. and Freixas, X. (2000) 'Equity, Bonds and Bank Debt: Capital Structure and Financial Market Equilibrium under Asymmetric Information', *Journal of Political Economy*, 108, 324–51.

Boot, A. and Thakor, A.V. (2000) 'Can Relationship Banking Survive Competition?', *Journal of Finance*, 55, 679–713.

Bordo, M.D. (1990) 'The Lender of Last Resort: Alternative Views and Historical Experience', *Federal Reserve Bank of Richmond Economic Review*, Jan/Feb, 76, 18–29.

Borio, C. and Filosa, R. (1994) 'The Changing Borders of Banking: Trends and Implications', *BIS Economic Paper, No. 43*, December.

Boyd, J.H. and Prescott, E.C. (1986) 'Financial Intermediary-Coalitions', *Journal of Economic Theory*, 38, 211–32.

Brealey, R. (1999) 'The Asian Crisis: Lessons for Crisis Management and Prevention', *Bank of England Quarterly Bulletin*, August, 285–96.

Brealey, R. *et al.* (2000) 'Financial Stability and Central Banks', a report for the Central Bank Governors' Symposium, Centre for Central Banking Studies, Bank of England.

Brenton, P., Scott, H. and Sinclair, P. (1997) *International Trade*, Oxford University Press, Oxford.

Briault, C. (1997) *Discussant to F. Bruni*, in *Towards More Effective Monetary Policy*, I. Kuroda (ed.), Macmillan, London, 379–86.

Briault, C. (1999) 'The Rationale of a Single Regulator', *Occasional Paper, No. 2*, Financial Service Authority, London.

Brouwer, H. (2000) *Report on Financial Stability*, available at the website: http://ne.eu.int/newsroom

Brownbridge, M. and Kirkpatrick, C. (2000) 'Financial Sector Regulation: Lessons of the Asian Crisis', *Development Policy Review*, forthcoming.

Bruni, F. (1997) 'Central Bank Independence in the European Union', in *Towards More Effective Monetary Policy*, I. Kuroda (ed.), Macmillan, London, 341–69.

Bryant, J. (1980) 'A Model of Bank Reserves, Bank Runs and Deposit Insurance', *Journal of Banking and Finance*, 4, 335–44.

Buchs, T.D. (1999) 'Financial Crisis in the Russian Federation: Are the Russians Learning to Tango?', *The Economics of Transition*, 7, 687–716.

Calomiris, C. (1997) *The Postmodern Safety Net*, American Enterprise Institute, Washington, DC.

Capie, F., Goodhart, C., Fischer, S. and Schnadt, N. (1994) *The Future of Central Banking: The Tercentenary Symposium of the Bank of England*, Cambridge University Press, Cambridge.

Caprio, G. (1997) 'Safe and Sound Banking in Developing Countries: We're not in Kansas Anymore', *Policy Research Paper, No. 1739*, World Bank, Washington.

Caprio, G. and Klingebiel, D. (1996) 'Bank Insolvency: Bad Luck, Bad Policy, and Bad Banking', in M. Bruno and B. Pleskovic (eds) *Annual Bank Conference on Development Economics*, World Bank.

Cardoso, E. and Goldfajn, I. (1998) 'Capital Flows to Brazil: the Endogeneity of Capital Controls', *IMF Staff Papers*, 45, 161–202.

Claessens, S., Dooley, M.P. and Warner, A. (1995) 'Portfolio Capital Flows: Hot or Cold?', *World Bank Economic Review*, 9, 1, 153–74.

Cole, H.L. and Kehoe, T.J. (2000) 'Self-fulfilling Debt Crises', *Review of Economic Studies*, 67, 91–116.

Cole, R.A. and Gunther, J.W. (1995) 'Separating the Likelihood and Timing of Bank Failure', *Journal of Banking and Finance*, 19: 1073–89.

Cooper, R.N. (1999) 'Should Capital Controls be Banished?', *Brookings Papers in Economic Activity*, 89–141.

Cordella, T. and Yeyati, L. (1997) 'Public Disclosures and Bank Failures', *IMF Working Paper WP/97/96*, Washington.

Cornett, M.M. and Tehranian, H. (1994) 'An Examination of Voluntary Versus

Involuntary Security Issuance by Commercial Banks', *Journal of Financial Economics*, 35, 99–122.

Corrigan, E.G. (1990) *Statement Before US Senate Committee on Banking, Housing and Urban Affairs*, Washington, DC.

Corrigan, E.G. (1990 and 1991) *Statements by President Gerald Corrigan of Federal Reserve Bank of New York before the United States Senate Committee on Banking, Housing and Urban Affairs*, May.

Corsetti, G., Pesenti, P. and Rabini, N. (1998) 'What Caused the Asia Currency and Financial Crisis?', Banca D'Italia, Temi di Discussione, December.

Courtis, N. (1999) *How Countries Supervise their Banks, Insurers and Securities Markets*, Central Banking Publications, London.

Crockett, A. (1996) 'The Theory and Practice of Financial Stability', *De Economist*, 144, 4, 531–68.

Cukierman, A. (1992) 'Central Bank Strategy, Credibility and Independence: Theory and Evidence', MIT Press, Cambridge, MA.

Dale, R. (1996) *Risk and Regulation in Global Securities Markets*, Wiley, London.

Davies, H. (1997) 'Financial Regulation: Why, How and by Whom?' *Bank of England Quarterly Bulletin*, February, 107–12.

Davis, E.P. (1999) 'Financial Data Needs for Macroprudential Surveillance – What are the Key Indicators of Risks to Domestic Financial Stability?', *Handbooks in Central Banking Lecture Series, 2*, Centre for Central Banking Studies, Bank of England.

De Bandt, O. and Hartmann, P. (1998) 'What is Systemic Risk Today?', *Risk Measurement and Systemic Risk: Proceedings of the Second Joint Central Bank Research Conference*, Bank of Japan, November, 37–84.

De Bonis, R., Giustiniani, A. and Gomel, G. (1999) 'Crises and Bail-Outs of Banks and Countries: Linkages, Analogies, and Differences', *The World Economy*, 22, 1, 55–86.

De Krivoy, R. (2000) *Collapse: The Venezuelan Banking Crisis of 1994*, Group of Thirty, Washington, DC.

Demirgüç-Kunt, A. and Detragiache, E. (1998a) 'Financial Liberalization and Financial Fragility', in B. Pleskovic and J.E. Stiglitz (eds) *Annual World Bank Conference on Development Economics*, 1997, World Bank.

Demirgüç-Kunt, A. and Detragiache, E. (1998b) 'The Determinants of Bank Crisis in Developing and Developed Countries', *IMF Staff Papers*, March.

Demirgüç-Kunt, A. and Detragiache, E. (2000) 'Does Deposit Insurance Increase Banking System Stability?', *IMF Working Papers WP/00/3*, Washington.

Demirgüç-Kunt, A. and Huizinga, H. (2000) 'Market Discipline and Financial Safety Net Design', World Bank Policy Research Working Paper, April

Dewatripoint, M. and Tirole, J. (1994) *The Prudential Regulation of Banks*, MIT Press, Cambridge, MA.

Di Noia, C. and Di Giorgio, G. (1999) 'Should Banking Supervision and Monetary Policy Tasks be Given to Different Agencies?', *International Finance*, 2, 3, November, 361–78.

Diamond, D.W. (1984) 'Financial Intermediation and Delegated Monitoring', *Review of Economic Studies*, July, 393–414.

Diamond, D.W. and Dybvig, P. (1983) 'Bank Runs, Deposit Insurance, and Liquidity', *Journal of Political Economy*, 91, 401–19.

Diamond, D.W. and Rajan, R.G. 'A Theory of Bank Capital', *Journal of Finance*, forthcoming.

Dixit, A.K. (1997) 'Investment and Employment Dynamics in the Short Run and the Long Run', *Oxford Economic Papers*, 49, 1–20.

Dooley, M.P. (1996) 'A Survey of Literature on Controls Over International Capital Transactions', *IMF Staff Papers*, 43, 639–87.

Dornbusch, R. (1986) 'Special Exchange Rates for Capital Account Transactions', *World Bank Economic Review*, 11–33.

Dow, J. (2000) 'What Is Systemic Risk? Moral Hazard, Initial Shocks and Propagation', Unpublished paper, London Business School, January.

Dowd, K. (1992) 'Models of Banking Instability: A Partial Review of the Literature', *Journal of Economic Surveys*, 6, 107–32.

Dubouchet, T. (2000) 'Les organes de supervision bancaire au sein de l'UEM', extract, 346–97, from *Doctoral Thesis, Economics Department, Université Lumière Lyon 2*, on 'La Politique Micromonétaire'.

Dunbar, N. (2000) *Inventing Money*, John Wiley & Sons, Chichester.

Ediz, T., Michael, L. and Perraudin, W. (1998) *Bank Capital Dynamics and Regulatory Policy*, Bank of England.

Edwards, F.R. (1996) *The New Finance: Regulation and Financial Stability*, The AEI Press, Washington.

Edwards, S. (1998) 'Capital Flows, Real Exchange Rates and Capital Controls: Some Latin American Experiences', *NBER Working Paper 6800*.

Eichengreen, B., Tobin, J. and Wyplosz, C. (1995) 'Two Cases for Sand in the Wheels of International Finance', *Economic Journal*, 105, 162–72.

Enoch, C., Stella, P. and Khamis, M. (1997) 'Transparency and Ambiguity in Central Bank Safety Net Operations', *IMF Working Paper, WP/97/138*.

Estrella, A. (1998) 'Formulas or Supervision? Remarks on the Future of Regulatory Capital', *Federal Reserve Bank of New York, Economic Policy Review*, October.

Euro-Currency Standing Committee (1997) 'Report of a Task Force on the Implications of Structural Change for the Nature of Systemic Risk', Paper discussed at ECSC meeting, December.

European Central Bank (2000) *Monetary Policy-Making Under Uncertainty*, Proceedings of the Conference on 3–4 December 1999, pamphlet, ECB, Frankfurt.

European Union Economic and Financial Committee (2000) *Report on Financial Stability*, Brussels ('Brouwer' Report).

Evanoff, D. and Wall, L. (2000) 'Subordinated Debt and Bank Capital Reform', paper presented at Western Economic Association International Conference, Vancouver, June.

Evans, H. (2000) 'Plumbers and Architects: A Supervisory Perspective on International Financial Architecture', *Occasional Paper, No. 4*, Financial Services Authority, London, January.

Falkena, H. and Llewellyn, D.T. (2000) *The Economics of Banking*, SA Financial Sector Forum, Johannesburg.

Farrell, G.N. (2000) 'An Empirical Analysis of South Africa's Financial Rand Exchange Rate System 1985–95', University of Birmingham Ph.D. Thesis.

Favero, C., Freixas, X., Persson, T. and Wyplosz, C. (2000) *One Money, Many Countries*, CEPR, London.

Ferguson, R. (2000) 'Alternative Approaches to Financial Supervision and Regulation', *Journal of Financial Services Research*, 17, 1, 297–303.

Financial Services Authority (FSA) (2000) 'A New Regulator for the New Millennium', pamphlet.

Financial Stability Forum (2000) *International Guidance on Deposit Insurance – A Consultative Process*, FSF Working Group, June.

'Financial System Inquiry Final Report' (Wallis Report) (1997) 'Financial Safety', Australian Government Publishers Service, March.

Fischer, K. and Gueyie, J. (1995) *Financial Liberalisation and Bank Solvency*, University of Laval, Quebec.

Fischer, S. (1999) 'On the Need for an International Lender of Last Resort', Paper prepared for the American Economic Association and the American Finance Association Meetings, IMF, mimeo.

Flannery, M. (1996) 'Financial Crises, Payment System Problems, and Discount Window Lending', *Journal of Money, Credit and Banking*, 28, 804–24.

Flannery, M. (1998) 'Using Market Information in Prudential Bank Supervision: A Review of the US Empirical Evidence', *Journal of Money, Credit and Banking*, August, 273–305.

Fleming, J.M. (1974) 'Dual Exchange Rates and Other Remedies for Disruptive Capital Flows', *IMF Staff Papers*, 21, 1–20.

Flood, R.P. and Garber, P.M. (1984) 'Collapsing Exchange-rate Regimes: Some Linear Examples', *Journal of International Economics*, 17, 1–13.

Flood, R.P. and Marion, N. (1998) 'Perspectives on the Recent Currency Crisis Literature', *NBER Working Paper 6380*.

Flood, R.P. and Rose, A.K. (1999) 'Understanding Exchange Rate Volatility Without the Contrivance of Macroeconomics', *Economic Journal*, 109, F660–72.

Freixas, X., Giannini, C., Hoggarth, G. and Soussa, F. (2000) 'Lender of Last Resort? What Have We Learned Since Bagehot?', *Journal of Financial Services Research*, 18, 1, 63–84.

Freixas, X., Parigi, B. and Rochet, J.C. (1998a) 'Systemic Risk, Interbank Relations and Liquidity Provision by the Central Bank', Mimeo, IDEI.

Freixas, X., Parigi, B. and Rochet, J.C. (1998b) 'The Lender of Last Resort: A Theoretical Foundation', Mimeo, IDEI.

Freixas, X. and Rochet, J.C. (1997) *Microeconomics of Banking*, MIT Press, Cambridge, MA.

Fries, S., Raiser, M. and Stern, N.H. (1999) 'Stress Test for Reform: Transition and East Asian Contagion', *The Economics of Transition*, 7, 535–67.

Fry, M.J. (1995) *Money, Interest and Banking in Financial Development*, 2nd edn, Johns Hopkins University Press, Baltimore.

Fry, M.J., Goodhart, C. and Almeida, A. (1996) *Central Banking in Developing Countries: Objectives, Activities and Independence*, Routledge, London and New York.

Fry, M.J., Julius, D., Mahadeva, L., Roger, S. and Sterne, G. (2000) 'Key Issues in the Choice of Monetary Policy Framework', in L. Mahadeva and G. Sterne (eds) *Monetary Policy Frameworks in a Global Context*, Routledge, London and New York, 1–216.

Fry, M.J., Kilato, I., Roger, S., Senderowicz, K., Sheppard, D., Solis, F. and Trundle, J. (1999) *Payment Systems in Global Perspective*, Routledge, London and New York

Fry, M.J. and Sinclair, P. (1996) 'Monetary Integration in Central and Eastern Europe: How to Proceed?' in H. Siebert (ed.) *Monetary Policy in an Integrated World Economy*, Mohr, Tuebingen.

Furfine, C. (1999) 'Interbank Exposures: Quantifying the Risk of Contagion', *Bank For International Settlements Working Paper, No. 70.*

Garcia, G. (1999a) 'Deposit Insurance: A Survey of Actual and Best Practices', *IMF Working Paper WP/99/54*, Washington.

Garcia, G. (1999b) 'Deposit Insurance: Obtaining the Benefits and Avoiding the Pitfalls', *IMF Working Paper*, August.

Garcia, G. (2000) 'Deposit Insurance and Crisis Management', *IMF Working Paper WP/00/57*, Washington.

Garcia, G. and Plautz, E. (1988) 'The Federal Reserve: Lender of Last Resort', Ballinger, Cambridge, MA.

Genotte, G. and Pyle, D. (1991) 'Capital Controls and Bank Risk', *Journal of Banking and Finance*, 15, 805–24.

George, E.A.J. (1994) 'The Pursuit of Financial Stability', *Bank of England Quarterly Bulletin*, February, 60–6.

George, E.A.J. (1997) 'Are Banks Still Special?', *Bank of England Quarterly Bulletin*, February, 113–18.

Gertler, M. and Gilchrist, S. (1994) 'Monetary Policy, Business Cycles, and the Behaviour of Small Manufacturing Firms', *Quarterly Journal of Economics*, 109, 309–40.

Giannini, C. (1999) 'Enemy of None but a Common Friend of All? An International Perspective on the Lender of Last Resort Function', *Princeton Essays in International Finance*, No. 214.

Glaessner, T. and Mas, I. (1995) 'Incentives and the Resolution of Bank Distress', *World Bank Research Observer*, 10, 1, 53–73.

Godlayn, I. and Valdes, R. (1997) 'Capital Flows and the Twin Crises: The Role of Liquidity', *IMF Working Paper*, 97/87, July.

Goldstein, M. and Turner, P. (1996) 'Banking Crises in Emerging Economies', *BIS Economic Papers, No. 46*, BIS, Basel.

Goodfriend, M. and Lacker, J.M. (1999) 'Limited Commitment and Central Bank Lending', *Federal Reserve Bank of Richmond Working Paper, 99–2.*

Goodhart, C.A.E. (1996) 'Some Regulatory Concerns', *Swiss Journal of Economics and Statistics*, 132, 613–35.

Goodhart, C.A.E. (1999) 'Myths About the Lender of Last Resort', *International Finance*, 2, 3.

Goodhart, C.A.E. (ed.) (2000) *Which Lender of Last Resort for Europe?*, Central Banking Publications, London.

Goodhart, C.A.E., Hartmann, P., Llewellyn, D.T., Rojas-Suarez, L. and Weisbrod, S. (1998) *Financial Regulation: Why, How and Where Now?*, Routledge, London.

Goodhart, C.A.E. and Huang, H. (1999) 'A Model of the Lender of Last Resort', *LSE Financial Markets Group Discussion Paper, dp0131.*

Goodhart, C.A.E. and Schoenmaker, D. (1993) 'Institutional Separation Between Supervisory and Monetary Agencies', *LSE Financial Markets Group Special Paper*, No. 52.

Goodhart, C.A.E. and Schoenmaker, D. (1995) 'Should the Functions of Monetary Policy and Bank Supervision be Separated?', *Oxford Economic Papers*, 39, 75–89.

Goodhart, C.A.E. and Schoenmaker, D. (1998) 'Institutional Separation Between Supervisory and Monetary Agencies', in C. Goodhart (ed.) *The Emerging Framework of Financial Regulation*, Central Banking Publications Ltd, London.

Gorton, G. (1988) 'Banking Panics and Business Cycles', *Oxford Economic Papers*, 751–81.

Gorton, G. and Winton, A. (1996) 'The Social Costs of Bank Capital', *Proceedings of the Conference on Bank Structure and Competition*, Federal Reserve Bank of Chicago.

Greenspan, A. (1994) Testimony on banking regulation, before the United States Senate Committee on Banking, Housing and Urban Affairs, 2 March.

Greenspan, A. (1998) 'Our Banking History', Remarks by Chairman Alan Greenspan Before the Annual Meeting and Conference of the Conference of State Bank Supervisors, Nashville, Tennessee, 2 May.

Grilli, V., Masciadaro, D. and Tabellini, G. (1991) 'Political and Monetary Institutions and Public Financial Policies in the Industrial Economies', *Economic Policy*, 6, 341–92.

Grilli, V. and Milesi-Ferretti, G-M. (1995) 'Economic Effects and Structural Determinants of Capital Controls', *IMF Working Paper WP/95/31*.

Grossman, G. and Helpman, E. (1992) *Innovation and Growth in the Global Economy*, MIT Press, Cambridge, MA.

Group of Thirty (G–30) (1997) 'Global Institutions, National Supervision and Systemic Risk', pamphlet, G-30, Washington, DC.

Guttentag, J. and Herring, R. (1983) 'The Lender of Last Resort Function in an International Context', *Princeton Essays in International Finance*, No. 151, May.

Hall, S. and Miles, D. (1990) 'Monitoring Bank Risk: A Market Based Approach', Discussion Paper, Birkbeck College, London, April.

Halme, L. (2000) 'Bank Corporate Governance and Financial Stability', in L. Halme, C. Hawkesby, J. Healey, I. Soapar and F. Soussa, *Selected Issues for Financial Safety Nets and Market Discipline*, Centre for Central Banking Studies, London.

Hammond, P.J. (1990) 'Theoretical Progress in Public Economics: a Provocative Reassessment', *Oxford Economic Papers*, and in P. Sinclair and M. Slater (eds) *Taxation, Private Information and Capita*, Oxford University Press, 1991, 6–33.

Hancock, G. and Wilcox, J.A. (1998) 'The Credit Crunch and the Availability of Credit to Small Business', *Journal of Banking and Finance*, 22, 983–1014.

Haubrich, J.G. (1996) 'Combining Bank Supervision and Monetary Policy', *Economic Commentary*, 11, 1–9.

Haubrich, J.G. and Wachtel, P. (1993) 'Capital Requirements and Shifts in Commercial Bank Portfolios', *Federal Reserve Bank of Cleveland Economic Review*, 29, 2–15.

Hawkesby, C. (2000) *Central Bank and Supervisors: The Question of Institutional Structure and Responsibilities*, Centre for Central Banking Studies, May.

Heffernan, S.A. (1986) *Sovereign Risk Analysis*, John Wiley & Sons, Chichester.

Heffernan, S.A. (1996) *Modern Banking in Theory and Practice*, John Wiley & Sons, Chichester.

Heller, H.R. (1991) 'Prudential Supervision and Monetary Policy', in J.A. Frenkel and M. Goldstein (eds) *International Financial Policy: Essays in Honour of Jacques J. Polak*, International Monetary Fund, Washington, DC, 269–81.

Hellman, T.P., Murdock, K. and Stiglitz, J.E. (2000) 'Liberalization, Moral Hazard in Banking, and Prudential Regulation: Are Capital Requirements Enough?' *American Economic Review*, 90, 147–65.

Hellwig, M. (1995) 'Systemic Aspects of Risk Management in Banking and Finance', *Swiss Journal of Economics and Statistics*.

Hoggarth, G., Reis, R. and Saporta, V. (2000) *Costs of Banking Instability: Some Empirical Evidence*, Bank of England.

Humphrey, T. (1989) 'The Lender of Last Resort: The Concept in History', *Federal Reserve Bank of Richmond Economic Review*, Mar/Apr, 8–16.

International Accounting Standards Committee (1997) 'Accounting for Financial Assets and Financial Liabilities', discussion paper.

International Monetary Fund (1998) 'Chapter 4: Financial Crises: Characteristics and Indicators of Vulnerability', *World Economic Outlook*, May.

International Monetary Fund (1999) *Code of Good Practices on Transparency in Monetary and Financial Policies: Declaration of Principles*, IMF, Washington.

Jackson, P. *et al.* (1999) *Capital Requirements and Bank Behaviour: The Impact of the Basel Accord*, Bank for International Settlements, BIS, Basel.

James, C. (1991) 'The Losses Realised in Bank Failures', *Journal of Finance*, September, 1223–42.

Jayaratne, J. and Strahan, P.E. (1996) 'The Finance–Growth Nexus: Evidence from Bank Branch Deregulation', *Quarterly Journal of Economics*, 111, 639–70.

Jensen, M.C. (1989) 'The Eclipse of the Public Corporation', *Harvard Business Review*, 67, 61–74.

Johnston, R.B. and Tamirisa, N.T. (1998a) 'Economic Effects and Structural Determinants of Capital Controls', *IMF Working Paper WP/98/181*.

Johnston, R.B. and Tamirisa, N.T. (1998b) 'Why Do Countries Use Capital Controls?', *IMF Working Paper WP/98/181*.

Jones, D.S. and King, K.K. (1995) 'The Implementation of Prompt Corrective Action: An Assessment', *Journal of Banking and Finance*, 19, 491–510.

Kaminsky, G. and Reinhart, C. (1998) 'The Twin Crises: The Causes of Banking and Balance of Payments Problems', *International Finance Discussion Papers*, No. 554, Board of Governors, Federal Reserve System.

Kaminsky, G.L. and Reinhart, M.R. (1999) 'The Twin Crises: The Cause of Banking and Balance of Payments Problems', *American Economic Review*, 89, 473–500.

Kane, E. (2000) 'Dynamic Inconsistency of Capital Forbearance: Long Run vs Short Run Effects of Too-Big-To-Fail Policymaking', paper presented to IMF Central Banking Conference, Washington, DC, June.

Kaufman, G. (1990) 'Resolving, Recapitalizing, and Restructuring Insolvent Banks and Banking Systems', in Yoon Hyung and Kim (eds) *Restructuring Korea's Financial Market*, Korean Development Institute, Seoul.

Kaufman, G. (1991) 'Lender of Last Resort: A Contemporary Perspective', *Journal of Financial Services Research*, 5, 95–110.

Kaufman, G. (1994) 'Bank Contagion: A Review of the Theory and Evidence', *Journal of Financial Services Research*, 18, 123–50.

Kaufman, G. (1996) 'Bank Failures, Systemic Risk, and Bank Regulation', *Cato Journal*, 16, 1, Spring/Summer, 17–45.

Kaufman, H. (2000) *On Money and Markets*, McGraw-Hill, New York.

Kim, D. and Santomero, A.M. (1988) 'Risk in Banking and Capital Regulation', *Journal of Finance*, 43, 1219–33.

Kim, M.S. and Kross, W. (1998) 'The Impact of the 1989 Change in Bank Capital Standards on Loan Loss Provisions and Loan Write-Offs', *Journal of Accounting and Economics*, 25, 69–99.

King, M.A. and Goodhart, C.A.E. (1987) 'Financial Stability and the Lender of Last Resort: A Note', *LSE Financial Markets Group Special Paper Series*, Special Paper No. 2.

King, R.G. and Levine, R. (1993) 'Finance, Entrepreneurship and Growth: Theory and Evidence', *Journal of Monetary Economics*, 32, 513–42.

Klein, M. and Giovanni, O. (1999) 'Capital Account Liberalization, Financial Depth and Economic Growth', *NBER Working Paper 7384*.

Konskenkyla, H. (2000) 'The Nordic Countries' Banking Crises and the Lessons Learned', paper presented at FDIC Conference, Washington, DC, September.

Krivoy, R. de (2000) *Collapse: The Venezuelan Banking Crisis of 1994*, Group of Thirty: Washington, DC.

Krugman, P. (1979) 'A Model of Balance of Payments Crises', *Journal of Money Credit and Banking*, 11, 311–25.

Kupiec, H. and O'Brien, J. (1997) 'The Pre-Commitment Approach: Using Incentives to Set Market Risk Capital Requirements', *Finance and Economics Discussion Series*, No. 1997–14, Federal Reserve Board, Washington, DC, March.

Laidler, D. (1998) 'Monetarism, Microfoundations and the Theory of Monetary Policy', *Working Paper No. 88076*, The Centre for the Study of International Economic Relations, University of Western Ontario.

Lane, T. (1993) 'Market Discipline', *IMF Staff Papers*, March, 55.

Lane, W.R., Looney, S.W. and Wansley, J.W. (1986) 'An Application of the Cox Proportional Hazards Model to Bank Failure', *Journal of Banking and Finance*, 10, 511–31.

Lang, W. and Robertson, D. (2000) 'Analysis of Proposals for a Minimum Subordinated Debt Requirement', paper presented at Western Economic Association International Conference, Vancouver, June.

Lannoo, K. (1999) *Challenges to the Structure of Financial Supervision in the EU*, Centre for European Policy Studies (CEPS), Brussels.

Laurens, B. (1997) 'The Use of Standing Facilities in Indirect Monetary Management: Country Practices and Operational Features', Operational Paper, International Monetary Fund, April.

Levine, R. (1997) 'Financial Development and Economic Growth: Views and Agenda', *Journal of Economic Literature*, 688–726.

Levine, R. (1999) 'Law, Finance, and Economic Growth', *Journal of Financial Intermediation*, 8, 8–35.

Lindgren, C.J., Garcia, G. and Saal, M. (1996) *Bank Soundness and Macroeconomic Policy*, International Monetary Fund, Washington.

Llewellyn, D.T. (1999) 'The Economic Rationale of Financial Regulation', *Occasional Paper*, No. 1, Financial Services Authority, London.

Llewellyn, D.T. (2000) 'Regulatory Lessons from Recent Banking Crises', *De Nederlandsche Bank Discussion Paper*, Amsterdam.

Louis, J.-V. *et al.* (1995) *Banking Supervision in the European Community – Institutional Aspects*, Editions de l'Université de Bruxelles, Brussels, Report of a Working Group of the ECU Institute Composed of J.V. Louis, Chairman, I. Begg, E. Garcia de Enterria, N. Horn, E. de Lhoneux, L.G. Radicati di Brozolo, R. Smits and J. Stoufflet.

Lucas, R.E. (1992) 'On Efficiency and Distribution', *Economic Journal*, 102, 233–47.

McCallum, B. (2000) 'Theoretical Issues Pertaining to Monetary Unions', in F. Capie and G.E. Wood (eds) *Currency Unions: Theory, History, Public Choice*, Palgrave, London, forthcoming.

McCloskey, D.N. (1970) 'Did Victorian Britain Fail?' *Economic History Review*, 23, 446–59.

McDonough, W.J. (1998) 'Statement Before the Committee on Banking and Financial Services, US House of Representatives', Washington, DC.

McKinnon, R.I. and Oates, W.E. (1966) *The Implications of International Integration for Monetary, Fiscal and Exchange Rate Policies*, International Finance Section, Princeton University, Princeton, New Jersey.

Mahadeva, L. and Sterne, G. (eds) (2000*) Monetary Policy Frameworks in a Global Context*, Routledge, London.

Mangano, G. (1998) 'Measuring Central Bank Independence: A Tale of Subjectivity and of its Consequences', *Oxford Economic Papers*, 50, 468–92.

Mankiw, N.G. and Whinston, M.D. (1986) 'Free Entry and Social Inefficiency', *Rand Journal of Economics*, 17, 48–58.

Mantousek, R. and Taci, A. (2000a) 'Banking Regulation and Supervision in Associative Countries', in D. Green (ed.) *Banking and Financial Stability in Central Europe*, Edward Elgar, forthcoming.

Mantousek, R. and Taci, A. (2000b) 'The Assessment of the Costs and Benefits of the Small and Medium Sized Commercial Banks Within the Czech Banking Sector', in J.Hoelscher (ed.) *Financial Turbulence and Capital Markets in Transition Countries*, Macmillan, forthcoming.

Marion, N. (1999) 'Some Parallels Between Currency and Banking Crises', in P. Isard, A. Razin and A.K. Rose (eds) *International Finance in Turmoil: Essays in Honor of Robert P. Flood*, IMF and Kluwer, Dordrecht.

Mendoza, O.G. (1995) *Crónica Involuntaria de una Crisis Inconclusa*, Editorial Planeta de Venezuela, Caracas.

Merton, R.C. (1995) 'Financial Innovation and the Management and Regulation of Financial Institutions', *Journal of Banking and Finance*, 19, 461–81.

Miller, M.H. (1995) 'Do the MM Propositions Apply to Banks?' *Journal of Banking and Finance*, 19, 483–9.

Mishkin, F.S. (1997) 'The Causes and Propagation of Financial Instability: Lessons for Policy Makers', in *Maintaining Financial Stability in a Global Economy*, Federal Reserve Bank of Kansas City, Kansas City.

Mitchell, J. (2000) 'Theories of Soft Budget Constraints in the Analysis of Banking Crises', *The Economics of Transition*, 8, 59–100.

Modigliani, F. and Miller, M.H. (1958) 'The Cost of Capital, Corporation Finance and the Theory of Investment', *American Economic Review*, 48, 261–97.

Montiel, P. and Reinhart, C. (1999) 'Do Capital Controls and Macroeconomic Policies Influence the Volume and Composition of Capital Flows?' Mimeo, University of Maryland.

Morris, S. (2000) 'Contagion', *Review of Economic Studies*, 67, 53–78.

Morris, S. and Shin, H. (1998) 'Unique Equilibrium in a Model of Self-fulfilling Currency Attacks', *American Economic Review*, 88, 587–97.

Morris, S. and Shin, H. (1999) 'Risk Management with Interdependent Choice', *Financial Stability Review*, Bank of England, November, 141–50.

Mullineux, A. and Sinclair, P. (2000) 'Oligopolistic Banks: Theory and Policy Implications', Paper to be presented to Royal Economic Society and Queensland Financial Stability Conferences, June–July 2000.

Myers, S.C. (1977) 'The Determinants of Corporate Borrowing', *Journal of Financial Economics*, 5, 146–75.

Myers, S.C. and Majluf, N.S. (1984) 'Corporate Financing When Firms Have Information That Investors Do Not Have', *Journal of Financial Economics*, 13, 187–222.

Nakaso, H., Hattori, M., Nagae, T., Hamada, H., Kanamori, T., Kamiguchi, H., Dezawa, T., Takahashi, K., Kamimura, A., Suzuki, T. and Sumida, K. (2000) 'Changes in Bank Behaviour during the Financial Crisis: Experiences of the Financial Crisis in Japan', paper presented to IMF Central Banking Conference, Washington, DC, June.

Neely, C. (1999) 'An Introduction to Capital Controls', *Federal Reserve Bank of St Louis Review*, November/December, 13–30.

Newbery, D. and Stiglitz, J.E. (1984) 'Pareto Inferior Trade', *Review of Economic Studies*, 51, 1–12.

Obstfeld, M. (1986) 'Rational and Self-fulfilling Balance-of-Payments Crises', *American Economic Review*, 76, 72–81.

Obstfeld, M. (1996) 'Models of Currency Crises with Self-fulfilling Features', *European Economic Review*, 40, 1037–47.

Obstfeld, M. (1998) 'The Global Capital Market: Benefactor or Menace?' *Journal of Economic Perspectives*, 12, 4, 9–30.

Obstfeld, M. and Taylor, A. (1998) 'The Great Depression as a Watershed: International Capital Mobility over the Long Run', in M. Bordo, C. Goldin and E. Whites (eds) *The Defining Moment: the Great Depression and the American Economy in the Twentieth Century*, 353–402.

Oliner, G. and Rudebusch, G. (1993) 'Is There a Bank Credit Channel to Monetary Policy?', *Working Paper*, Federal Reserve Board of Governors.

Pauli, R. (2000) 'Payments Remain Fundamental for Banks and Central Banks', *Bank of Finland Discussion Papers*, 6/2000.

Peek, J., Rosengren, E.S. and Tootell, G.M.B. (1999) 'Is Banking Supervision Central to Central Banking?', *Quarterly Journal of Economics*, 114, 2, 629–53.

Peek, J., Rosengren, E. and Tootell, G. (1998) 'Does the Federal Reserve have an Informational Advantage? You can Bank on it', *Working Paper No. 98-2*, Federal Reserve Bank of Boston, April.

Petersen, M.A. and Rajan, R.G. (1994) 'The Benefits of Firm–Creditor Relationships: Evidence from Small Business Data', *Journal of Finance*, 49, 3–37.

Powell, A. (2000) 'Safety First Monetary and Financial Policies for Emerging Economies', *IMF MEA Conference Papers*, IMF, Washington.

Prati, A. and Schinasi, G. (1999) 'Financial Stability in European Economic and Monetary Union', mimeo.

Prendergast, C. (1993) 'The Provision of Incentives in Firms', *Journal of Economic Literature,* March, 7–63.

Prowse, S. (1997) 'Corporate Control in Commercial Banks', *Journal of Financial Research*, 20, 509–27.

Rajan, R.G. and Zingales, L. (1998) 'Financial Dependence and Growth', *American Economic Review*, 88, 559–86.

Reid, M. (1982) *The Secondary Banking Crisis, 1973–75: Its Causes and Course*, Macmillan, London.

Reinhart, C. and Smith, T. (1997) 'Temporary Capital Controls', Mimeo, University of Maryland.

'Report on Financial Stability' (Brouwer Report) (2000) issued by the Economic and Financial Committee under Informal Ecofin, April.

Richardson, J. and Stephenson, M. (2000) 'Some Aspects of Regulatory Capital', *Occasional Paper*, No. 7, FSA, London, March.

Rochet, J.C. and Tirole, J. (1996) 'Interbank Lending and Systemic Risk', *Journal of Money Credit and Banking*, 28, 733–62.

Rodgers, P. (1997) 'Changes at the Bank of England', *Bank of England Quarterly Bulletin*, 37, 241–6.

Rogoff, K. (1985) 'The Optimal Degree of Commitment to an Intermediate Target', *Quarterly Journal of Economics*, 100, 1169–89.

Romer, P.M. (1990) 'Endogenous Technological Change', *Journal of Political Economy*, 98, S71–102.

Rossi, M. (1999) 'Financial Fragility and Economic Performance in Developing Countries: Do Capital Controls, Prudential Regulation and Supervision Matter?' *IMF Working Paper WP/99/66*.

Saapar, I. and Soussa, F. (2000) *Financial Consolidation and Conglomeration: Implications for the Financial Safety Net*, Centre for Central Banking Studies, Bank of England, May.

Sachs, J., Torrell, A. and Velasco, A. (1996) 'Financial Crises in Emerging Markets: The Lessons from 1995', *Brookings Papers 1*, Brookings Institution, Washington.

Salant, S.W. and Henderson, D. (1978) 'Market Anticipations of Government Policies and the Price of Gold', *Journal of Political Economy*, 86, 627–48.

Salop, S. (1979) 'Monopolistic Competition with Outside Goods', *Bell Journal of Economics*, 10, 141–56.

Santomero, A. and Hoffman, P. (1998) 'Problem Bank Resolution: Evaluating the Options', *The Wharton School Financial Institutions Center Discussion Paper*, 98–05.

Saunders, A. and Wilson, B. (1996) 'Contagious Bank Runs: Evidence from the 1929–1933 Period', *Journal of Financial Intermediation*, 5, 409–23.

Schaefer, S. (1990) 'The Regulation of Banks and Securities Firms', *European Economic Review*, 34, 587–97.

Schinasi, G., Drees, B. and Lee, W. (1999) 'Managing Global Finance and Risk', *Finance and Development*, 36.

Schoenmaker, D. (1996) 'Contagion Risk in Banking', *LSE Financial Markets Group Discussion Paper*, No. 239.

Schwartz, A. (1995a) 'Coping with Financial Fragility: A Global Perspective', *Journal of Financial Services Research*, September.

Schwartz, A. (1995b) 'Systemic Risk and the Macroeconomy', in G. Kaufman (ed.) *Research in Financial Services*, 7, 19–30, JAI Press, Greenwich.

Shadow Financial Regulatory Committee (USA) (1993) Statement on 'The Proposed Federal Banking Commission', No. 100, December.

Shadow Financial Regulatory Committee (USA) (1998) Statement on 'The Federal Reserve Board and Prudential Supervision', No. 153, December.

Sharpe, A. (1990) 'Asymmetric Information, Bank Lending, and Implicit Contracts – A Stylised Model of Customer Relationships', *Journal of Finance*, 45, 1069–87.

Shiller, R. (2000) *Irrational Exuberance*, Princeton University Press, London.

Simone, F. and Sorsa, P. (1999) 'A Review of Capital Account Restrictions in Chile in the 1990s', *IMF Working Paper WP/99/52*.

Simons, K. and Cross, S. (1991) 'Do Capital Markets Predict Problems in Large Commercial Banks?', *New England Economic Review*, May, 51–6.

Simpson, D. (2000) 'Cost Benefit Analysis and Competition', *in Some Cost Benefit Issues in Financial Regulation*, Financial Services Authority, London.

Sinclair, P. (1990) 'The Economics of Imitation', *Scottish Journal of Political Economy*, 37, 113–44.

Sinha, R. (1999) 'Corporate Governance in Financial Services Firms', *Loughborough University Banking Centre Paper No. 121/98*, Loughborough University.

Slovin, M.B., Sushka, M.E. and Polonchek, J.A. (1993) 'The Value of Bank Durability: Borrowers as Bank Stakeholders', *Journal of Finance*, 48, 247–66.

Soussa, F. (2000) 'Too Big to Fail: Moral Hazard and Unfair Competition?' in L. Halme et al. (*op cit*).

Stephen, D. and Fischer, M. (2000) 'On Internal Ratings and the Basel Accord: Issues for Financial Institutions and Regulators in the Measurement and Management of Credit Risk', Paper presented at IMF Central Banking Conference, Washington, DC, June.

Szego, G. (1997) 'A Critique of the Basel Regulation or How to Enhance (Im)moral Hazard', Paper presented at the Conference on Risk Management and Regulation in Banking, Bank of Israel, Jerusalem, 15–17 May.

Taylor, M. (1995) 'Twin Peaks: A Regulatory Structure for the New Century', pamphlet, Centre for the Study of Financial Innovation, CSFI, London, December.

Taylor, M. (1996) 'Twin Peaks: How to Reform the UK's Regulatory System', pamphlet, CSFI: London, October.

Taylor, M. and Fleming, A. (1999) 'Integrated Financial Supervision: Lessons of Northern European Experience', International Monetary Fund draft paper, September 1999.

Thakor, A.V. (1996) 'Capital Requirements, Monetary Policy, and Aggregate Bank Lending: Theory and Empirical Evidence', *Journal of Finance*, 51, 279–324.

Thomson, J.B. (1991) 'Predicting Bank Failures in the 1980s', *Federal Reserve Bank of Cleveland Economic Review*, 27, 9–20.

Thornton, H. (1802) 'An Enquiry into the Nature and Effects of the Paper Credit of Great Britain', Treasury and Civil Service Committee (1995) 'Sixth Report: The Regulation of Financial Services in the UK, Volume II', HC 1994–5, 332 II.

Tobin, J. (1978) 'A Proposal for International Monetary Reform', *Eastern Economic Journal*, 4.

Treasury and Civil Service Committee (1995) 'Sixth Report: The Regulation of Financial Services in the UK, Volume II', HC 1994–5, 332 II.

Treynor, J.L. (1972) 'The Trouble with Earnings,' *Financial Analysts Journal*, 28, 41–3.

Tuya, J. and Zamalloa, L. (1994) 'Issues on Placing Banking Supervision in the Central Bank', in T.J.T. Balino and C. Cottarelli (eds) *Frameworks of Monetary Stability: Policy Issues and Country Experiences*, IMF Institute of Monetary Affairs Department, IMF, Washington.

Vickers, J.S. (1986) 'Signaling in a Model of Monetary Policy with Incomplete Information', *Oxford Economic Papers*, 38, 443–55.

Vickers, J.S. and Yarrow, G.K. (1988) *The Economics of Privatization*, MIT Press, Cambridge, MA and London.

Volcker, P. (1984) 'The Federal Reserve Position on Restructuring of Financial Regulation Responsibilities', *Federal Reserve Bulletin*, 70, 547–57.

Wallis Committee Report (1997) *Financial System Ingiving: Final Report*, Australian Government Publishing Company, Canberra.

Wallman, S. (1999) 'Information Technology Revolution and its Impact on Regulation and Regulatory Structure', in R. Littan and A. Santomero (eds) *Brookings–Wharton Papers on Financial Services*, Brookings Institution Press, Washington.

White, W. (1998) 'The Coming Transformation of Continental European Banking?', *BIS Working Paper*, No. 54, Basel.

Index